BATTLE OF
CRETE

BATTLE OF
CRETE

GEORGE FORTY

Ian Allan
PUBLISHING

First published 2001
This edition 2009

ISBN 978 0 7110 3446 4

Published by Ian Allan Publishing

an imprint of Ian Allan Publishing Ltd, Hersham, Surrey KT12 4RG.
Printed and bound in the UK by CPI Mackays, Chatham, Kent ME5 8TD.

Code: 0907/B2

Please visit the Ian Allan website at:
www.ianallanpublishing.com

Contents

Introduction

'. . . Others hold that Daedalus, by means of his wings, returned to the island of Minos, whose fleets upon the sea were powerless to prevent this ingenious invasion, and that there he overthrew the King.'

Ex-German paratrooper, Baron von der Heydte, used this quotation from Greek mythology to open his own story of the German invasion of Crete. He titled his book *Daedalus Returned*, clearly likening the mythical Greek architect and sculptor, who was said to have built the Labyrinth for King Minos of Crete, to the parachute and glider-borne soldiers of the Fallschirmjäger. Daedalus had fallen out of favour with King Minos and had been imprisoned, so the wings he had made out of wax and feathers were to effect the escape of himself and his son Icarus from prison on the island. As the story goes, they both escaped but Icarus flew too near the sun and his wings melted, causing him to fall into the sea and drown – a fate that would befall many of the modern-day 'birdmen' in the attacking German force.

The seizure of the island of Crete by the Germans in late May 1941 was the first major military operation ever to be carried out solely by airborne forces acting on their own without any ground support. Having achieved local air superiority, they were able to air-land a sizeable force of well-equipped paratroops, who, in spite of considerable opposition from a numerically larger but less well-equipped Allied force, were, after savage fighting, able to achieve complete success. Their victory was all the more remarkable considering that the Allies had full knowledge of the German plans and controlled the seas around the island with superior naval forces. However, in this instance, German airpower was able to inflict heavy casualties on the Royal Navy and thus to isolate the island. This meant that not only could it not be properly reinforced, but also subsequently that, while part of the garrison could be safely rescued, many would be drowned when the rescuing ships were themselves bombed and sunk. As the German report on the battle rightly comments, 'In this trial of strength, air power won a decisive victory over a naval force in restricted waters.' It is interesting therefore to see that one of the direct results of Operation 'Merkur' was that Adolf Hitler was so shaken by the losses sustained by his 'secret weapon', that he discounted any future use of airborne troops on such a grand scale. The Allies, however, came to the entirely opposite conclusion, being so impressed with the German success that they rapidly began to build up their own airborne forces virtually from scratch. Allied airborne troops would go on to have their own successes and failures later in the war.

The Germans saw Crete as being very important strategically to the British for three main reasons: first, while in British hands, the island was ideally placed to maintain naval and air superiority in the eastern Mediterranean; second, it could serve as a springboard for landings on the Balkan coast; third, it was a potential airbase for Allied bombers attacking the Romanian oilfields. And, of course, it would become equally important to the Germans for all the same reasons in reverse, while being an ideal place from which to support Rommel's ground offensive onto Egypt and the Canal Zone. Viewed from either side, therefore, it was a prize worth fighting for.

A fair number of books have already been written about the battle for Crete, so what makes this one special? I like to think that it is because it follows the 'At War' style, namely that it tells the story of the short bloody campaign mainly through the eyes of those who actually took part on both sides, irrespective of rank or position; so it really does get to the hearts and minds of the sailors, soldiers and airmen who fought in this savage battle, displaying incredible courage and determination to win out against all odds.

As in Channel Islands at War, I have closed the book with a section entitled: 'What is left to see', so that visitors to the island will know where to find the monuments, etc, that remain. For many years they have been visited by the survivors of both sides, men like the UK Cretan Veterans' Association and their Commonwealth, Greek and German contemporaries, who have made yearly pilgrimages to remember their fallen comrades. Hatred and animosity largely forgotten, they spend precious hours remembering the brave young men – and women, too – who fought and died in the battles and the years of occupation which followed.

2001 will see the last officially organised visit by the veterans, although I have no doubt that many will continue to visit this beautiful island which holds so many memories and such a special place in their lives. I salute them all and dedicate this book to their memory.

George Forty
Bryantspuddle, Dorset, December 2000

Acknowledgements

I have so many people to thank for kindly supplying me with photographs and material in the preparation of this book, that I am bound to leave someone out. If I have done so, then I apologise humbly to them and would ask their forgiveness.

I don't think that I have ever received as much material for any of my books since the early days of Desert Rats at War, which I began in the early 1970s – and there were a lot more veterans around in those days and memories were sharper. Nevertheless, I have been staggered by the response, especially from the British and New Zealand Cretan veterans' associations. I have had to be selective purely because of the finite size of the book, but am delighted that I was able to persuade my publishers to increase the size of the book! This is also one of the first occasions when I have used the Internet to contact people on the other side of the world, and it has been a revelation.

My grateful thanks, therefore, go to:
Mrs Marilyn Abraham of New Zealand, who made numerous contacts for me in the Land of the Long White Cloud; the Aircrew Association; Horace Baber, late Royal Marines; C. J. Bartle, Secretary No 80 Squadron RAF Association; R. Bramley, Editor The Turret; Lawrence Brooksby, for all his excellent help with translations; Lt-Col Andrew W. Brown MBE, late A&SH; W. B. Buck, late Northumberland Hussars; Chris Buist, late RM; Hoddy Buswell, late RM; Tom Caselli, late Commandos (Layforce); Gnr Cole, NH; John C. 'Syd' Croft, late RA; John H. Dart, Curator, The Welch Regiment Museum; Fred Dashfield, late RM; Brian L. Davis, some of whose marvellous collection of photographs are included; Ken

Dawson, late Northumberland Hussars; Defence & Military Attaché Staff, British Embassy, Athens (in particular, the late Brig Stephen Saunders); Mr Manolis Doulgerakis, Dinos Heraklion; Lt-Col Alastair Scott Elliot, RHQ A&SH; Lt-Col David Eshel, late Israeli Defence Forces; Herr Gottfried Emrich, late Fallschirmjäger; Herr Ewald Feldhaus, late Fallschirmjäger; Maj-Gen Michael Forrester CB, CBE, DSO, MC, late Queens; John Forty; Mrs Iris France, who kindly allowed me to use her late husband's reminiscences; Herr Felix Gaerte, late Fallschirmjäger; Geschichte der 5 Pz Div; Wg Cdr Bill Goldfinch, late RAF; Ted Grogan; Paul Handel; E. N. Harrison, No 228 Squadron Association RAF; Hellenic Army General Staff, Military History Directorate; Hellenic Tourism Organisation; Rex Hey, late RAOC and REME; Cliff Hoare, late RHants; Wg Cdr E. A. Howell OBE, DFC, late RAF; IWM Dept of Photographs for the large selection of photographs which have been included; IWM Dept of Printed Material – for Cretan Crazy Week by the late Maj-Gen Freddie Graham; IWM Dept of Sound Archives for extracts from its amazing tape collection; Allan A. Jackson, late Royal NZ Artillery; A. J. F. Jenkins; George Katsanevakis, Prefect of Canea; Basil Keeble; Herr Sebastian Krug, Fallschirmjäger; Wg Cdr Henry Lamond, late RAF; Lt-Col Bill Laxton MC, late RM; Norman Lees, Secretary No 37 Squadron Association, RAF; Lt-Col Stephen Lindsay, RHQ The Black Watch; Wg Cdr Tony Main OBE, late RAF; Mrs Jill McAra, who sent me her family letters from the late Lt Ed McAra and Lt-Col Jack McNaught; James McNally, RA; the staff at MOD, Whitehall Library for their never-failingly wonderful service; Ken Moss, Secretary, UKCVA; David Musther, late RAF; Capt A. Newring, Editor, Globe & Laurel; No 30 Squadron RAF; Col Geoffrey Norton TD, JP, DL, Y&L; The Nottingham Sherwood Rangers Yeomanry; Michael Payne; Lt-Col Adrian Peck OBE, late QOH; John Pidgeon; Wg Cdr G. R. Pitchfork MBE, BA, late RAF; Ian Powys; John F. Price,

Chairman, UKCVA; RAF Museum, Hendon; RAF Personnel Management Agency; Bruce Robertson; Col Hugh Sandars, Managing Trustee, The QOH Regiment Museum; Herr Eugen Scherer, late Fallschirmjäger; Bill Siddle, late Northumberland Hussars; Bob Sollars, late RM; Peter Starling, The Curator, RAMC Museum; Georg Marcus Stiehl, 1 Kameradschaftsleiter, Kameradschaft Sturmregiment im Bund Deutscher Fallschirmjäger eV; Col Anthony Swallow OBE, Royal Tigers' Association, RLeics; Lord Terrington; Herr Hans Teske, late Fallschirmjäger; Ralph Thompson, 15/19 KRH and Northumberland Hussars, Discovery Museum; Alexander Turnbull Library, Wellington, New Zealand; Herr Werner Wagenknecht; Bruce Welch, late 19th Battalion NZEF; Herr Helmut Wenzel, late Fallschirmjäger; Mrs B. Wilson, Commonwealth War Graves Commission.

Chronology

1940

28 October
Italian forces invade Greece.

29 November
Churchill tells Eden, who is visiting MELF, to press for British troops to garrison Crete.

1 December
Greek Government invites British to occupy Suda Bay. On orders from GHQ, the Cretan Civil Guards are organised.

13 December
Adolf Hitler issues War Directive No 20 for the invasion of Greece – Operation 'Marita'.

1941

26 March
British heavy cruiser HMS *York* torpedoed in Suda Bay, by Italian explosive speedboats.

28 March
Naval battle off Cape Matapan – RN sinks the Italian cruisers *Fiume*, *Pola* and *Zara* and two destroyers, thus confirming the Royal Navy's pre-eminence in the Mediterranean.

3 April
The 2nd NZ Division deployed in Greece.

6 April

Germans launch simultaneous attacks on Greece and Yugoslavia.

17 April

Churchill, in a message to Wavell about the war in Greece, stresses the need for the Imperial force not to remain there against the wishes of the Greek C-in-C, and thus expose the country to devastation, so gives his approval for an evacuation to take place, but ends with the words: 'Crete must be held in force, and you should provide for this in the redistribution of your forces. It is important that strong elements of the Greek Army should establish themselves in Crete, together with King and Government. We shall aid to maintain defence of Crete to the utmost.'

18 April

Wavell orders evacuation of Greece (Operation 'Demon'). Crete warned of possibility of airborne attack.

21 April

Greece agrees to German terms for an Armistice.

23 April

The Greek political leadership (HM The King, the Prime Minister and others) transfer to Crete.

24/25 April

Evacuation of British and Allied troops from Greece begins.

25 April

Adolf Hitler issues War Directive No 28 for the invasion of Crete by air – Operation 'Merkur' – to be under command of Generalleutnant Kurt Student, Commander of XI Fliegerkorps.

28 April

Maj-Gen Freyberg evacuated with his troops from Greece to Crete.

30 April

Germans have occupied all the Greek mainland. Some 25,000 Allied troops have been evacuated to Crete. Wavell visits Crete and appoints Maj-Gen Freyberg as C-in-C Crete Garrison.

THE AERIAL BOMBARDMENT BEGINS

1 May

Start of three weeks of heavy aerial bombardment of Crete by the Luftwaffe.

10 May

Wavell advises Churchill that he has sent six Infantry tanks (Matilda Mk IIs) and 15 light tanks (Light Mk VIs) to Crete and that they will arrive in the next few days.

14 May

Heavy German air attacks on Heraklion and Maleme airfields in the morning. Force 'A' (commanded by Vice-Adm Pridham-Wippell) sails from Alexandria that afternoon to cover waters west of Crete. Wellington bombers raid airfields in Greece (Hassani and Menidi).

16 May

2nd R Leics taken to Crete on board cruisers of Force 'B' (HMS *Gloucester* and *Fiji*). Heavy German air attacks on Heraklion and Maleme airfields in the morning, also at Suda Bay and Canea. Force 'C' (King) and Force 'D' (Glennie) ready to sweep the Aegean.

17 May

Suda Bay bombed in the morning by Stukas, also heavy raids continue on Heraklion and Maleme airfields. RAF attack enemy aircraft on Greek airfields (Hassani, Argos and Maloi). All cruisers and destroyers recalled to Alexandria to refuel and replenish.

18 May

More heavy raids on Suda Bay, also on Maleme and Heraklion airfields. Wellingtons raid Hassani and Eleusis airfields. HMS *Glengyle* lands 700 men of the A&SH at Tymbaki. First VC to be awarded to the Mediterranean Fleet (to PO Sephton, a director gunlayer on HMS *Coventry* of Force 'C').

19 May

Low-flying machine gun attacks and continual bombing of the airfields at Maleme and Heraklion all day. Suda Bay dive-bombed and Force 'A1' (Rear-Adm Rawlings) relieves Force 'A' to the south-west of Crete.

THE AIRBORNE ASSAULT BEGINS

Tuesday 20 May

Heavy bombing at Suda and Maleme precedes glider and para landings. 10,000 paras land, but sustain heavy casualties so that only 6,000 are still in action by last light. Of their four main objectives – Maleme, Galatas/Canea, Rethymnon and Heraklion – they have only managed to establish a firm perimeter at Maleme. Forces 'A1' (Rawlings), 'B' (Rowley) and 'D' (Glennie) move to west of Crete; Force 'C' (King) moves to south of Kasos Strait.

Wednesday 21 May

Three British destroyers bombard Scarpanto airfield before

dawn. Heavy bombing in Maleme-Canea area. More troop carriers land despite heavy casualties, the Germans concentrating west of Maleme airfield and near Canea. By the late afternoon, they are in control of Maleme airfield, and a counter-attack by two NZ battalions fails. Elsewhere, at Rethymnon and Heraklion, the defenders have more success with their counter-attacks. At sea, RN patrol to the north and north-west of Crete with cruisers and destroyers. HMS *Juno* sunk by air attack. During a night engagement, RN destroy an enemy troop convoy of caiques carrying men of 5 Gebirgs Division on their way to Crete.

Thursday 22 May

NZ troops counter-attack before dawn reaches Maleme airfield, but they are forced to withdraw. Situation gets worse and they have to withdraw to a shorter line leaving the Germans in complete control of Maleme airfield, so that they can bring in large numbers of reinforcements (about 12,000). NZ troops fall back towards Galatas. At Heraklion the situation is still well in hand. Many German aircraft destroyed. Force 'C' encounters a convoy south of Milos and is heavily attacked by the Luftwaffe, HMS *Naiad* and HMS *Carlisle* both damaged. Joined by Force 'A1' in Kithera Channel, HMS *Greyhound*, HMS *Gloucester* and HMS *Fiji* are sunk, HMS *Warspite* and HMS *Valiant* are both hit.

Friday 23 May

A corrupt signal that ships are short of ammunition causes Cunningham to order all naval forces to withdraw at 0400hrs to Alexandria to replenish. NZ troops ordered to withdraw towards Suda Bay, new line formed east of Maleme-Canea area suffers from very heavy air attacks. Germans continue to bring in reinforcements in troop carriers. An ultimatum to the British and Greek defenders at Heraklion to surrender is rejected. More caiques are sunk by HMS *Kelly* and HMS *Kashmir* to the north of the island; they are both later sunk by Stukas. HM The King of Greece leaves Crete on HMS *Decoy*. RAF drop medical supplies and stores to troops at Heraklion and Rethymnon. Blenheims bomb Maleme airfield at first light. Five MTBs sunk in Suda Bay by air attack.

Saturday 24 May
Before first light HMS *Jaguar* and HMS *Defender* unload ammunition. At Suda Bay RAF sends Wellington bombers to bomb Maleme (three are lost), and Hurricanes (five aircraft) to strafe enemy positions at Heraklion. Army HQ Canea has to transfer to Naval HQ Suda Bay, due to heavy bombing. Fighting continues in Maleme-Canea area. Ammunition shortages, especially for the Greek troops at Heraklion. The C-in-C (Adm Cunningham) advises the Chiefs of Staff that the scale of enemy air attacks is such that the Navy cannot operate in daylight.

Sunday 25 May
Germans try to break through at Galatas and capture it, but it is retaken by British and NZ troops. 2Lt Charles Upham's gallantry at Maleme and in subsequent actions result in the award of his first VC – he will be awarded a second later in North Africa. Allied garrisons at Rethymnon and Heraklion are cut off. Germans advance inland and occupy Kandanos. Considerable resistance from Cretan civilians (unexpected by the Germans) leads to executions, pillage and burning of villages. British cruisers and destroyers sweep the north coast of Crete before dawn. At dawn, Wellington bombers drop medical supplies at Rethymnon. Luftwaffe continues air attacks west of Canea all day, whilst troop carriers continue to land reinforcements. Some 24 Ju52s are destroyed on Maleme airfield by British aircraft bombing and machine gunning the strip, but seven aircraft are lost (three Hurricanes, three Blenheims and one Maryland).

Monday 26 May

British cruisers and destroyers make another sweep of the north coast. The line which had been held in the Canea-Maleme sector is broken and defenders have to withdraw on Canea, the Germans entering Perivolia and Galatas. At Heraklion, however, men of the A&SH supported by two Matilda Mk II tanks break through from the south and seal off a large number of the enemy. Freyberg decides on a withdrawal to Sphakia on the south coast from which troops will be taken off by sea. HMS *Formidable* and HMS *Nubian* badly damaged by enemy aircraft in an attack on Vice-Adm Pridham-Wippell's force.

Tuesday 27 May

Before dawn HMS *Abdiel* and two destroyers disembark 'Layforce' – 750 Special Forces (commandos) – at Suda Bay. Early in morning, Wavell signals Churchill that Crete is no longer tenable. Chiefs of Staff subsequently order evacuation and the garrison receives Wavell's approval to evacuate. New defence line formed, called '42nd Street', west of Suda Bay. As the Germans advance, NZ and Australians launch a bayonet charge inflicting heavy casualties. The Allied Force, albeit now in some confusion, starts to withdraw south over the White Mountains and across Askifou Plain towards Sphakia as new defence line collapses. Maj-Gen Weston appointed to command the rearguard. Germans secure control of Suda Bay and Canea, but Heraklion still holding out. AOC MEC promises as much fighter protection to RN as possible during the evacuation.

Wednesday 28 May

Force 'B' (three cruisers and six destroyers) leaves Alexandria for Heraklion to evacuate garrison, while Force 'C' (four destroyers) heads for Sphakia, where main withdrawal is still directed from a joint Military and Naval HQ in a cave near the beach. More enemy paratroops arrive in the Heraklion area. RAF Wellingtons bomb Maleme and Scarpanto airfields. HMS *Ajax* bombed that evening and has to be detached from Force 'D' to return to Alexandria. Italian troops occupy the area of Lasthi. Sgt Alfred Hulme awarded the VC for actions on the 28th and for his part, earlier, in the counter-attack at Galatas.

Thursday 29 May
Before first light 700 troops are embarked at Sphakia and 4,000 at Heraklion; however, HMS *Imperial* sunk on leaving. Force 'B' is heavily bombed throughout the day, HMS *Orion* and HMS *Dido* are both damaged and HMS *Hereward* is sunk. Rearguard still carrying out an orderly withdrawal, but Sphakia is heavily bombed and strafed. Forces 'B' and 'C' arrive in Alexandria, whilst Force 'D' on its way to Sphakia. Germans now in control of Rethymnon and Heraklion.

Friday 30 May
Before first light, Force 'D' embarks some 6,000 men at Sphakia and arrives at Alexandria that afternoon, but HMAS *Perth* hit en route. Force 'C' on its way back to Sphakia. RAF bomb Maleme, Scarpanto and Rhodes. Rearguard now only a few miles from Sphakia. Rethymnon Garrison surrenders to the Germans.

Saturday 31 May
Final evacuations from Sphakia by RN before dawn, Force 'C' embarking some 1,500 men. Fighter cover for Force 'C' knocks down four enemy bombers. Gen Freyberg and Capt Morse RN taken off by Sunderland flying boat, whilst Weston remains in command in Crete. He estimates that there are still some 9,000 troops left to be evacuated in the

Sphakia area. Force 'C', with HMS *Phoebe*, HMS *Abdiel* and three destroyers, is sent to make final lift. Admiralty told that the evacuation will cease after dawn on 1 June. Weston told by Wavell that the capitulation of all troops left on Crete will take place on 1 June. Gen Student issues orders regarding the execution of civilians.

Sunday 1 June
Force 'D' embarks nearly 4,000 men at Sphakia; HMS *Calcutta* is sunk by a dive-bomber on its way to meet Force 'D', which arrives at Alexandria late that afternoon. Weston passes on message about capitulation to senior officer left on Crete and returns to Egypt by flying boat as ordered.

CRETE AFTER ITS CAPTURE

1944
April
The abduction of Gen Kreipe.

May
The razing to the ground of the villages of Kamares, Lokhria, Margarikari and Saktouria and the neighbouring parts of the Nome of Heraklion in reprisal for assisting guerrillas.

1 December
German troops on Crete withdraw to Suda Bay and coastal positions.

1945
12 May
Surrender of remaining German troops on Crete.

Glossary

1Welch	1st Battalion The Welch Regiment
2A&SH	2nd Bn Argyll and Sutherland Highlanders
2BW	2nd Black Watch
7RTR	7th Royal Tank Regiment
A&SH	Argyll and Sutherland Highlanders
AA	Anti-aircraft
ADMS	Assistant Director Medical Services
ADOS	Assistant Director Ordnance Services
ADST	Assistant Director Supplies and Transport
AMPC	Auxiliary Military Pioneer Corps
AOC	Air Officer Commanding
AQMG	Assistant Quartermaster General
A/Tk	anti-tank
Aust	Australian
AVM	Air Vice-Marshal
Bde	Brigade
Bdr	Bombardier
BGS	Brigadier General Staff
Bn	Battalion
Bty	Battery
BW	Black Watch
Cav	Cavalry
coy	Company
CRA	Commander Royal Artillery
CRE	Commander Royal Engineer
CRS	Casualty Reception Station
Def	Defence
Det	Detachment

Div	Division
DZ	drop zone
EOT	Hellenic Tourism Organisation
ETA	estimated time of arrival
Fd	Field
Feldwebel	German equivalent of Company Sergeant-Major or Sergeant (RAF)
FJR	Fallschirmjägerregiment; eg 6./2FJR
FM	Field Marshal
Gefreiter	German equivalent of Lance Corporal or Aircraftsman 1st Class
General der Flieger	German equivalent of Air Marshal
Generalfeldmarschall	German equivalent of Field Marshal or Air Chief Marshal
Generalleutnant	German equivalent of Lieutenant-General or Air Vice-Marshal
Generalmajor	German equivalent of Major-General or Air Commodore
Generaloberst	German equivalent of General or Air Chief Marshal
GHQ	General Headquarters
GOC	General Officer Commanding
Grossadmiral	German equivalent of Admiral of the Fleet
hy	Heavy
I/JG26	Jagdgeschwader (day fighter)
Inf	Infantry
Kapitän zur See	German equivalent of Captain (Royal Navy)
KRH	King's Royal Hussars
LAA	Light AA
LAC	Leading Aircraftsman
LAD	Light Aid Detachment
LL	Luftlande
M and V	meat and vegetables

MEC	Middle East Command
Med	Medium
MELF	Middle East Land Forces
MG	Machine gun
Mk	Mark
MNBDO	Mobile Naval Base Defence Organisation
MOA	Marine Officers Attendant
MT	Motor Transport
MT	Motoscafo Turismo Italian MTB
MTB	Motor Torpedo Boat
NZ	New Zealand
Oberfeldwebel	German equivalent of Sergeant-Major or Flight Sergeant
Obergefreiter	German equivalent of Corporal or Leading Aircraftsman
Oberst	German equivalent of Colonel or Group Captain
Oberstleutnant	German equivalent of Lieutenant-Colonel or Wing Commander
OKW	Oberkommando der Wehrmacht
Operation 'Merkur'	(Mercury)
PO	Petty Officer
QOH	The Queen's Own Hussars Regt
RA	Royal Artillery
RAD	Reichsarbeitsdienst
RAMC	Royal Army Medical Corps
RAOC	Royal Army Ordnance Corps
RAP	Regimental Aid Posts
Regt	Regiment
Reichsmarschall	German equivalent of Marshal of the RAF
REME	Royal Electrical and Mechanical Engineers
RHants	Royal Hampshire Regiment
RLeics	The Royal Leicestershire Regiment
RM	Royal Marines

RTR	Royal Tank Regiment
Sec	Section
Sigs	Signals
SOE	Special Operations Executive
UKCVA	UK Cretan Veterans' Association
Unteroffizier	German equivalent of Corporal (RAF)
Waffenbehälter	Weapons container
Y&L	The York & Lancaster Regiment
VC	Victoria Cross

1

Crete – The Island

Crete (Kriti in Greek) is the fifth largest island in the Mediterranean and largest of the islands that form part of modern Greece. Long and narrow – 152 miles long on its east-west axis and varying in width from 7.5 to 35 miles – it has an area of some 3,190 square miles. Its spine is made up of three massive mountain ranges, covering two-thirds of the island's surface. In the far west are the Lefka Ori, or White Mountains, whose highest peak is Pahnes at 8,042 ft. In the centre is the Ida or Psiloritis range, with Mount Idhi (Ida) just making the claim as being the island's tallest mountain at 8,058 ft. In the east is the Dikti range, which reaches a height of 7,045 ft. At the very eastern end of Crete are the lower hills of the Sitia range at around 3,000 ft. There are a total of 57 peaks over 6,000 ft, many of which are covered with snow throughout the winter. In some places the mountains run steeply down to the sea, but on the north coast of the island the slope is more gradual, providing for a number of good, natural harbours – the best being at Suda Bay – and coastal plains on which the main towns of Canea, Rethymnon and Heraklion – to use the usual English versions of their names – are located. [1]

In the centre of the southern side of the island is the Messara Plain, the largest flat area on Crete, which extends for some 18 miles. There are a few small rivers, numerous mountain torrents – fed by springs – that rush through precipitous ravines down to the sea, and some seasonal watercourses which become dried up wadis in the hot season. The harbours on the southern coast are small and few in number. They are also exposed to southern winds of gale force and are also of only limited use because of sudden shelving.

The climate varies between temperate and tropical, with some 25in of rain in the winter, while the summers are hot and dry. In May the weather is generally bright and clear, hot during the day, but cold at night. Encyclopaedia Britannica classifies its landscape as being 'dominated by characteristic Mediterranean scrub (maquis and garigue); olives, carobs and orange trees are cultivated'. Agriculture has always been the economic mainstay of the island's population, which now numbers over half a million (536,980 in 1991), with vineyards, lemon, olive and orange groves being the mainstays, whilst goats and sheep are grazed on the one-fifth of the island which is unfit for cultivation. Tourism is now very important and a growing source of foreign currency.

The island is today divided into four prefectures (Nomes)–Hania, Rethymnon, Heraklion and Lasithi, each with an administrative capital and being further subdivided into provinces. Canea, which was the capital, and Heraklion, which is now the capital, are the only two places of any size. Situated only 108 miles away from Athens, Crete is the gateway to Greece and the Aegean on the one side, and to Africa on the other, so its occupation has long been seen as being vital to anyone wishing to dominate the area – hence its turbulent history of invasion and occupation by foreign forces. However, it has never been an easy place to conquer, the mountains in particular providing an ideal place for a resistance movement to operate. This has bred a fiercely partisan spirit amongst the Cretans, which many invaders have discovered to their cost.

By 3000BC the Bronze Age Minoan civilisation flourished, being named after the legendary ruler King Minos. Centred on Knossos, it was at its peak in the 16th century BC, when it traded widely with the rest of the eastern Mediterranean, its distinctive sculpture, pottery, fresco paintings and metalwork being highly prized. One 'visitor' to the island – Baron von der Heydte, who commanded a battalion of German

Fallschirmjäger during the invasion wrote:

'In addition to contemporary habitations, one may discover, at any time and anywhere, tokens of bygone days. One's foot may suddenly kick against some ancient masonry hidden in the undergrowth ... betoken that once upon a time – who knows when? – man has lived and fought here, toiled and worried.' [2]

Crete has a history of being occupied by the foreign nations, including the Romans whose army conquered the island in 67BC and made it a part of the province of Cyrenaica in North Africa. In AD395 it became part of the Eastern Roman Empire, and over 400 years later the Arabs gained control over certain areas of Crete from about AD824; fighting between Arabs and Byzantines continued for several centuries thereafter. Next came the Crusaders, who in 1204, after the Fourth Crusade, sold the island to Venice. The rise of the Ottoman Empire saw the Venetians and Turks fight for control of the island, culminating in 1699 when the city of Candia (now Heraklion) was taken by the Turks after a long siege. Crete stagnated under Turkish rule and there were constant uprisings until the Turks were expelled by Greece in 1898. The island was finally united with Greece in 1913. The islanders had never abandoned their Orthodox religion and Greek language throughout these difficult years, remaining fiercely independent despite everything – as the next conquering army would soon discover to its cost!

Crete also posed health problems for European invaders as a contemporary German survey pointed out: 'Water could only be consumed in a filtered condition. Leprosy, Aleppo boil and Malaria are characteristics of the sub-tropical zone and render the life for Europeans unpleasant.' However, the report does conclude on a more positive note, 'But a Gebirge (mountain troop) or Fallschirmjäger (paratrooper) does not worry about these things. The command gives the order and if it means getting the devil out of hell, the order will be executed!'

Maj J. W. Stewart-Peter of the 2nd Black Watch was just one of the many British soldiers for whom Crete held a strange and lasting fascination. His battlefield reminiscences of the fighting around Heraklion are to be found in a later chapter; however, he also wrote the following description of 'that lovely isle' as he called it:

'Crete, that lovely isle – indeed that demi-paradise, is peopled by heroes and by heroines. The southern counterpart of Finland – they were poor in the worldly sense, but none richer in the spiritual. Crete is an island in which everything is beautiful, with the exception of the Syrian descendants in the environs of its towns, and the treatment of horses and mules. The configuration of the island is grandly and diversely impressive, its setting magnificent. Its flora must be nearly unsurpassed for variety and brilliance. Its fauna is limited – but made up for by its birdlife. Every living thing, from its rare orchids and alpine plants–through its apple green and furry spiders – its toads coloured green and gold surpassing the wrappings of Messrs Louis Roederer's excellent champagne corks–to the smoky grey sweep of the Montagu harriers quartering the rocky hills, was beautiful.

'I say was, because today as I write the Hun is therein and viewed through whatever rose-tinted Vichy spectacles – he is not beautiful. The people are a simple but proud peasantry – making the barest of livings by the hardest of work; but in them I saw civilisation in its real sense. They were not greedy, they did not normally hate – but they showed when the Hun came they could hate splendidly. They loved their church, with a primitive belief in the Supreme Being who endowed their life with the fruits of their labour. The Being who gave them rain and sun in due season and blessed their scant flocks with increase. The Being who coloured their glorious flowers and gave bouquet to their wines. They were poor people as the world knows riches – a man with the equivalent of £400 a year was a Croesus. They toiled all day, men, women and lads, in the olive groves, in the vineyards and shepherding in the hills.

'I only knew them when the war had taken the best of their young men and many of their middle-aged; when their sound and lusty mules and horses had been taken; "to Albania" to help the hardy Greeks, Cretans and Evzones,[3] to beat the wretched conscripted, but magnificently equipped, Italians, from the borders of Greece. They did not complain, but they did not rejoice. Calm, wide-eyed, kind and a little sorrowful, they kept on, placing their faith in God. Even when the Germans – who had terrified half Europe into submission without firing any shot save for those firing squads – threw themselves against them, the Cretans trusted in their God, themselves and the British.

'The women toiled on – weeded and pruned the vines; and, where mules were lacking, fallowed with broad hoes, from dawn to dusk, the broad acres between the olive trees. Their wine unsold, they did not complain, their fishing restricted, they grumbled not. Up in the hills the old Cretan bands–barely removed from the brigands who harassed the Turks – sharpened their Cretan knives and awaited with stout hearts the new foe–who might come from the air–a fresh and modern terror – but they were not afraid.' [4]

Military topography

To summarise on this background survey of Crete, I quote from the German report on the capture of Crete which summarises the topography, as at May 1941, most succinctly thus:

'The island of Crete is approximately 160 miles long and varies in width from 8 to 35 miles. The interior is barren and covered by eroded mountains which, in the western part, rise to an elevation of 8,100 feet. There are few roads and water is scarce. The south coast descends abruptly towards the sea; the only usable port along this part of the coast is the small harbour of Sphakia. There are hardly any north-south

communications and the only road to Sphakia which can be used for motor transportation ends abruptly 1,300 feet above the town. The sole major traffic artery runs close to the north coast and connects Suda Bay with the towns of Maleme, Canea, Rethymnon and Heraklion. Possession of the north coast is vital for an invader approaching from Greece, if only because of terrain conditions. The British, whose supply bases were situated in Egypt, were greatly handicapped by the fact that the only efficient port was in Suda Bay. The topography of the island, therefore, favoured the invader, particularly since the mountainous terrain left no other alternative to the British but to construct their airfields close to the exposed north coast.' [5]

Place names

There is a fair amount of diversity between modern Cretan place names, with those used during the war, also between various languages and the transliteration from Greek. We have tried to standardise, viz:

Antikithera – also Andikythera, Antikythera, Andikithira
Canea – also Hania, Chania, Xania, Khania
Heraklion – also Iraklion, Heraclion, Candia (historical)
Kithera – also Kythera, Kithira
Maleme – also Malemes
Rethymnon–also Rethymno, Retimo, Rethimnon, Rettymnon
Sphakia – also Sfakia
Suda – also Souda

Notes

1. Every map of Crete seems to have different spellings for town names, so I have tried to use those that seem to be most used in English language texts.

2. Baron von der Heydte; *Daedalus Returned* – Crete 1941; Hutchinson, 1958.

3. A soldier in an elite Greek infantry regiment.

4. Unfortunately most of the contents of Maj Stewart-Peter's diary went down to the bottom of the Mediterranean when the cruiser HMS *Orion* was sunk. However, I am grateful to the Black Watch Museum and Archives for allowing me to quote from what remains.

5. Quoted from The German Campaigns in the Balkans, Vol 15 of the Garland WWII German Military Studies.

2

Crete – The Italians Must Not Have It

'One salient strategic fact leaped out upon us – CRETE!
The Italians must not have it.
We must get it first – and at once.'
Winston Churchill [1]

In late October 1940, Anthony Eden was in Khartoum conferring with Generals Smuts and Wavell, when Churchill telegraphed him to say that he and Wavell should return to Cairo as soon as they could, because as the Prime Minister put it: 'We here are all convinced an effort should be made to establish ourselves in Crete, and that risks should be run for this valuable prize.' Churchill went on to say that he thought it was of 'prime importance' to hold the best airfield on the island and to establish a naval refuelling base at Suda Bay. Not only, he said, would the successful defence of the island be an invaluable aid to the defence of Egypt, but also he felt that the 'loss of Crete to the Italians would be a grievous aggravation of all Mediterranean difficulties'. Eden was to discuss matters with Smuts and Wavell, then, Churchill told him, he was not to hesitate in making proposals for large-scale action at the expense of other sectors and to work out what further aid would be required from the UK. Two days later Churchill records in his memoirs that, 'At the invitation of the Greek Government, Suda Bay, the best harbour in Crete, was occupied by our forces.' [2]

Great Britain and the Commonwealth stand alone

By the early spring of 1941, Great Britain and the Commonwealth had been standing virtually alone for over nine months against the might of the Axis war machine, ever since the capitulation of France the previous June. The one gleam of success in a seemingly endless catalogue of failure and defeat had come when the tiny Western Desert Force had triumphantly trounced the far larger Italian Tenth Army, driving it out of Egypt and Cyrenaica and causing it to surrender completely at Beda Fomm-Sidi Saleh on 5–7 February 1941 – a victory which was later described by historian Sir Basil Liddell Hart as being 'one of the most daring ventures and breathless races in the annals of the British Army'. Anthony Eden even coined a new version of Winston Churchill's famous Battle of Britain phrase, when he remarked, 'Never has so much been surrendered by so many to so few!'

Unfortunately, those heady days at the start of the year had been followed by a sudden change of fortunes with the arrival on the desert scene of the charismatic Generalleutnant Erwin Johannes Eugen Rommel and his Deutsches Afrika Korps. The 'Desert Fox', as he quickly became known to both sides, had swiftly turned the tables upon the British, pushing them out of Cyrenaica and back into Egypt. Wavell's forces opposing him had been considerably reduced because of the need to send troops to Greece, where a similar retrograde situation had emerged. The initial successes of the tiny Greek Army against the inept Italians had been followed by the highly successful German Operation 'Marita' against Greece and its British and Commonwealth allies. This was even now drawing to a close. It had taken the Germans just 24 days to complete the victory, the following being the main factors in their success (which did not bode well for the coming battle for Crete):

a the superiority of their ground forces, especially their tactical training, weapons and equipment.

b their supremacy in the air.

c   the inadequacy of the British expeditionary force – at that time in the Middle East they simply did not have enough men and material available to fight large-scale operations simultaneously in North Africa and in the Balkans. [3]

d   the poor condition of the Greek Army and its shortage of modern equipment.

e   the lack of co-operation between the British, Greek and Yugoslav forces caused by the total absence of a unified command.

f   the early collapse of Yugoslav resistance.

g   Turkey's continuing strict neutrality.

British Military Mission in Greece

At the time of the German invasion of Greece, Michael Forrester was a young captain in the Queen's Regiment (now Maj-Gen Retd, CB, CBE, DSO, MC and Vice-President of the UKCVA) and serving in Athens as a member of the British Military Mission which, together with an RAF contingent of two squadrons of Bristol Blenheim fighter-bombers, had been sent to Greece immediately following the Italian invasion from Albania. He recalls:

> 'Meanwhile in London, pressure from Winston Churchill and Anthony Eden was mounting to send a force from the Middle East to support the Greeks in the event of a German attack through Yugoslavia. And on 7 March, the first contingents of the Allied Expeditionary Force ('W' Force) consisting of 1st British Armoured Brigade, plus an ANZAC Corps under Gen Blamey and comprising 2nd New Zealand Division and 6th Australian Division, started to arrive. The C-in-C was Gen Sir Henry Maitland Wilson.
>
> 'The German attack on Yugoslavia and Greece started on 6 April and it soon became clear that with the bulk of the Greek Army facing the Italians in Albania, withdrawal by 'W' Force was inevitable. On 20 April, Gen Wavell flew to

Athens and, in view of the rapid progress made by the German forces, ordered the evacuation of the Allied Expeditionary Force from the beaches in the Athens area and also in the Peloponnese.

Life in the British Mission

'Experience in the Mission had proved fascinating. My appointment was GSO3 in the small General Staff Branch headed by Col Guy Salisbury-Jones (later Maj-Gen Sir Guy, GCVO, CMG, CBE, MC, HM Marshal Diplomatic Corps) formerly of the Coldstream Guards.

'The GSO2 was Maj Peter Smith-Dorrien, later tragically killed by the terrorist bomb at the King David Hotel in Jerusalem. Apart from a memorable visit to the Albanian front where I was privileged to see the Greek Army fighting the Italians in the Epirus Mountains, often above the snow line, I was in Athens liaising with Greek GHQ for which Prince Peter (King George II of Greece's young cousin) had been appointed Chief Liaison Officer to the British Mission. Throughout these months I had built up a huge admiration for the Greek Army, and also for the Greek people whose enthusiastic support for their Army at times manifested itself in the streets of Athens. And so it was that, during the third week of April, I realised that saying goodbye and leaving my friends to a German occupation was going to prove a painful and emotional experience, compounded by a feeling of guilt that it was we, the British, who, due to our intervention, were responsible for their plight.'

Meanwhile, in Crete

As we have seen, thanks to Churchill's foresight, there had been a British garrison on Crete since shortly after the Italian invasion of Greece in October 1940. We will go into the detail of the make-up and layout of the garrison in a later chapter; suffice it to say here that, initially, it was about a brigade plus in strength, which included the manning of three reasonable airfields and a naval refuelling base. It had formed the main supply base for British operations in Greece and the Balkans, and would later act as a 'collecting point' for many of the British and Greek servicemen evacuated from Greece. However, this increase in the number of troops on the island did not mean that the garrison was that much stronger or more able to deal with an enemy assault, because many of these new arrivals came without weapons, vehicles and equipment, and were generally in a parlous state, having carried out a difficult withdrawal through Greece.

From the German point of view, Crete represented a major strategic prize well worth fighting for, especially the Luftwaffe. Accordingly, in mid-April 1941 General der Flieger Kurt Student, the commander of XI Fliegerkorps, part of Gen Loehr's Luftflotte IV in the Balkans, presented a plan to Reichsmarschall Hermann Goering for the airborne invasion of Crete. On the same day, 15 April 1941, the Army High Command submitted to Gen Alfred Jodl, Chief of the Operations Section of the OKW, 4 a plan for the invasion of Malta. Five days later, after conferring with Student, Hitler decided in favour of Crete.

On 25 April 1941, Hitler issued Directive No 28. It began, 'The occupation of the island of Crete (Operation "Merkur") is to be prepared in order to have a base for conducting the air war against England in the Eastern Mediterranean.' From the Luftwaffe's point of view this was a very sensible and worthwhile aim, although its confidence was not entirely shared by the other two services. The Kriegsmarine, for example, while welcoming the opportunity to break the power of the British Mediterranean Fleet in the Eastern Mediterranean, still had considerable reservations about the fighting ability of the Italian fleet. The Heer's lack of enthusiasm stemmed from the conviction that the British would fight to the bitter end over this key position because it protected their North African flank and, in particular, the vital

Suez Canal. This might, they argued, require a higher proportion of highly trained troops to be diverted to what was at that time a secondary theatre of war, preventing them from being available for the next major offensive, namely the invasion of Russia. Hitler, however, made one major qualification in Directive No 28 and that was that the requirements for air transport should not be allowed to lead to any delay in the strategic concentration for Barbarossa, so clearly it would be up to the Luftwaffe to 'carry the ball'.

The author of the plan for the invasion of Crete was Generalleutnant Kurt Student (1890-1978). Commissioned in 1912, he became a pilot the next year and saw active service during the Great War, flying bombers and reconnaissance aircraft, before becoming a fighter pilot and leader of Jagdstaffel 9. He was awarded the Knight's Cross of the House Order of Hohenzollern, and on 20 June 1918 was promoted Hauptmann. He transferred back to the infantry postwar, but then joined the Reichswehr's newly formed aviation group (Truppenflieger Staffel 120) in April 1920. He was an interested observer at the Soviet air manoeuvres from 1924 to 1928, then in April 1938, he was promoted to Generalmajor and made commander of the 3rd Flieger Division. Three months later he became chief of the parachute and glider arm, forming (in secret) the first Fallschirmjäger battalion in 1938. This led on to the formation of 7th Flieger Division (its 'Air Division' title was deliberately chosen to disguise the fact that it was a parachute division), which he also commanded.

The new formation was not used in the invasion of Poland, as Hitler did not wish to divulge his 'secret weapon' too early. However, it was used to great effect in the subsequent assaults on Norway, Belgium and the Netherlands. Probably their most spectacular operation was the taking of the fortress of Eben Emael by just 500 glider troops on 10 May 1940, while some 4,000 Fallschirmjäger dropped around The Hague and Rotterdam. Student, who was personally directing operations, was wounded badly in the head and put out of action until January 1941. He was also awarded his Knight's Cross (12 May 1940) and on 2 September 1941, received the Golden Pilot's Badge with Diamonds, an award that was presented to only about 40 airmen. At the same time as he received this award from Goering he was told to investigate other possibilities for the use of airborne troops, and during the months that followed took over the forming and subsequent command of the Air Landing Corps, which was, again for security reasons, designated XI Fliegerkorps. His part in the Crete operation will be covered later, but his Fallschirmjäger would suffer grievous casualties which would disenchant Hitler to such an extent that they would not be used again in a major airborne operation, but instead fight as ground troops. Student would reach the rank of Generaloberst as commander of the 1st Fallschirmjägerarmee, fighting in the Reichswald and in the defence of the Rhine and suffering heavy losses. In April 1945, he was appointed C-in-C Army Group Vistula and later, when the this unit was cut off, surrendered to the British. After spending some years in prison, he returned to Germany, becoming president of the Association of German Parachute Troops in 1949, a post he held until his death on 1 July 1978. Student, although appearing slow and thoughtful, was an officer of exceptional ability and was considered by Hitler to be one of his most energetic generals. A measure of the respect in which his former enemies held him was his naming by the New Zealand Cretan Veterans' Association as their vice-president in 1962.

Rule Britannia!

From the outbreak of war, until the spring of 1941, the Royal Navy had been most successful in maintaining control over the eastern part of the Mediterranean – despite the fact that Mussolini looked upon it as his private Italian lake. In spite of the size and modernity of the Italian fleet, Britain still managed to defend Egypt and its all-important Suez Canal, while retaining its vital bases of Gibraltar in the western Mediterranean and Malta in the eastern. Alexandria was the main base, roughly half-way in between the two and, most significantly, only 60 air miles from Sicily. C-in-C of the British Mediterranean Fleet was Adm Sir Andrew B. Cunningham GCB, DSO, known by one and all (for obvious reasons) as 'ABC'. From the outset he had been determined to gain command of the Mediterranean and to keep it. A remarkable sailor, he was an inspiration to all – his often quoted warning that 'It takes the Navy three years to build a ship. It would take three hundred to rebuild a tradition', showed plainly that, in true Royal Naval tradition, he intended to take the battle to the enemy, despite the fact that the much larger Italian Navy had capital ships that were on the whole newer, faster and better armed. Once the French Fleet had been taken out of the equation at Oran, Alexandria and elsewhere, then he could turn his full attention to the Italians, whose apparent superiority hid a number of weaknesses. They were unaggressive, had no experience of night fighting and lacked any aircraft carriers. This had been Il Duce's deliberate policy, as he was convinced that his ships could be properly protected from attack by shore-based aircraft. The highly effective British carrier-borne raid on the main Italian naval base of Taranto on 11 November 1940, which hit and put out of commission some of the most important Italian warships, showed how wrong he was. This was followed in March 1941, by the battle of Matapan, where the battleship *Vittorio Veneto* (the only undamaged Italian battleship after Taranto) was badly damaged and the cruisers *Pola, Zara* and *Fiume* sunk. This victory confirmed the Royal Navy's power in the Mediterranean over the Italians.

Arthur John Stevens was an aircraft airframe fitter, also known as a rigger, who was trained specifically to look after the Westland Walrus light seaplane, normally carried on a catapult. He was serving on board HMS *Gloucester* and his 'action station', along with other members of 44 Mess, was as a member of the ammunition party for a 4in AA gun on the port side. His specific job was to transfer the 4in shells to the gun handler or to put them on the lower part of the gun or into the lockers that were adjacent to the guns. In a taped interview at the Imperial War Museum (10986/4) he talked about various actions in which his ship took part, one being Matapan.

> *'I can remember the* Gloucester *being detailed off to chase this particular Italian ... I believe it was the* Fiume. *It was brought to a standstill by gunfire and the* Gloucester *was detailed off to circle round it at that stage, and a signal was sent to the Italians to get their men off the ship ... Time was allowed for them to get away and then we were told to blow it out of the water, which we did ... it was a stationary target so it was easy meat ... I think there was tinfish [torpedoes] put into her to make sure she went down and her crew were picked up by a hospital ship as far as I understood.'*

Later HMS *Gloucester* took part in the Allied force to Greece: 'We'd been given the job of transferring quite a number of Australians to Greece ... And on two or three occasions we were 800 plus as a ship's company and we were transporting 600 army personnel ... our mess-decks were covered with soldiers playing cards, the Aussies were boys for playing cards. A lot of them were seasick. Eventually these chaps were landed in Greece.' More from Arthur Stevens later, when he had the traumatic experience of being sunk by bombing during the assault on Crete, while helping to deal with the seaborne part of the invasion, before his eventual rescue from the water by the enemy.

Enter the Luftwaffe. Although the Royal Navy was more than holding its own against the Italians, there was soon to be a new player in the game. This was the Luftwaffe, with its Junkers Ju87 Stuka and Ju88 bombers, which soon began to have a devastating effect upon British seapower. The aircraft carrier HMS *Illustrious* was one of the first casualties, being seriously damaged on 10 January 1941 in the Sicilian narrows. *Illustrious* managed to reach Malta and, subsequently, Alexandria, but was 'hors de combat' for a long time, and underwent extensive repairs in the USA. The day after *Illustrious* was hit, the cruiser HMS *Southampton* was dive-bombed and sunk. Adm Cunningham was, therefore, relieved when a new aircraft carrier, HMS *Formidable*, arrived from the South Atlantic on 10 March. He hoped it would enable him to put into practice his theories on how to deal with the new threat. This entailed having some 12 fighters in the air over the fleet flying combat air patrols, and a destroyer screen to put up an anti-aircraft 'umbrella barrage' over any particular ship that was attacked.

Unfortunately, matters were not helped by the grievous shortage of RAF aircraft, particularly after German success in the Balkans, when Axis aircraft were both more plentiful and more able to operate with impunity. This presented a growing threat to the Royal Navy. As Capt S. W. C. Pack rightly says in *The Battle for Crete*, 'Though Britain still held the sea, the Germans now had practically undisputed supremacy in the air and were in full control of Rumania, Bulgaria, Greece and many of the Aegean islands. They were also at the gates of Egypt.'

The fight against the odds

Air Chief Marshal Sir Arthur Longmore, the Air Officer C-in-C at Cairo, had precious little with which to counter the German threat. His command was vast, including Egypt, Sudan, Palestine and Trans-Jordan, East Africa, Aden and Somaliland, Iraq and its adjacent territories, Cyprus, Turkey, the Balkans, the Mediterranean and Red Seas and the Persian Gulf – an area some four and a half million square miles! To cover this vast area he initially had just 29 squadrons, totalling about 300 aircraft, half of which were based in Egypt and the rest spread between Palestine, the Sudan, Kenya, Aden and Gibraltar.

At the start of the war few of these machines could be

described as modern. The best of the bunch were probably the Sunderland flying boats that outfitted two of the four naval co-operation squadrons, and the Blenheim Is which comprised nine of the 14 bomber squadrons. The Blenheim I was an adequate bomber but with a short range that reduced its effectiveness considerably. The five fighter squadrons were made up of obsolescent Gloster Gladiators, while the tactical reconnaissance squadrons flew the almost defenceless Westland Lysander. Together these made up 18 of the 29 squadrons under his command, but the other 11 had an incredible assortment of outdated, obsolescent prewar aircraft.

Against this the Italian Regia Aeronautica had 282 aircraft based in Libya, 150 in Italian East Africa and 47 in the Dodecanese, while many of their 1,200 home-based aircraft could easily be moved down to airfields in Sicily and southern Italy. However, as with the Italian Navy, the RAF more than held its own initially. As the RAF history of the period comments, 'The enemy's timidity was astonishing enough in view of his superior forces.' [5] A more personal view comes from the diary, *A Summer's Journey*, of the late Aircraftsman Colin France:

'I joined 33 Squadron at Mersa Matruh on 14 March 1940, just less than five months after my 19th birthday. The Squadron was equipped with Gauntlets and Gladiators, biplanes which were taken into service in 1935 and 1937 respectively. A few weeks after my arrival I was admitted into the naval Hospital in Alexandria, the victim of an insect bite. After a week or so I was transferred to the Helmich hospital in Cairo. On being discharged from hospital I called at a barber's shop for a haircut and afterwards went to Heliopolis where I heard it was possible to get a lift in an aircraft to my unit in the Western Desert. Whilst engaged in this quest I was accosted by the Station Warrant Officer who told me to get my hair cut. It was useless to argue as I had been given an order, so off again I went to the Station barber's shop.

'I was very fortunate and obtained a lift in an old Vickers Valencia biplane. The first one I boarded developed a fault and I was transferred to another. Soon I was winging my way over the Western Desert where a sandstorm was raging. Whilst I had been in hospital, the Italians had decided to commence their warlike activities on the Libya/Egypt border and consequently 33 Squadron moved somewhere to the rear of Mersa Matruh on about 17 June 1940. I found them after a couple of hours at Qasaba. The Italians, I believe, were somewhere in the vicinity of Sidi Barrani, a little way up the solitary coast road from Mersa Matruh. On 25 June we moved to Heluan in Cairo where we were refitted with Hurricane Is. After conversion we moved to Fuka in the desert on 22 September where our squadron was engaged in support of Gen Wavell and his 30,000 men and the rout of a superior force of Italians. It was during this offensive that one of our pilots, "Deadstick" Dyson, shot down six Italian CR42 biplanes in 15 minutes.

'At the end of January 1941 we embarked on a troopship, manned exclusively by RAF personnel, landed in Piraeus and then went on to Eleusis, an aerodrome to the north of Athens, on 1 February. We shared the airfield with Blenheims of 30 Squadron and a few Greek aircraft. We moved to Larissa in northern Greece on 4 March, the day after the town had been devastated by an earthquake, followed the same night by a bombing attack by five SM79s. We experienced a few tremors the day we arrived. I had a respite from the war – a weekend in Volos and a few visits to Larissa including chatting up a pretty Greek girl in the cemetery there, sitting on a tombstone while a friendly Greek interpreted for us!

'As the Germans advanced into Greece we came under constant attack from Messerschmitt Bf109s. I remember one particular attack by five of them. There was very little warning of these raids and consequently our aircraft were often caught on the ground. We lost two aircraft taking off, but some were in *the air and dogfights ensued over the airfield. One Bf109 did not seem to care what he aimed at, so all the airmen concentrated their rifle and machine gunfire on him. We were successful and he was forced to land. All the time he was circling to land, his guns blazed away at the ground staff. When his aircraft landed some distance from the airfield we all ran towards him with the sole intention of shooting him. However, we were beaten to it by some officers who reached him by car and took him into protective custody. He was jumping about – we thought with rage, but evidently he had been shot in the foot.*

'The Germans were relentless in their advance and we were ordered to pack up and move out. Many were the rumours circulating as to our destination, but we knew we were moving in the direction of Athens. The convoy proceeded very slowly as many other units were under similar orders. We were constantly harassed by Bf109s who strafed the road, and the odd Stuka who dropped his "eggs" on the road to delay our progress further. It was after one of these bombardments that I received my first (and only) issue of rum in the Royal Air Force, but it was very welcome.

'The road was packed with vehicles as we proceeded towards Lamia. All had the same idea, peace and safety and somewhere to have a night's sleep. I arrived at Eleusis on 18 April but many of the squadron continued on to Argos and Megara in the Peloponnese, then on to Patras and Egypt. I stayed in Eleusis a little longer, helping build pens for the few remaining aircraft and also destroying equipment, thus denying its use to the enemy.'

Little had changed on the British side when, as Colin France has just explained, it was decided to send help to the Greeks (they had only 72 aircraft in total, so were glad of a little assistance). A mixed squadron (No 30) of Blenheims was sent to defend Athens, to be followed shortly afterwards by two more Blenheim squadrons (Nos 84 and 211) and two fighter squadrons (No 80 and No 112). The last of these was due to re-equip, so handed over its Gladiators to the Greeks. The British force was headed by AVM J. H. D'Albiac, and his four squadrons did extremely well, No 80, for example, claiming the destruction of 42 enemy aircraft in combat for the loss of only six.

More modern aircraft had started to arrive in theatre, but only in small numbers. The legendary Gloster Gladiator biplanes Faith, Hope and Charity that had so successfully defended Malta against all the Italian onslaughts, were joined by four Hawker Hurricanes at the end of June 1940. More Hurricanes then arrived at Alexandria, having been successfully flown off the converted training carrier HMS *Argus* at the other end of the Med. These operations did not always go smoothly. For example, in November 1940, 12 Hurricanes and a Skua flew off Argus, but only the Skua and four of the Hurricanes arrived (and their petrol tanks contained 12, 4, 3 and 2 gallons of petrol respectively).

A land, sea and air battle
While this book is mainly about the land battle on Crete, I hope this early chapter has convinced the reader that it cannot be viewed in isolation. The sea and air battles were an integral part of the whole and, as the quote from Capt Pack emphasised, while the Royal Navy could reign supreme on the high seas, the Luftwaffe had control in the skies above, which negated much of the British naval superiority. German airpower would ensure that they were able to invade Crete by air, but British seapower would ensure that this invasion could not be supported from the sea. Who would win this unique tri-service battle? Whatever the final outcome it would undoubtedly be a close run thing.

Notes

1. Quote taken from Winston Churchill's *History of the Second World War Volume 2 Their Finest Hour.*
2. Ibid.
3. The Greek C-in-C, Gen Papagos, had strong misgivings about the strength of the British assistance – initially all that was offered was a single artillery regiment and some armoured cars. He is on record as saying that he considered that British intervention would 'not only fail to produce substantial military and political results in the Balkans, but would also from a general Allied point of view, be contrary to the sound principles of strategy.'
4. The Oberkommando der Wehrmacht was the German Forces High Command which Hitler had formed in 1938 to replace the war ministry. Its main task was to correlate and supervise the individual strategy of the three service HQs.
5. The Royal Air Force 1939-1945 Vol 1 The Fight at Odds.

3

The Garrison Assembles

First arrivals

The first British troops to arrive on Crete did so in autumn 1940, under orders from C-in-C Middle East, Gen (later FM) Sir Archibald Wavell KCB, CMG, MC. Known as 'Creforce', they basically comprised 14th Infantry Brigade, commanded by Brig O. H. Tidbury. The brigade had been serving in Palestine under Brig G. Dawes before the war. On 26 July 1940, Brigade HQ was disbanded in Egypt and re-formed as HQ Creforce on 30 October 1940 under Brig Tidbury. Just before the invasion, on 27 April 1941, Tidbury handed over command to Brig B. H. Chappel, who would remain in command until 30 May 1941 when HQ Creforce ceased to function. [1]

After Crete 14th Infantry Brigade would move to India, where it was redesignated 14th Air Landing Brigade and saw service in Burma. In Crete the brigade initially consisted of:

2nd Battalion York & Lancaster Regiment (2Y&L)
2nd Battalion Black Watch (2BW)
15th Coast Artillery, RA
52nd LAA Regiment, RA
42nd Field Company, RE
a Royal Signals Section
189th Field Ambulance (enlarged to function as a 50-bed hospital)

The two regular infantry battalions guarded the fine harbour and naval refuelling depot at Suda Bay – the 2Y&L responsible for the main approaches, while 2BW guarded the nearby town of Canea, until moving to Heraklion in spring 1941. Prime Minister Winston Churchill saw Suda Bay as another 'Scapa Flow', so was most anxious to make it into a heavily defended naval base. The forces available, in particular the air cover, were rather too thin for this, although they were perfectly adequate to deal with any threat posed by the Italians.

Creforce co-operated with the local Cretan forces on the island. The resident 5th (Cretan) Division was some 7,000 men strong, and there were as many again reservists and 1,000 paramilitary policemen. These local forces would have been of considerable value to the defence of the island, but most were taken away to fight on the mainland, transferring to the Epirus front in November 1940. There they fought bravely in the bitter winter. Also on the island were some 15,000 Italian POWs, situated in camps near Canea. They were starving and their uniforms were in tatters. They did not require much guarding, because of the belligerent attitude towards them of the local population – one can guess that they were probably safer inside the barbed wire.

One of the first British arrivals was Rex Hey, a motor vehicle mechanic in the RAOC [2] who now lives in Randburg, South Africa. Rex was a member of the Light Aid Detachment (LAD), attached to the 52nd LAA Regiment, RA [3] recruited mainly from the Burnley, Nelson and Colne area of Lancashire.

'I'm starting this story from our camp in Egypt, where we were being prepared to move into the desert – "Up the Blue" in the Army slang of the day. We had been waiting for some time for our vehicles which had just arrived along with crates of equipment ... The crates had been unpacked and the Bofors Light AA guns had been thoroughly degreased, oiled and reassembled. We reached the point when we were ready to move apparently to support the desert army and then suddenly, to our

astonishment, we received instructions to recrate all the spares and equipment, strip all the guns and regrease them as we would be going on a sea voyage!

'We had no indication at all of our destination – which was not unusual – and could only think that it would be the Far East, but we were completely wrong, of course. We were told we would be informed of our destination when we were aboard ship ... Following the usual delays of loading and eventually embarking, we left the dockside, moved out of the harbour and into the open sea. Our destination was still the subject of much rumour and conjecture, but as promised, once we were on our way, Col Mather, CO of the 52nd LAA, came on the ship's tannoy and announced that we were going to the island of Crete in the Aegean Sea. I don't think any of us had ever heard of Crete before or indeed of the Aegean Sea. We were then told that it would not be a long voyage and it was our task to take over the island. We were also advised that there was quite a possibility that the Italians might have beaten us to it and that in that case we would have to fight our way ashore! This news did little to lighten our spirits as neither the LAA nor the Ordnance Corps were trained as infantry, so not unnaturally there was considerable apprehension throughout the ship ... As we left the land behind, we joined a convoy of merchant ships with a Royal Navy escort. It was tremendously encouraging to be in the middle of dozens of our ships stretching as far as one could see, only days after Mussolini had proclaimed that the Mediterranean was an Italian lake in which the enemy would not dare to sail. I clearly remember that the only worries we had were a submarine warning and the sight of Italian planes at a great height, but neither caused any problems.

'After some otherwise uneventful hours we caught the first sight of our destination, the White Mountains of Crete. We approached what turned out to be Suda Bay with some misgivings after the colonel's warning, as we were neither trained nor equipped for any sort of armed landing. However, we *sailed serenely into the huge natural bay of Suda, and eventually to a small dock area – I think there were two piers for unloading. It was like arriving at the Isle of Man. There could never have been a more peaceful landing. The weather was spring-like, with a gorgeous blue sea and a cloudless sky. It was our first experience of Crete, and the smell of the wild thyme and other herbs pervaded the whole island – I can smell it as I write. We docked without any problem and worked solidly for the whole day (and following days) to unload as much equipment as we could. It really was all hands to the pumps. Then, in the evening, we moved away from the dock area. It didn't take long to realise that the island was undeveloped, one could say primitive. There was no preparation for our arrival, so things were rather chaotic to say the least. We had been warned of the possibility of air attacks, but to our relief they didn't happen. Eventually we moved to the headland above Suda Bay to what I believe was an old, abandoned prison, where we had to settle down as best we could for the night. My first brush with Lt Newman occurred as we arrived at the prison. Apparently the CO's staff car (a Humber Snipe) would not start when it was unloaded and was stuck at the docks. Lt Newman, as head of the RAOC on the island, was in a bit of a panic about this and asked me to accompany him to the docks. When we had examined the vehicle he said, "Well, Hey, what do you think is the problem?"*

"I think it is an electrical problem and I'm not an electrician," I replied.

"Don't split hairs," he retorted, "you are an MV fitter Class 1, so do something about it!" I checked it over again and said hopefully, "I think it's a bad battery connection … If we clean the terminals and pack them with a bit of tin I feel it will be OK."

"Ridiculous!" he said. I looked at him and asked him if he wanted me to do as I suggested. "Get on with it, Hey," he said brusquely.

'I had had similar problems with the taxis and coaches working with my father. When Lt Newman heard it start he

came back very impressed with my diagnosis. "Good show, Hey!"
he said and from then on I was his favourite mechanic and he
took me on all inspections of the battery vehicles. Apparently he
was an electrical engineer and was clueless where vehicles were
concerned. On the inspections I would walk around the vehicle
checking all the greasing points (which he was very keen on) and
on one occasion, with some pleasure he said, "Hey, you've missed
an important one here." I looked at it and said, "Sir, that is not
a grease point, it is the dust cap off the compressor."
 "Oh," he said, and walked away!'

The LAD personnel stayed for a couple of nights at the prison
while they unloaded their equipment and looked for more
suitable accommodation in and around Canea. Eventually they
found an abandoned builder's yard with a small office attached.
It was cramped for the workshop section which now had a
complement of some 30 men, but they had to make do. While
there, they experienced their first air raid:

'. . . *not very pleasant, but we had become fairly experienced*
after France and this was quite a small raid, which caused
little damage, but nonetheless one of the Signal Corps lost a
foot. Fortunately he was the only casualty and was sent back to
Egypt on the next ship out ... the end of his war I imagine.
 'We managed to organise ourselves fairly well in these
premises after minor alterations. There was an amusing
incident here in our early days. The single toilet was the
continental type with a hole in the floor and places on each side
for one's feet. Everyone complained about this and it was
agreed that something should be improvised. The job was
given to my friend Eric Lacey, and although not by any means
a handyman (or a soldier!) Eric was certainly a man of ideas.
He built a wooden box and placed it over the hole in the floor.
On top of the box was a seat, but it had a square hole, which
was easier for Eric to make. This looked OK, but it was

rapidly found that it was most uncomfortable to sit on as the edges of the square hole were rather sharp (plus the possibility of splinters). So Eric duly rounded off the edges and it was fairly satisfactory, except it was now discovered that the hole in the seat did not line up with the hole in the floor, which meant there was a build-up of you-know-what in the concrete basin below. As this one toilet was to serve thirty men, correcting this was a matter of some urgency. Eric was asked to do something about it. Ingenious as ever, he obtained an empty petrol can, cut a piece of tin out of it, and made a deflector which fitted at an angle on the underside of the seat. This worked extremely well except that if you were near the lavatory when it was in use, you could clearly hear the first – can I say it? – turd hit the tin deflector as it bounced into the hole in the floor! I wonder if it is still there – who knows?

'On a more serious note, one of the mechanics and I had been working on a Bren carrier engine in the confined space of the small garage. We had kept the doors closed with the engine running as we tuned it, and the next thing we remembered was lying outside the garage on the ground, while attempts were made to bring us round. I have been extremely careful with carbon monoxide fumes ever since, but if one ever wanted to depart this mortal coil it would be a wonderfully easy way to go. The day after this incident I had to take the carrier out on test, and decided to go through the small town of Canea. I am sure that not many people who read this story will have driven a Bren carrier – neither had I up to this point. For your information, the steering is controlled by two levers protruding from the floor, one for right turns and one for left. The steering relies on judicious use of these levers which, in fact, apply the brakes on either side, thus forcing the vehicle into the desired direction. Unfortunately for me it was market day in Canea, which narrowed the already narrow streets and I had never driven a carrier before. I soon discovered it was the easiest thing in the world to "oversteer", and unless great care

was taken it would turn almost at right angles. Inevitably in my inexperience I did exactly this and took a couple of fruit stalls with me. There was much screaming and shouting by the stall owners, which I didn't understand, but there was no doubt about their feelings! They were duly compensated.

'Canea was delightful, completely unspoilt by any form of commercialism, especially the little, almost biblical, fishing port. Primitive to a degree, it was not difficult to imagine one had been whisked back to Bible days. The little harbour cafes or tavernas were a new experience. As with everything else, they were quite primitive but so welcoming. Always on the table were plates of mandarin oranges and sliced tomatoes. The food was quite basic but good and extremely cheap – at first. The owners rapidly realised we had money to spend. When we first arrived it was possible to buy around 20 oranges for the equivalent of a shilling, but very quickly we would be lucky to obtain half a dozen for the same price. The cost of food also rocketed. The booze, generally Greek, was potent and good, particularly the spirits, which we rapidly learned to treat with some caution. Ouzo was lethal if one overdid it, but as I'm not one to over-imbibe, I had no problems. One evening at one of the harbour cafes I spotted rice pudding on the menu. A particular favourite of mine, I ordered it without question – at the first spoonful I thought I would be ill. It was rice pudding alright, but made with olive oil! Most of the cooking was done with olive oil and the pastries were superb – chips were always cooked in it and never the slightest flavour. Olive oil in my mind took me back to the days of my childhood when it was forced down one's throat for various illnesses. Of course we quickly discovered that olives were the main source of revenue for the island.

'There had been no apparent preparations for our arrival and the equipment was moved to any available location until we got organised … 52nd LAA Regiment had three batteries, but one did not come with us to Crete and from what we heard

followed the original plan and joined the desert force. We had been warned about air raids, but had no serious problems whilst unloading … The officers were obviously investigating various positions for siting the guns, but I knew next to nothing about these plans – my world was the workshop and from my point of view I should have been involved just in the servicing and maintenance of the vehicles. However, I should have known better as I had already been involved with the maintenance and indeed with minor modifications to the Bofors guns in France.

'From our point of view the first priority had been locating premises from which we were able to work, but we soon found there was an even greater priority than this – the island had no fortifications at all, either from sea or air attack. The only defence from the air raids was any warship that happened to be in Suda Bay. There were many famous ships, with what appeared to us in those early days as a frightening level of armament. They seemed indestructible. Their presence was a double-edged weapon as the very fact they were there drew air attacks. I can still see those majestic ships – the Barham, *the* Warspite, *the* York *(more about the* York *later), the* Exeter, *the* Ajax, *the* Gloucester *and the* Kelly, *and frequent visits from various aircraft carriers. In our ignorance we felt pretty secure with these wonderful ships around us, but their visits were short and we obviously desperately needed some protection from enemy aircraft.*

'One day we were virtually conscripted for a special job along with some of the Gunners. We were transported across the bay to a chosen spot where we met a rather fearsome-looking naval commander, complete with luxurious beard (very much like the sailor on the old Capstan cigarette tin). We were immediately left in no doubt who was going to be in charge; he certainly exuded authority. In brisk, no nonsense terms, he told us what we were there for: we were to build a jetty so that goods and equipment could be ferried across the bay instead of

taking the long and time-consuming journey around the bay by road. Crete is a volcanic island and we had to build the jetty from the indigenous rocks, of which there certainly was an ample supply. The problem was that we had to break up suitable large lumps from the area surrounding us – we had wondered what the pickaxes were for and now we knew! For several days this work continued. We worked up to our waists in the water positioning the rock under our friend's direction. It was hard work, but strangely satisfying as we watched the jetty taking shape. There was no complaint about the commander's authority, he got "stuck in" with the rest of us and in no time commanded our respect. The jetty was quite impressive when finished and certainly served its purpose in the weeks and months that followed.

'We had begun to get visits from the Luftwaffe as our preparations had obviously been spotted from the air, but the job had continued with occasional frantic rushes for cover. There were other frightening occasions when an air raid started during the boat crossing from Suda. In the middle of the bay in a small boat it always felt that you were the target. In actual fact the targets were almost always the docks or the ships anchored in the bay, or our "jetty", but whichever way one looked at it, we were in the middle with no assurance we would not be the next target. I have often heard people say that they got used to air raids; well, I never did.

'We were advised, no instructed, that we would be installing the guns on the opposite side of the bay. I made a half-hearted protest that I had no experience at all of gun fittings as I was strictly a motor vehicle fitter, but that didn't wash and the Ordnance section as a whole was involved in this vital work. And vital work it certainly was. I will make no bones about it, I dreaded those trips across the bay as it was more than obvious the Luftwaffe was not going to stand idly by as we prepared the gun sites. Installing the guns was a most hazardous business. First of all, of course, the proposed gun sites had to be levelled and this meant a lot of pick and shovel work. Nobody was free from this really hard manual labour. One blessing was that the weather was perfect and we soon acquired a beautiful all-over tan. We created large concrete bases into which were embedded "rag bolts" with their heads deep in the cement and the thread standing out, positioned ready for the gun base to be lowered onto; large nuts would hold the bases securely in position. By this time the Stukas had found us. We had experienced them in France, but that didn't make them any more pleasant. They would arrive with a fighter escort of Bf109s to protect them – completely unnecessary as there were none of our fighters in evidence – circle around the chosen target and then one of them would peel off and go into his dive. One by one the others would follow, with their "Banshee" screaming. [4]

'The Stukas were specialised dive-bombers, the actual aiming being done by diving directly at their target, releasing their bombs at the chosen height, so close sometimes to the target that it seemed impossible for them to recover from the dive. The courage of the pilots was unbelievable. If there were warships in the bay, as there generally were, the intensity of the fire from their anti-aircraft guns was incredible. The sky seemed to be a solid mass of shell bursts through which the Stukas made their dive. It seemed absolutely impossible that they could survive, but I never actually saw one shot down. Following their dive, they would leave the action, flatten out and skim along the water below the bursting shells. They did an awful amount of damage, and the frustrating thing was that they would have been sitting ducks against fighter aircraft as they had neither the speed or manoeuvrability for aerial combat. At that time all we seemed to have was a couple of old Gloucester Gladiators, a couple of Fairey Fulmars and a Swordfish. If the Swordfish was in the air when the attack took place, it immediately and frantically came down. All the British aircraft were virtually obsolete and hadn't the slightest

*hope of surviving against the far superior planes of the
Luftwaffe. So the Germans had it all their own way, except
for the intense fire from the warships which, incredible as it
seemed, had little effect. They had the gun emplacements pin-
pointed, but the main targets for the moment were ships
unloading or in the harbour.'*

The hazardous undertaking of emplacing the guns in their
positions was then undertaken; in some cases the concrete
hadn't been given long enough to set and once the nuts were
tightened the bolts began to pull out, leading to pandemonium!
Rex explains that if this happened the installation had to be
halted until the concrete had set, and then started again; they
were constantly under attack from the dive-bombers, although
he cannot remember any casualties to the crews, but as he puts
it: 'diarrhoea reached endemic proportions!'

Another first arrival was Hoddy Buswell, a sapper in 42nd
Field Company, RE, who had arrived at Suda Bay on the
evening of 5 November 1940 and then landed the next
morning and moved to the nearby village of Tsikalaria. He told
me that the unit tasks had been,

*'. . . building workshops, storage huts, water supply, pits for
petrol storage, additional accommodation – eg a hospital, a
light railway, repairing roads, strengthening bridges and
improving Maleme airfield. Then another section took on
similar work at Heraklion, also defensive installations as
required. Built "42nd Street" which was a low lying road to
our headquarters through the olive groves – it's still there
today, only now it has a tarmac surface. The only way to the
Akrotiri peninsula was via Canea, so we punched a road off
the Suda-Canea road to Akrotiri and called it "Rhodesia
Way" after Lt Lowenson, our section lieutenant ... It wasn't
long before we were visited by the "screaming Stukas" and
they concentrated on the Suda Bay area where we were*

working. It became a regular pattern, early morning and late afternoon, we became so accustomed to the raids that we even complained if they were late!'

Edward Telling was a member of the 15th Coast Artillery Regiment, and like Rex Hey he was a fitter. His first task on landing at Suda Bay was to help in the installation of some 4in guns. He also was billeted at the old prison, which he describes as not having cells, but rather 'sort of long dormitories and, apart from the fact that they had no windows, quite reasonable'. The guns had to be manhandled into position as there were no cranes or specialised equipment. In a tape he recorded for the Imperial War Museum he talks about this:

'. . . *literally man-handling because we had no equipment.*

I mean we had no cranes, so it was all done by man-handling. We had an extremely good master gunner who was in charge who was called Master Gunner Juniper. He really knew all about it and taught us how to handle heavy objects, use gins [a three-legged ad hoc crane with a pulley at the top], slings and what have you. We worked under his supervision.' [5]

Edward Telling had this to say about the Cretans: 'They were marvellous people. From the time we got there they helped us ... they are absolutely marvellous people. They helped us throughout the 10 days of the battle and what they did was nobody's business. I never came across any hostility towards us at all.'

The following quotation is taken from an article in the December 1996 edition of The Red Hackle. It was taken from the memoirs of the late Maj Richard Fleming, who, in 1939 at the age of 25, had taken over command of D Company 2BW. They moved to Palestine, then to British Somaliland in the summer of 1940, and then on to Egypt in late August 1940. Now they were on their way again.

'We were embarked at Port Said in late November on HMS York for where we knew not. But once away we knew it was to be the island of Crete.

'Whilst proceeding along the north coast of the island, Keith Dick-Cunningham – another superb character – and I were very hospitably shown the ship's Holy of Holies, ie the bridge. However, very shortly after our arrival up there, we were politely requested to descend therefrom, as Italian aeroplanes had been spotted coming at the ship from three different directions. Descend we did quite rapidly, as the ship started to dance about from one direction to another. The planes were firing torpedoes. Keith and I looked over the side and literally saw a monster cruising alongside, missing us by not more than 15 yards. Hats off to our Captain, whose skilful navigation had avoided all three attacks.

'Disembarking at Suda Bay, which even as early as then had had quite a few air attacks, the battalion was billeted in schools and the like, west of the town. My D Company was well housed and everything was fun. Archie Wilder was my second in command and we shared a cottage, being looked after by a dear landlady.

'Nothing much was done at that stage, but we did do quite a lot of digging defensive positions against possible attack from the sea. The Cretans were so pleased to have us among them and were hospitable almost to a fault. I do remember one couple who had invited me into their cottage saying, "This is the greatest privilege of our lives, to be able to entertain a real British officer in our home."

'One morning, after what I expect was a fairly heavy drinking night, I was feeling somewhat ill and asked Archie Wilder how he was feeling. He took one look and got me off to see our quack, Gibson, who straight away diagnosed jaundice and arranged for me to go to the one and only hospital, which was situated at the Villa Ariadne, Knossos, near Heraklion away to the east of the island. I was laid off work for perhaps three weeks and during that period the battalion moved away from Canea and Suda Bay to be placed as a guard for the Heraklion airfield.'

Basil Keeble of Ipswich was a member of 189th Field Ambulance, RAMC and well remembers the Villa Ariadne:

> '*We had to deploy and reinforce our own units as attacks were expected on all major areas of military concentration. Heraklion was one area which needed reinforcing, so a small unit of our 189 Field Ambulance was despatched to the area to man a CRS.6 I myself and this small unit from Khalepa near Canea, moved to the Heraklion area and following several moves which included a cave by the airport and a large warehouse in the harbour area, further large houses were considered but these positions were all too vulnerable to attack, so we travelled inland to Knossos, south of Heraklion, to occupy a large villa (Ariadne) within the palace of Knossos, an area which Sir Arthur Evans the archaeologist had excavated and the villa was where he lived. Here we settled to establish the CRS and to make it suitable for the reception of casualties.*'

14th Infantry Brigade

Wavell himself visited Crete on 13 November and apparently considered the garrison was sufficient with just the Italians to worry about. At that time there were the two battalions of 14th Infantry Brigade, together with some eight heavy and 12 light AA batteries. In fact, there was quite a strong school of thought that the garrison on Crete was something of a waste of time and that every soldier or weapon sent there was one less available for use elsewhere in the Middle East. However, when the Greek forces on the island were reduced to under 1,000 (and not all had rifles), the brigade was brought up to full strength by the arrival of a third infantry battalion – 1st Battalion The Welch Regiment (1Welch). The army garrison would remain at this level until the arrival of the troops evacuated from Greece. On the naval side, however, there was a major development with the arrival of the Royal Marines' Mobile Naval Base Defence Organisation (MNBDO) in April

1941. However, even before the end of November it had become very clear that the entire island would have to be defended and not just Suda Bay and the limited area around it and to the west. Therefore, the garrison would have to be split – hence the dispatch of the Black Watch to Heraklion as Maj Richard Fleming has already mentioned.

MNBDO No 1

This excellent organisation was commanded by Maj-Gen E. C. Weston, Royal Marines, who was the very first officer to actually carry out a comprehensive military survey of the island, which he undertook in early April. His report, which he produced on 15 April, over a week after the German invasion of Greece, accepted the fact that the Germans would attempt to capture the island, but that their attack would probably come by sea, although it would be covered by heavy air bombing and strafing and, possibly, some parachutists might be used. He estimated that the enemy forces would probably be a lightly equipped brigade of some 3,000 plus, but that they might assault both ends of the island, so as well as the strong infantry brigade group required to defend the Suda-Maleme area, another similar force was needed for Heraklion. This latter brigade group could be Greek forces, if they were available. He also recommended additional AA protection.

While much of his appreciation was sound, it is perhaps a pity that he made such a low estimate of the size of the potential enemy invasion force and, even more importantly, anticipated that it would mainly be a seaborne invasion. This is understandable, as very few British officers had any experience of an airborne invasion whatsoever and could not have imagined the daring German plan to invade mainly from the air, let alone know how to deploy their forces properly against such an eventuality. The need to guard against the threat of a seaborne invasion would dog all subsequent planning, command and control – even during the battle. Thus it would seriously dictate the deployment of troops from then on, and may have been a major reason for the apparent inaction of Maj-Gen Freyberg, the final commander of Crete, when the invasion started.

The MNBDO had arrived in the Middle East at the beginning of the year, and was designed to provide coastal, ground and AA protection for temporary harbours/ports which the Royal Navy wished to use. In addition, it also contained a landing and base maintenance group which was able to improve docking facilities and provide logistics for a naval base. It was, therefore, ideal for the improvement of Suda Bay, which Adm Cunningham wished to use as a secure forward base in order to ease some of the strain on his ships which had to operate over a considerable distance away from their main base at Alexandria. 'It was 420 sea miles by the shortest route from Alexandria and nearer 500 by the west-about route. German-held Piraeus, almost due north of Maleme and Suda, was only 170 sea miles away from Crete.' [7]

At full strength an MNBDO contained about 8,000 men including engineers and mechanics, transport and crane drivers, armourers and gunners, surveyors and draughtsmen, bricklayers, masons, carpenters, plumbers, painters, decorators and camouflage modellers, miners, blacksmiths, tinsmiths and even divers. However, MNBDO 1 was not complete as only the advanced groups arrived before the German invasion began. These were the Landing and Maintenance Group, the Transport Company, the Signals Company, the Searchlight Regiment and one of the AA regiments – some 2,200 men in all.

Lt-Col Bill Laxton MC, now of Richmond, British Columbia, was second-in-command of the Signals Company of MNBDO 1, and landed in Suda Bay on the morning of 9 May 1941. He was still busy 'setting up shop' some 11 days later when the German assault began. More later about this gallant officer, who was severely wounded in action in the Galatas area, while clearing the enemy from an AA battery which had been overrun. One of his men was Horace Baber, RM. He had joined the Royal Marines in February 1938, aged just 17. After training he served on the battleship HMS *Royal Oak* and was lucky to be picked up by a patrol boat when she was sunk with the loss of some 850 of the crew. He writes:

'I was burnt in the explosions, but managed to reach the upper deck. I dived off the bottom as she was going over, was picked up by a patrol boat and transferred to Invergordon Naval Hospital for medical treatment. Early in 1940 I did a course at Portsmouth as a Royal Marine signaller and was sent to Dover for the Battle of Britain. The situation eased at the end of 1940, and in early 1941 I embarked for the Middle East via South Africa. In early March, we were embarked for Crete, enduring a torpedo attack by Italian bombers on the way – a portent of things to come! We landed at Suda Bay docks and were quickly dispersed into the olive groves for fear of enemy air attacks. Our uniforms were still as for peacetime – tropical tunics with brass buttons which were to be kept "highly polished!" Our marine force was about 2,000 strong and the first thing that happened was a kit inspection, for which the brasses on our equipment had to be highly polished. We were attacked by German aircraft who must have seen the glint of brass from above. After that incident all brasses had to be left dull.*

'The day of dispersal came and we were sent as a signal detachment to the Akrotiri peninsula. We took over a villa as our headquarters, overlooking Suda Bay and the docks. Our main job was to provide telephone lines to the AA and coastal artillery gun positions ... Our marine organisation was called the Mobile Naval Base Defence Organisation No 1 and our main job was to land from ships to form advanced naval bases. We were a self-contained force consisting of marine battalions as infantry, gunners and all sorts of specialists as required. This also included naval personnel. In dire straights we reverted to our role as basic infantry (and this included having to unload ships at the docks as well as our signalling duties).'

Thin on the ground

No RAF squadrons were permanently based on the island until April 1941, so the RAF was in a parlous state on Crete, even before the final withdrawal from Greece. The only aircraft they could eventually muster were 12 Bristol Blenheim bombers, 12 Gloster Gladiators and six Hurricanes, together with a further six obsolescent Fleet Air Arm aircraft. This meagre force had to operate out of two partly finished aerodromes at Maleme (an existing Fleet Air Arm airfield) and Heraklion and a landing ground at Rethymnon, while work was supposedly in progress at Pedalia, Kastelli, Messara Plain and Kassamos Kasatelli. The only problem was that there was just one engineering officer who was hampered by a lack of building materials, tools and transport. In addition, once Rommel had cleared the British out of Cyrenaica, no longer could they expect fighter cover from Derna. It had to come from the old Western Desert fields over 300 miles away, as compared with the Germans whose newly captured airfields on mainland Greece were less than 120 miles away. There was very little of anything available for this 'rear area' despite the fact that it would become of prime importance once Greece had fallen.

On 17 April, ACM Sir Arthur Longmore, the AOC-in-C, appointed Gp Capt G. R. Beamish as Senior Air Officer Crete. Before then the highest ranking airman on the island had been a flight lieutenant. Sqn Ldr (later Wg Cdr, OBE, DFC) Edward Howell was typical of the handful of pilots on Crete before the invasion. He arrived in early May, having taken over command of No 33 Squadron (Hurricanes) a few days previously. An experienced Spitfire pilot, he had never flown a Hurricane before, and didn't want any of his new squadron to know. He had to learn the hard way, and faster than he had hoped, because just a day or so after his arrival he had to 'scramble' with the other Hurricanes as he graphically explains in this extract from his book *Escape to Live*:

'I opened the throttle and saw a string of five Messerschmitts coming in over the hill firing at me. It seemed an age before my wheels came off the strip. I went straight into a turn towards the approaching 109s, my wing tip within inches of the ground. The faithful old "Hurrybus" took it without a murmur, the enemy flashed past and I went over instinctively into a steep turn the other way.'

Howell was, for the moment, concentrating on practical things – such as getting the undercarriage up, closing the hood, switching on the gunsight and the firing button, but then:

'. . . enemy aircraft kept diving at me in threes and fives. They were travelling fast and did not stay to fight. They just had a squirt at me and climbed away out of range again. It kept me fully occupied with evasive action. Out of the corner of my eye I saw two aircraft diving earthwards in flames. One was a Hurricane. There was no sign of the other. I was alone in a sky-full of Jerries ... Just level with me and about a mile away, two 109s were turning in wide line-astern formation. I headed in their direction ... I drew in closer and closer with an eye on my own tail to make sure that I was not jumped. I restrained myself with difficulty. It is only the novice who opens up at long range. My own teaching! I went right in on the tail of the second 109 until I was in close formation with him. I was slightly below him and his slipstream was just above me. I could have lifted my nose and touched his tail with my prop. I dropped a little and pulled up, with my sight on his radiator. I pressed the firing switch and the Hurricane shook and shuddered as 10,000 rounds a minute poured from the guns into him. Bits broke away and a white trail burst from his radiator as the coolant came pouring out. He turned slowly to the right in a gentle dive.'

Edward Howell then made the mistake of following the stricken enemy aircraft down to confirm it as a kill, until he suddenly realised that the other Messerschmitt was on his tail! 'I realised my mistake and pulled quickly up into a turn to port. I flick-rolled over into a steep turn the other way and found myself coming in from the enemy's quarter. I opened up to full throttle and gave him a burst. He dived away to port and I followed, this time with an eye open behind me.' The dogfight continued until eventually Howell ran out of ammunition and the enemy aircraft headed for home, 'certainly full of holes'.

Howell tried to land at Maleme, but the Bofors guns were putting up too much flak, so he turned east and went to Rethymnon, refuelled and rearmed, then returned to his home base. 'A crowd gathered round me as I taxied in to the refuelling pens. Everyone had assumed that I had been shot down. They had seen my 109 come down and they were delighted that I had opened my score. We had accounted for six Bf109s and had lost the other two Hurricanes shot down in flames.' They had also one more Hurricane destroyed on the ground – a mass of charred wreckage – the Fleet Air Arm had lost all their Fulmars, destroyed on the ground, as well as two of their Gladiators. As Howell rightly puts it, 'The prelude to invasion had entered upon its last phase.'

The torpedoing of HMS *York*

Earlier on, some weeks before this air action, on the night of 25/26 March 1941, the Italians had launched a daring raid on Suda Bay, using explosive speedboats – *Motoscafo Turismo* (MT), which had been invented in World War 1, and consisted of small speedboats packed with explosives with a single crewman steering from the aft. On approaching the target, the steersman would set the controls and then escape on a small liferaft, leaving the boat to crash into its target. The unit which operated these weapons was known as 'X MAS', their distinctive shoulder patch being a skull clutching a rose in its teeth! On that night the torpedo boats *Crispi* and *Sella* carried six MTs close to the entrance to Suda Bay. Having successfully negotiated the harbour entrance, they attacked the British ships there. These included the heavy cruiser HMS *York*, which was hit twice, and the tanker *Pericles*, which was hit once and sank. The *York* was badly damaged, her boilers and engine room flooded, with no power available to her main guns. Beached, she would be used as an AA platform while her crew was employed ashore. All six of the Italian steersmen survived, were taken prisoner and were later awarded the *Medalgia d'Oro*.

One of the crew of HMS *York* was Chris Buist of Bury St Edmunds, then an RM gunner. He told me:

> *'I was the watch of duty below decks in the early hours of 26 March 1941, when there was a terrific bang and a sheet of flame shot right through our mess deck and the ship lifted up in the air. Everything went black as we lost all power – no lights at all – just total darkness. When daylight came, we saw that the stern of the vessel was underwater from the catapult to the quarterdeck and we lost all our stores of food. The officers' cabins were also flooded. The captain put off all the ship's company to live in tents ashore and afterwards we salvaged what we could from the ship. The 4in guns, for example, were taken ashore and mounted to use against enemy aircraft. At first the living conditions were pretty grim, as we had no food or water until we could arrange for rations from the Army. We also lost some of our uniforms and equipment.'*

The evacuation from Greece

While the garrison on Crete had been busy with its own affairs, the war in Greece had escalated to alarming proportions. Once again, the Allies were losing. Field Marshal List's Twelfth Army had attacked the Metaxas Lines on 6 April. By the 23rd, after heavy fighting, the Greeks had been forced to surrender. The British and Commonwealth troops, who had been hastily sent there from North Africa, were compelled to withdraw and attempt to escape. Outflanked and outnumbered, they fought their way back to the southern ports and eventually managed to evacuate four-fifths of their force, although this meant leaving some 11,840 behind together with masses of weapons, vehicles and equipment. Of those evacuated some 18,850 were taken to Crete (5,299 from the UK, 6,451 Australians and 7,100 New Zealanders). Their arrival would considerably strengthen the garrison numerically, although they brought few weapons other than their personal arms – and not all even had these.

Although it is not entirely relevant to our story, the experiences of these troops as they withdrew through Greece serve as quite a good lead-in to the battles that would follow on Crete. Our source is James McNally, a member of 64th Medium Regiment, RA, which was equipped with a mixture of 4.5in guns and 6in howitzers. They had been sent over from Egypt to Greece and *en route* the ship carrying the vehicles developed a fire in the bunkers. The captain was quite put out when he was told that the vehicles were carrying all the first line ammunition! The drivers had to spend the rest of the voyage shovelling coal, but they reached Piraeus safely. After a day outside Athens, when all the vehicles were repainted to match the Greek scenery, they started moving up Greece. He writes:

'On arrival at Kozani on the fourth day, 234th Battery less C Troop was detached and put under command of Col Panagopoulos, CRA of the Greek Force covering the road to Veroia and Salonika. The remainder of the regiment continued further north to positions near Edessa. The Greeks were most helpful with guides, ponies, mules, etc, and in introducing us to Ouzo – dangerous stuff in more than a small quantity – and Rosina – wine treated with resin, an acquired taste. Here we remained until a few days after the Germans invaded Greece. Then the Greeks blew the road and *disappeared. We were now covering the Florina Gap, and had inflicted numerous casualties on the Germans, but were soon ordered back behind the River Aliakmon. We then moved on to Domodossola and then back by way of Thermopylae and the coast of Kiffissokouri. One troop, supporting 2nd New Zealand Division, remained in action at Thermopylae as long as it could before destroying the guns.*

'*Driving a Matador* [8] *with a 6in howitzer in tow down through the passes was very hairy – they had been bombed, so there were boulders and rubble blocking the way. One false move, losing control, hitting a boulder and we were over the side – hundreds of feet drop. We got to the bottom of one pass and veered to the right. I wasn't too happy, intuition perhaps telling me we were going the wrong way. I pulled into a farm to turn around and the family came out screaming and shouting. We didn't understand them but we knew they didn't want a 6in gun there. I backed in, then pulled out, heading back the way we had come.*

'*The bombing was terrible, especially the dive-bombing. Eventually, we were ordered to destroy the guns and vehicles, just saving some of the lighter ones to carry personnel back to Athens. We let the oil and water out, left the engines running with a weight on the accelerator pedal, slit the tyres and did as much damage as possible. We destroyed the gunsights and blew the guns up. We left with just a side pack, shaving gear and rifle (in an artillery unit only drivers were issued with rifles). It was a long trek back without food or water, continually bombed and strafed, taking cover anywhere. The beautiful villages we had passed through on the way up were now razed to the ground and the people gone. The CO, Lt-Col Syer, was killed in a bombing raid during a detour around a town and Maj Hunt took command. Eventually we had to abandon our vehicles as we ran out of petrol, so we carried on trudging towards Piraeus. Here there was complete devastation, ships on fire, others sunk. We found some tinned food –*

*Maconochie's Stew – I thoroughly enjoyed it! More waiting,
then a ship moved in – all aboard and away!'*

Another member of the 64th was John C. 'Syd' Croft. He
suffered badly from the chronic skin disease psoriasis and,
while in Greece, it took a turn for the worse as he recalls:

*'Nothing serious, but my ointment had run out and I needed
a new jar to ease the terrible irritation. The rest of the
regiment, together with the RAP and the regimental doctor
at RHQ, were in the Vevi area to the west of Lake Petersko
waiting for the Germans to advance through the Monastir
Gap. Because RHQ was difficult to reach along the narrow
mountain roads, my troop commander decided to send me
down the valley road in a 15cwt truck to a very small hospital
in the nearby village of Kozani. This hospital was no bigger
than a small British village hall and was crowded with beds
filled with wounded Greek soldiers and civilians. Although I
was only a lowly lance-bombardier, the Greek Army doctor
and his orderlies decided at once to treat me as an honourable
and welcome guest and patient, insisting I stayed in the
hospital for a couple of nights. I was allocated the one and only
single room. Meanwhile, the troop truck had to return, the
driver promising to pick me up in a couple of days.*

*'But within those two days the Germans had struck. The
troop moved into the Florina valley (as I discovered much later
on) and was unable to collect me. Within hours the Stukas had
dive-bombed Kozani because it was an important crossroads
and also lay across the main Allied supply route. Before I
realised what had hit us, I was helping with the civilian
casualties now pouring into the hospital. As the battle
progressed and the Germans got nearer, the Greeks decided to
evacuate the walking wounded Greek soldiers and myself to
Larissa. We were put on an old motor coach and then began a
most hair-raising experience as the driver sped through the*

*mountains at a reckless speed. If anyone spotted an enemy
aircraft, the driver would try to stop on a suitable bend, taking
shelter as close as he could to the cliffside.*

'*We arrived safely at Larissa, where I found a British LAA
unit with a Bofors gun. The OC happened to be an old school
friend of mine, and he gave me a really nourishing hot meal and
a most welcome cup of tea. He said he couldn't accommodate me
nor had he any jobs or vacancies in his unit, and so he arranged
to put me on the night train from Larissa to Athens. When I
arrived, I contacted the Station RTO who then arranged for me
to go to a British Army hospital in the city. I was only there a
few days but while there received coal tar baths, ointment and
sun lamp treatment for my skin problems. It was almost as
though there was no war on at all – except for the daily air raids
on Athens airport. We could clearly see these across the city from
the upper windows of the hospital.*'

Then one day, John Croft and the other patients were put on a
train and taken as far as Megara, where they left the train as it
was about to be bombed. After deciding to go to Corinth to try
to catch a boat, they met other soldiers hurrying back from
there who explained that German parachutists had landed, so
they decided to return to Athens. He was now with a group of
four or five others all looking for some way of escape.
Fortunately, they met up with some New Zealanders who gave
them a lift back to Athens in a carrier.

'*We passed through Athens around midnight. How the driver
found his way through the city I do not know. But I do
remember the brave Greek people lining the streets and
wishing us good luck. It was terrible. It was like leaving a
sinking ship with most of the passengers still on board. I heard
later that the Germans entered the city some six or seven hours
after we passed through.*'

Soon after leaving Athens the carrier ran out of fuel, but John was lucky enough to be given a lift by a passing Australian ambulance, but they were hit by the Luftwaffe and had to walk once again. Apart from the clothes he stood up in he had lost everything except for his gasmask case, in which he carried his few valuables, his folding Ensign camera and photographs, etc.

> *'It was already getting dark, but somehow or other we managed to reach a small port – Rafti – and we didn't have to wait long before we made out the shapes of Royal Navy destroyers creeping slowly into the harbour and moving alongside the jetty. I clambered up the net to the top where sailors grabbed me and dumped me down onto the deck of the ship. We were hustled through doors, down ladders into crowded mess decks where we were soon refreshed with a lovely hot cup of cocoa.*
>
> *'Everybody was very tired, and it was a case of putting our heads down on our arms on the mess tables and grabbing a little sleep. It seemed no time at all before we reached, in the dawn of yet another day, a harbour which I later discovered was Suda Bay on the island of Crete. The destroyer tied up after landing, and we were taken to a nearby reception camp where names, numbers and units were recorded before giving us a dish (in my case a tin) of stew consisting of M and V (meat and vegetables), army biscuits and a "tin" of hot tea. Most of us were without mess tins or mugs and salvaged empty M and V tins etc, which made good mess tins and mugs when one was hungry and thirsty. Later, we were told to go to a certain numbered tree in the olive grove and stay there until called. I was there for a day or two before I was eventually called and told my battery had been located.'*

John Croft rejoined 'D' Troop, 234 Medium Battery on 1 May 1941, after being parted from them for some 20 days.

More from John later, but now it is time to turn to the

Commonwealth forces from Australia and New Zealand, who made up such a large proportion of the troops sent to Greece (17,125 Australians and 16,720 New Zealanders as compared with 19,206 UK troops). One of these Commonwealth soldiers was Lt Edmund John McAra, who would sadly be killed in Crete in the battle for Hill 107 at Maleme, an action which will be described later. This extract from the letters which he sent home from Greece and Crete vividly describes what the Kiwis had to go through, and I am most grateful to his daughter-in-law, Mrs Jill McAra, for sending them to me. The first was written 'Somewhere in Greece' on 20 April 1941 (and begins with the comment that he has heard that all previous outward mail had been destroyed by the bombing):

'Dearest Heart,

I'm afraid the newspaper headlines the past few days must have worried you at times but, as you see, I've come through it all safe and well, the reputation of the mortars secure; and all still bright and shining old dear! Well, to go back to the beginning, we were just settling nicely into our roost on "Gibraltar", as we called our crag from its resemblance to its big brother. I can't, of course, go into details of the battalion's situation, but roughly you can imagine a long, steep sided ravine running up into a mountain. Across its foot passes a road, crossing the stream that brawled down the ravine, Gibraltar rose sheer between the opposing slopes, forming the only position from which guns could be brought to bear on the bridge and riverbed beyond. That to the left, up which wound the road, was held by B, with D in line behind them; only a few odd men were in reserve (the "de-horsed" carrier platoon and the pioneers).

'In front of us we could see for 1,000 yards down the river bed, which then swung left beyond the ridge held by B and out of sight. The wedge of dead ground into which the rifle companies could not fire, was the weakest point of our front, as

once the enemy penetrated the bridge they could work up the gullies either side of Gibraltar and take us in the rear. The hillsides were so steep, rocky and bush-covered that infiltration of that kind had every chance of success. Gibraltar itself had obviously been a natural stronghold from earliest times; ruins of houses and old fortifications were to be found all over it; hidden by masses of flowering trees, white and pink, for all the world like some Japanese cherry grove – a dream-like place in the warm sun, with butterflies, flowers and a soft wind; the great wall of snow-covered peaks in a half circle towering above us in the clear blue heavens.

'*Down in the gully was an exquisite stone bridge, rising to a single keystone, all so covered with moss that it seemed like a natural feature. The whole place breathed the past history of a great people – it wasn't Thermopylae, but you felt Thermopylae would have been just like that! If you can imagine the rock as a crouching lion, Smith's gun (mortar) pit would be at the mane, and Spenne's on the haunches; both dug in on the short rear slope that fell away almost sheer to the torrent far below. We carried in a ton and a half of bombs, a terrific task up the rear face, hoisting ourselves by ropes up a rock crevice; but to use one of the tracks along the front face would have been crazy.*

'*At one time McAra slipped and went skidding down, only missing going over by one of the others bracing himself in the way. We built a cookhouse on the rock ledge where I slept and soon made ourselves extremely comfortable. The day after all our work on the pits was completed, a sudden order came to get out that night, as the left flank, miles away, was giving. So, with curses we lowered all the ammo down the cliff again, and had just finished loading the first truck when the order was cancelled as some other units had gone in and restored the line. The men were worn out, so I decided to leave Smith's gun [mortar] on the rock and use the second team as a carrying party only. Next morning we were just on the point of settling down to breakfast (bully and biscuit hash) when all of a sudden the Vickers guns on C Coy's ridge opened up. We dropped everything and fairly flew into the gun pits, pulses hammering with excitement until the wicked stutter of the machine guns and the beat of the pulse were as one! They were firing at long range at some armoured cars, and no other sign of the approaching enemy was seen; but in an hour or two the first shells began to come over. Amid the soft green of the deciduous trees crowding the hillside behind us, balloons of blue smoke rose slowly through the leaves, followed an instant later by metallic clangs. Our own 25pdrs, hidden in the valleys, opened up in reply, the lay of the ground being such that all the shells fired by both sides fairly parted our hair as we lay behind the crest of the rock. The sound as of brazen wings beating their inevitable way overhead was uncanny in the sunny morning. All day long the firing continued, searching ridges and gullies, but the countryside below us spread silent and empty, full of the colours of spring; the little white villages shining in the distance; no life in the roads or fields. None of us slept that night, watching the black shadows of the ravine mouth, and dawn found us cold and tired in the pits. A couple of days before I had gone down the river and made what's called a compass traverse of the area, so that by using a few aiming marks on the river bank, I could work out a fire-plan that the guns (mortars) would be able to follow day and night, once the night aiming lamps were set up; so it was only a matter now of fire-orders.'*

Ed goes on to explain the subsequent battle in considerable detail, a battle in which his mortars played a significant part, but eventually they had to pull back and begin a long and painful withdrawal. He wrote:

'I shall never forget the scene. We were busy loading our two trucks by the roadside when the first of the rifle companies came along the road on their way back – rain beating into their faces and glistening on groundsheets and helmets as they trudged

slowly by – the weary, dragging pace of exhausted men – they looked real front-line soldiers that morning ... While we waited in the now pouring rain, Freyberg turned up in his car and walked among the men, chatting here and there; a quiet-spoken fellow with a cheering inflexibility of purpose about him. He came up to where I was standing and gave us an interesting little picture of his side of the show ... While we were scrambling into the 3-ton Chevrolets, that eventually came for the brigade, the intelligence officer came across and warmly congratulated yours truly on our morning's shoot, but the compliment I valued most came from tough Lt Laurence as he led his tired platoon past ours. Seeing our guns he called, "I could kiss those mortars but since they look rather oily I'll lift my tin bowler to them instead!" – which he ceremoniously did to the great gratification of the crews!

'Without lights driving was a constant strain on all responsible for keeping the route – the Tommy drivers had already been continuously on the road for 48 hours – and my poor devil constantly nodded over the wheel. Someone up in front turned right instead of left (none of us had maps); we lost the road and became involved with retiring artillery columns on a road edged with deep ditches and fluid with mud. What a nightmare it all was – the bus in front overturned and we had to extricate cut and shaken men in pitch darkness – vehicles were ditched and abandoned; the wildest rumours flew of German armoured divisions ahead! A wan dawn found disorganised transport still on the road and a terrible sense (happily unfounded) of disaster in the minds of all ... Never, never shall I forget those aged peasant women – they stood in their humble clothes, with their life histories written in poignant fullness in their wrinkled old faces, weeping for us as we trudged by – I heard one rough lad mutter, "By Jesus, they are the first women I've seen cry over this poor bastard." ... Once more we dug in on a new line; were moved out to allow formation of a two, instead of one, brigade front, and dug in all over again; the men almost

physically finished and rations reduced to a handful of dry biscuit and bully – how one longed for tea, hot and sweet, gallons of it – it grew to an absolute craving. Of the scenes that we saw on that retirement there are many I cannot tell you of yet – that last day we passed through a town that had been bombed to rubbish only half an hour before, the planes still visible in the distance as we went through the smoke and dust-filled streets where bodies of civilians and Greek soldiers lay in the listless, terrible detachment of death, and the only living were a number of Aussies in full possession of the town's liquor supply ...'

By the 23rd they had reached the coast not far from where they had landed, lying hidden from the German planes – the only aircraft they ever saw. They had to endure constant bombing and strafing then:

'How we cursed, longed and prayed for just one squadron of Spitfires! We surely understand Dunkirk now! ... Next day the same bombing by planes just beyond the range of our Brens, but what a thrill came later! The morning was gloriously sunny; towering cumulus clouds resting on the blue shadowed hills across the silken sheen of the inlet where several German bombers were leisurely pounding the peaceful harmless villages we had passed through. Then they vanished among the hills, leaving one of their number to continue the filthy job of terrorisation – it was no more than that. Suddenly everyone looked up at an unmistakable chatter of machine guns, faint and high up in the shining clouds. Someone yelled and pointed to the German who was now speeding flat out above the quiet hills and sea. From behind and above him were dropping three speeding arrows, tiny but unmistakable. Everyone went mad! "Hurricanes! Go get the bastard! They've got him – they've got him!" Away along the mountains on both flanks you could hear the cheering as a thread of smoke lengthened behind the doomed, fleeing plane.

"Bup-bup-bup," came another faint stutter of guns and a sudden flash of yellow broke the dark shape of the German as he went over in a slow, perfectly curving dive, faster and faster in a thickening blur of smoke. It was like a Derby finish – men leaping in the air, hoarse with excitement as the black shape hit the sea, exploded for a second time and vanished, leaving a blur of flame on the water as the oil burnt out. Up in the smoke spun the white speck of a parachute, slowly descending to the water as the only member of the crew to get out settled to a watery death. The three planes circled once and then away – fierce and free as eagles and the excitement died down in a tumult of discussion. Alas we saw those planes no more and in the late afternoon the bombing was as bad as ever.

'*We said goodbye to Greece last night, travelling a final 20 miles to the small bay where we were to be picked up ... Our two trucks went off with the rest of our battalion transport down a hollow where the drivers drained the oil and water, revving up the engines till they seized. The feeling was quite foolish and irrational but I felt like a ploughman watching his horses being taken away to the slaughter house as our two faithful V8s rolled away. Squat and powerful, they had carried loads of double their capacity over all the fearful roads of Greece until they seemed to have achieved a personality of their own ... At dusk we piled into the remaining trucks and set off on our last few miles ... in the villages the people stood silently watching us go by, but none but the children raising any greeting, and only the most self-controlled of men could have been free from a sense of bitterness and defeat – barely a month in Greece, coming with such high hopes and now haring out as fast as the trucks could take us ... but everything seemed to have been just a fortnight too late ... A high-walled steamer loomed up over us, and one by one we scrambled up the steep ladder to her deck, fumbling along to a curtained doorway – I remember realising I was shuffling along like an old man and said to myself, "Here, here, this won't do," but I was past paying any attention to me! We herded down into the holds, crammed with officers and men as though on our way to a saleyard, then those wonderful sailors came pushing great pails of hot cocoa, navy cocoa – thick and sweet. I sat on the deck with a great pudding bowl full in my hands and lapped away in physical ecstasy, feeling as though reviving from the dead. The kindness of those sailors and their mothering way with the dog-tired troops made one want to weep in one's silly feeble state. The Navy has been father, mother and all to us all the way.'*

They were attacked from the air *en route* to Crete, but eventually, about mid-afternoon saw their destination, '. . . the blue hills and snowy mountains, backbone of a large island lying across our course. We entered a small harbour, with the ruins of ancient fortifications at the mouth and the white houses of a small town among a few trees.'

And the Aussies

Bill Bracht was a member of the crew of the Australian cruiser, HMAS *Perth*, which accompanied the British cruiser HMS *Orion* to go to rescue some of the last troops from Greece. As normal, they did not know their destination until they had left Alexandria, when the captain briefed everyone over the ship's loudspeakers. He explained how they were going to take off the rearguard, and that at 2330hrs that night they would be standing off the shore at Salamis to effect this rescue. As the Germans were known to have motor torpedo boats stationed at Piraeus, it was essential that there was no noise. He further told them that the ship would be closed up at full action stations from 1900hrs. Bracht recalled,

'We were at our destination at the appointed time, and as soon as we flashed the signal to shore, scores of small boats came towards us. Soon we had hundreds of soldiers, to our surprise they were Australians, clambering up the nets and as they

arrived on deck they were taken to the mess decks where they were given scalding tea and a hot meal.' [9]

By 0200hrs, they had taken on some 400 soldiers, which was all they could manage, so then they headed for Crete at full speed, leaving HMS *Orion* still loading. During the journey the soldiers told him about their experiences during the difficult withdrawal and how the Germans had continued to advance 'like machines in columns. Bullets wouldn't stop them ... The only time they broke ranks was when the Maoris got among them with bayonets – they don't like steel.' On arrival at Suda Bay at around 1100hrs they watched the soldiers go ashore and he comments that 'at least they had rested for about nine hours and eaten well and so were a little happier and ready to meet whatever awaited them'.

Leaving Athens and Greece

We left Capt Michael Forrester, a member of the British Military Mission in Athens, in Chapter 2. Like all the rest of the British and Commonwealth forces, the mission would have to leave Greece. First, however, they had to leave Athens:

'The British Mission left Athens during the afternoon of 24 April. I remember travelling in a staff car with Col Salisbury-Jones along roads filled with weary marching Allied soldiers. Our Greek Army driver tried using side-lights to help him avoid those marching, only to attract the odd shot from disheartened soldiers, fearful of air attack. We crossed the bridge at Corinth which links the Peloponnese with the mainland of Greece not long before it was captured by German Fallschirmjäger, and arrived at Nauplion where we joined up with Headquarters "W" Force, which was awaiting evacuation by Royal Navy warships and Sunderland flying boats. The atmosphere was tense: sounds of small-arms fire came from the hills to the north. I remember a long narrow jetty at the end of

which was gathered a small group of officers including the unmistakable figure of Gen "Jumbo" Wilson, who stood with his suitcase beside him. Then up the jetty, fast moving, came the BGS, Sandy Galloway, who joined the group to report that he had just received a signal saying that the expected Sunderland had been delayed and that it was not possible to give a new ETA (estimated time of arrival). "So what in these changed circumstances, do you, Commander-in-Chief, wish to do?" To which Jumbo quietly replied: "I will do what many soldiers have done before me – I'll sit on my kit and wait!"

'I have already mentioned my feelings on leaving Athens and having taken in the scene at Nauplion, I found it difficult to come to terms with the thought of an orderly evacuation – I did not want to leave Greece without having done something active. So, having learned that an ad hoc evacuation point was being established at Monevasia, a small village about 25 miles north of Cape Malea (the southernmost point of the Peloponnese) I went to the transport area which contained the vehicles that had brought HQ "W" Force and others from Athens, selected a civilian car which I filled up with petrol from other vehicles. Col Salisbury-Jones, after listening sympathetically to my plan, gave his assent. At about midnight I set off with my batman, the faithful Albert Hursey, on the 150-mile drive to Monevasia. My aim was to complete the journey during the hours of darkness, thereby avoiding the attention of the Luftwaffe but, due to the mountainous roads, this was not to be, and at first light we were still some 25 miles short of our destination. Nevertheless, despite the attention of one determined Bf109, we reached Monevasia unscathed.

'Monevasia was a small fishing port surrounded by olive groves covering the area up to the foot-hills. I quickly found the Beachmaster, who had already organised some 50 men, mostly Australian and New Zealand soldiers with two or three officers including one British, into small groups. They were to lie low in the olive groves and move forward to embark on a caique crewed by Greeks. *The voyage to Crete was to take three nights, the first to the island of Kithera, the second to Antikithera and the third to Kastelli in the Kisamos Gulf of Crete. We were given the impression that the Greek captain would be in complete charge of the caique.*

'*The day passed without incident, and at dusk we embarked on the caique when I noticed there were several Greek civilians, men and women, on board. The majority of the soldiers went below. Having chosen to rest on deck, I awoke about midnight with an uneasy feeling that all was not well: this was confirmed by a glance at the North Star which told me that we were sailing almost due east. I went up forward to find the Captain drunk, sprawled over the tiller and making no sense. A quick calculation, based on my rather large-scale map, suggested we were several hours out to sea with rather fewer hours left in which to get back to land before dawn and the Luftwaffe would be up in the skies.*

'*With the help of two huge Australians we disposed of the captain by dropping him into the arms of those in the hold. Then there seemed no alternative but to take over as captain and with the help of my prismatic compass, but without knowing our position, I set a westerly course, hoping to hit Kithera. At first light I was concerned that there was no land in sight. I therefore decided to clear the deck: all soldiers were to go below, or lie under tarpaulins out of sight, and I positioned the women, who fortunately were wearing bright clothing, in the bow. It wasn't long before we heard the drone of aircraft: a Bf110 appeared and flew around us in a wide circle, before making a low-level approach. As it grew nearer the women responded magnificently by waving their hands, handkerchiefs and scarves. The plane flew over us having a good look, turned to fly over a second time, and as it did, hands came out from the cockpit acknowledging the waving by the women. We breathed again.*

'*About mid-morning we saw land ahead and entering a small bay found our way into a narrow creek with thick vegetation, under which we were able to conceal the caique. Contact with the local people revealed that we were not in Kithera, but back on the mainland at Cape Malea and that "the Germans were not far away!" There was nothing to do but to lie low – locals reported that the Germans were getting closer, but we were not disturbed. At last light, we slipped out on course, determined by my prismatic compass, for Kithera, which we reached under cover of darkness. Here we repeated the lying up process until dusk, when we set out for Antikithera.*

'This, an even smaller island, we reached during darkness and once again found cover for the caique and ourselves to lie up, hidden from aerial reconnaissance. Again, at last light, we set out, this time on the last leg of our voyage to Crete, and entered the head of the Kisamos Gulf as dawn was breaking on 30 April. We beached the caique at Kastelli and reminded by the absence of anyone around of the threat from the air, lost no time in disembarking and dispersing without celebration, in search of our respective units.'

The garrison commander

A summary of the British, Commonwealth and Greek defenders who were now assembled on Crete can be found in Appendix 1. All that remains is to say a word or two about the new garrison commander – Maj-Gen Bernard Freyberg VC, DSO, CMG (later Lt-Gen Baron Freyberg of Wellington VC, GCMG, KCB, KBE, DSO) who was appointed by Wavell on 30 April 1941. Known as 'Churchill's Salamander', this remarkable soldier had been born in London in 1889, but two years later had emigrated with his parents to New Zealand. He had become a living legend when, in 1915, he had swum ashore in the Dardanelles to light false beacons as part of a plan to disguise the chosen landing beaches to the Turks. This exploit won him an immediate DSO. The following year in November 1916, then a lieutenant-colonel, he was awarded the VC while serving in France for 'utter contempt for danger and splendid personal gallantry'. By the end of the Great War, aged only 28, he was an acting brigadier, with a VC, DSO and two bars, a CMG and nine war wounds! Buildings and even streets in New Zealand towns and cities had been named after him, and his statue erected in Wellington. However, peacetime saw him reduced to his substantive rank (lieutenant-colonel). He commanded 1st Battalion, The Manchester Regiment from 1929 to 1931 and then was appointed AQMG Southern Command, before joining the War Office. He retired from the British Army in 1934, aged only 45, but was recalled to the colours when war was declared, becoming GOC Salisbury Plain District. At the end of 1939, the New Zealand Government invited him to assume command of the Second New Zealand Expeditionary Force, which he accepted; shortly afterwards, he took his newly formed force to Egypt.

Freyberg was an imposing figure, over six feet tall and built with the physique of a rugger forward, confident and assured. 'Tiny' Freyberg, as he was called, was quickly accepted by all ranks of the force. He was well used to the informality of ANZAC troops – one of his biographers telling how, when a British general complained of an absence of salutes from the New Zealanders, he told him that they would 'always wave back!' On their arrival in the Middle East, he had wished to have time to train his division properly before they were committed to battle; this was to prove impossible as 1940 progressed from disaster to disaster. The three brigades of his 2nd NZ Division (4th, 5th and 6th) departed for the Middle East at three-to four-monthly intervals; then 5th Brigade was diverted to the UK for anti-invasion duties after the fall of France and remained there until early 1941. Just as he was getting his division together in the Middle East, the situation in the Balkans worsened. Churchill agreed to send troops to aid the Greeks and, although the German invasion had yet to take place, the NZ division found itself on the way to Greece. By the end of March most of the division was there, and on 5 April

1941, Freyberg's division became part of Lt-Gen Thomas Blamey's I Australian Corps. Subsequently, they would be faced with a difficult withdrawal, as already touched upon, and by late April they would have been evacuated – leaving behind over 1,600 men to become POWs, plus masses of transport and spiked guns. Freyberg himself (after having had nine staff cars shot from under him) would leave Greece on 28 April – having disregarded an order to leave five days earlier. However, instead of going to Egypt and being given the chance to regroup and retrain his battered brigades, he – plus many of his soldiers – found themselves in Crete, with just their uniforms and personal weapons. The 4th and 5th NZ Brigades had sustained nearly 900 casualties in the fighting in Greece, 291 being killed in action. Bloody but unbowed, they licked their wounds and waited for the next German onslaught, which obviously was only a matter of days away.

Gen Freyberg was, initially, an unwilling commander of the Allied forces in Crete. As I have explained, all he wanted to do was to get himself and his shattered troops back to Egypt, where they could re-equip and train properly. However, it was not to be. Churchill and his advisors did not consider that either Royal Marine Maj-Gen E. C. Weston of MNBDO 1 or Brig B. H. Chappel, the present commander of Creforce, to be the right man for the job. The unanimous choice was 'Tiny' Freyberg. However, he would have to be persuaded and the New Zealand Official History of World War 2 gives this description of a meeting between Freyberg and Wavell on Crete on 30 April, in which they quote Freyberg's own words:

'We met in a small villa between Maleme and Canea and set to work at 1130. Gen Wavell had arrived by air and he looked drawn and tired and more weary than any of us. Just prior to sitting down Gen Wavell and Gen Wilson had a heart-to-heart talk in one corner and then the C-in-C called me over. He took me by the arm and said, "I want to tell you how well I think the

New Zealand Division has done in Greece. I do not believe any other Division would have carried out those withdrawals as well." His next words came as a complete surprise. He said he wanted me to take command of the forces in Crete and went on to say that he considered Crete would be attacked in the next few days. I told him I wanted to get back to Egypt to concentrate the division and train and re-equip it, and I added that my government would never agree to the division being split permanently. He then said that he considered it my duty to remain and take on the job. I could do nothing but accept. With that over we sat down round the table on the flat-topped roof in the open air under an awning. The only subject on the agenda was the defence of Crete ... There was not very much to discuss. We were told that Crete would be held. The scale of attack envisaged was five to six thousand airborne troops plus a possible seaborne attack. The primary objectives of this attack were considered to be Heraklion and Maleme aerodromes. Our object was to deny the enemy the use of Crete as an air and submarine base.' [10]

The die was cast.

Notes

1. Creforce actually had two other commanders between Tidbury and Chappel; initially there was Maj-Gen M. D. Gambier-Parry (later to be captured by the Germans complete with his entire headquarters at Mechili on 8 April 1941, while he was commanding 2nd Armoured Division) who took over in January 1941, only to be replaced in February 1941 by Brig A. Galloway when he went to his short divisional command.
2. In the early days of the war, the RAOC was responsible for all vehicle and equipment repairs and it was not until Army Order 70 of 1942 was published, that the Corps of Royal Electrical and

Mechanical Engineers was formed and took over the provision of specialist electrical and mechanical servicing and repairs.

3. Not all the regiment went to Crete; at least one battery stayed in North Africa.

4. The Ju87 Stuka dive-bomber was fitted with a 'screamer' which the pilot switched on when he opened his dive brakes.

5. IWM Department of Sound Records Accession No 10978/3.

6. The CRS was where field ambulance vehicles would bring casualties from the Regimental Aid Posts (RAPs).

7. S. W. C. Pack: *The Battle for Crete*; Ian Allan.

8. The AEC Matador was a large 11-ton truck, the first 4x4 to be produced by the British in any quantity, and was designed to be an artillery tractor, although some were used as cargo vehicles. They were extremely reliable. 'The British Army is the most satisfied customer AEC ever had,' wrote C-in-C Middle East to the company during the North African campaign in 1942. I can personally vouch for their longevity as one of my troop leaders 'acquired' one in Aden in 1963 and used it as a runabout.

9. As quoted in *Crete 1941 Eyewitnessed*.

10. Taken from Gen Freyberg's report to the NZ Minister of Defence and quoted from *The Official History of New Zealand in the Second World War 1939-45 CRETE*, by D. M. Davin.

4

Operation 'Merkur'

Hitler's secret weapon

As has already been mentioned, Germany did not use its airborne forces in their proper role during the initial assault on Poland, but a few units were employed as ordinary infantry. The bulk was kept to be used as Hitler's 'secret weapon' in the attacks on Norway and Denmark, and then again, most effectively, against France and the Low Countries in May 1940. As we shall see, some of them were also used in Greece, but it would be on the island of Crete that their first major divisional operation took place. Before going into the details of the planning and preparation for Operation 'Merkur' it is relevant to look at how Germany became one of the leading countries in airborne warfare and what training had to be undertaken by the members of this revolutionary new arm.

Although the parachute had been invented in the 18th century, it was not used by service pilots until towards the end of World War 1, and its potential for landing airborne troops was not recognised until the inter-war period, even though Col Billy Mitchell, who had commanded the US Army Air Corps in France in 1918, had suggested using aircraft to break the deadlock of trench warfare. He had proposed that aeroplanes should be used to carry an attacking force over the trenches, to be dropped by parachute behind enemy lines. The idea was considered, then shelved and then forgotten, when tanks and armoured cars broke the deadlock on the ground and warfare became more fluid once again. Throughout the 1920s, parachutes did become more commonplace as the use of the aeroplane increased, but parachuting as a hobby was still confined to a small body of experts – everywhere, that is, except for the USSR, where parachute towers were erected in many large cities and anyone who showed an interest in parachuting was encouraged to learn how to jump.

Italy was the first nation to appreciate the full military potential of airborne forces and began experimenting with them in the mid-1920s. In November 1927, the Italians held their first ever practice drop demonstration over Cinsello, and the following year had formed a company of trained military paratroopers. The Russians had also appreciated the potential of the paratrooper, selecting men for training in 1929, forming their first parachute unit in 1930, and dropping a complete battalion in 1933. A year later they dropped a regiment of 1,500 men and by the mid-1930s were able to drop thousands of specialised paratroops, who were not only highly trained troops but also skilled saboteurs, capable of operating independently behind enemy lines. Impressed by such demonstrations, the Germans also began organising both paratroop and glider-borne forces. The Nazi Government had earmarked funds, and the new arm had the vociferous support of Reichsmarschall Hermann Goering, who was shortly to become head of the Luftwaffe. Born in 1893, the son of a minor diplomat, Goering had applied to attend aviation school at the start of the Great War, but had been rejected because he failed the entrance examination. He became an infantryman instead, and gained distinction for bravery. However, he suffered continually from arthritis, so found trench life unbearable until, through a friend, he managed to enter the air service. He proved to be a natural pilot, shooting down some 22 enemy aircraft, while winning Germany's highest award, the coveted 'Pour le Merite' (also known as the 'Blue Max'), and later commanding von Richthofen's elite squadron flying in a distinctive all-white aircraft. Postwar he became an ardent anti-communist and a strong supporter of Adolf Hitler. In 1933, when the Nazis came to power he was given wide controlling influences over establishing both a new air force and, at the same time, the infamous Gestapo. He quickly became drunk with power and far more interested in collecting as much land and loot as he could, so his grasp on his military duties began to diminish, with the result that the Luftwaffe lacked cohesive leadership at the beginning of the war.

However, one of Goering's many acts against the Communists had been to form a special unit within the Prussian police (of whom he was Chief of Police). Formed by a Maj Wecke, the new force became known as initially 'Police Group Wecke'. It was highly effective and rapidly gained a reputation as a crack unit, not only receiving its own standard, but in late 1933, being given the title 'Provincial Police Group Goering', which was later changed to 'General Goering Regiment'. As Goering controlled both the police and the air force, it was an easy matter for him to move this elite unit into the Luftwaffe. Then, in an order of 29 January 1936, Goering further directed that one of its battalions should be trained and equipped in the paratroop role, thus planting the first seeds that would develop into an airborne force some 11 divisions in size.

By early 1936, a Paratroop Training School had been established at Stendal-Bostel airfield, near Berlin. On 11 May 1936, Oberstleutnant Bräuer, CO of the 'Hermann Goering' Fallschirmjäger Bataillon, became the very first member of the new airborne force to make a parachute descent from the wing of an aircraft. This method was rapidly changed when it became clear that a much safer method was to leave from a side door of the transport aircraft.

At the same time as the Luftwaffe was getting involved in airborne warfare, so was the Heer, but without someone who had the ear of the Führer. Their progress, consequently, was slower and it was not until spring 1937 that permission was given for the OKH to raise a Paratroop Rifle Company. This is not the place to go into details as to how the army/air force rivalry was settled; suffice it to say that in June 1938, Generalmajor Kurt Student was charged with the formation of the first airborne division – to be known as the 7th Flieger Division, which would bring together the paratroop, glider and air transport units under one single command. The inclusion of glider-borne troops, using the DFS230 glider, was a most significant step, as would be shown in the invasion of the Low Countries two years later. With its home base at Tempelhof airfield, Berlin, the first order of battle of the new division was as follows:

Unit	Location	Commander
1st Battalion, 1st Parachute Rifle Regiment	Stendal	Lt-Col Bräuer
Parachute Infantry Battalion	Brunswick	Maj Heidrich
Air Landing Battalion	Berlin	Maj Sydow
Infantry Gun Company	Gardelegen	Lt Schram
Medical Company	Gardelegen	Maj Dieringshofen
Glider Detachment	Prenzlau	Lt Kiess
Signals Company	Berlin	Lt Schleicher
Training School	Stendal	Maj Reinberger [1]

In January 1941, it was decided to create a corps-sized formation, XI Fliegerkorps, which comprised:
Korps Truppen (Corps Troops)
7th Flieger Division – Fallschirmjägerregiment 1, 2 and 3
Luftlande Sturmregiment (air-landed assault regiment)
Flieger Führer (Flight Control)
22nd Infanterie Division (later Air Landing)

Special Instructions from the Führer
Hitler continued to take a personal interest in the development of the airborne forces and went so far as to issue 10 special instructions to the individual soldiers of his Fallschirmjäger. Although somewhat idealistic, they are translated here and have a distinct bearing on the way the troops fought on Crete:

1 You are the chosen warriors of the Wehrmacht. You must train to perfection, so that you can endure any hardship. To you the battle is the fulfilment of your training.

2 True comradeship must be your ultimate goal. Side by side with your comrades, you will conquer or die.

3 Beware of loose talk, it may be the death of you. Act, don't chatter.

4 Personal bravery and offensive spirit will win battles, so always be strong and resolute.

5 Conserve your ammunition when you fight; he who does not do so does not deserve the title Fallschirmjäger.

6 Never surrender – death before dishonour.

7 Always keep your weapons in tip-top condition, it must be 'first my weapon then myself'.

8 You must always clearly understand your mission, so that, if your commander is killed, you can take over and complete it to the best of your ability.

9 Fight the 'open' enemy with chivalry; however, do not show the guerrilla any quarter.

10 Stay wide-awake. Get yourself fighting fit and stay in condition – be as agile as a greyhound, as tough as old leather and as hard as Krupp's steel!

Basic training

Herbert Holewa, born in Silesia in 1918, served in the Luftwaffe Signals. In 1939 he volunteered for paratroop training and was transferred to airborne forces. In a series of interviews with the Imperial War Museum, he recorded his memories on tape (Accession No 12340). He had said that his paratroop training at Stendal was very, very hard. The paratroop arm wanted only the best and because some 16,000 men had volunteered and only 6,000 were needed, they could afford to be choosy, taking only the fittest and most able volunteers. He said that he was not frightened of jumping from an aircraft because the pre-jump training was very thorough and jumping soon became a matter of course. They started by using make-believe aircraft and jumping into a pit lined with peat, before progressing onto the real thing. He said that he did only about six to eight weeks at Stendal, then passed out and joined the newly formed nucleus of Sturmregiment 1 at Hildesheim. However, he was already a fully trained soldier and did not need the usual basic training. His first operational jump would be at Crete, so more from Herbert's tapes later.

In general terms, during the training of the would-be paratrooper great emphasis was put upon physical training, marching and agility. However, most volunteers had first to spend some three months improving their basic infantry skills, which included learning how to use enemy weapons and unarmed combat. The latter half of the course was on aircraft skills – such as learning how to do the special 'head-first dive' that was used to leave the transport aircraft (normally the Ju52). Also they had to learn how to pack a parachute, because every man would invariably pack his own 'chute before making operational jumps. After passing this phase of the course they took a 16-day parachute course during which they made a minimum of six 'live' jumps – packing their own parachutes before each one. It was a very compressed course and later, with hindsight, it had to be lengthened because there was too little time for the average recruit to learn everything properly.

The parachute course was followed for the successful students by a passing out parade, at which they were awarded their paratroop badge – a diving eagle surrounded by a wreath – and became a full member of a parachute unit. There was still much for the newly fledged paratrooper to learn at his unit, because the initial training did not include a night jump, nor had he carried out any tactical training – not even being taught how to rally after dropping in the DZ.

Uniform

In and out of barracks, the Fallschirmjäger wore the normal Luftwaffe uniform apart from his distinctive 'Storming Eagle' badge on the left breast (the eagle was gold-coloured, the wreath of oak and bay leaves was in oxidised silver; in its claws was a swastika). They wore the same yellow patches as other Luftwaffe troops on the collars of their jackets, but had regimental titles embroidered on their cuffs – dark green for the 7th Flieger Division and light green for the regiments (see below also for the special 'Crete' cuff-title).

What set the paratrooper apart was the combat dress. Instead of the usual German 'coal scuttle' helmet, the paratrooper's helmet was brimless (to prevent the parachute lines snagging), had a chinstrap which was attached to the helmet in three places (either side and at the back), was thickly padded with foam rubber and had a Luftwaffe eagle (facing forwards) on the left side. On his top half, the paratrooper wore a distinctive jump smock (Fallschirmschützenbluse). Designed prewar, the smock as worn in Crete was a 'step-in' garment with a central opening in the front and secured from neck to crotch by a heavy duty brass zipper (earlier models had buttons). Olive-green in colour and made of water-resistant gaberdine, it had a 'stand or fall' collar which could be worn buttoned-up or open, and the legs of the blouse came down to about mid-thigh. Each leg had a single brass press-stud with which the leg could be gathered and fastened. It also had four pockets – two on the chest and two horizontal ones on the thighs, all being closed by metal zips (under fly-fronted covers). The national emblem was worn on the upper right breast, while rank badges were worn on both upper arms of the smock.

The paratrooper's trousers were of field-grey woollen cloth, with two side and two hip pockets, two openings just above knee-level and a single fob pocket. The opening on the right-hand side above the knee was where the paratrooper kept his utility knife (known as a gravity knife) which was primarily there to enable him to cut loose from the parachute harness if he was being dragged along the ground by a strong wind. There were eight belt loops around the waist, and at the ends of the legs were short 'v' sections cut out and fitted with lengths of tape to enable the ends to be gathered in to give them a loose, baggy appearance. On their feet they wore special high-sided leather jump boots. Black leather gauntlet gloves were also issued – those for winter were fur-lined.

Other miscellaneous items included knee pads worn outside the trousers, or the earlier-pattern knee protectors, worn inside the trousers; also there were elbow pads. There was a special ammunition bandoleer which had to be looped around the neck, then ran down to the waistband where it was tucked in to the trousers. The bandoleer was for rifle ammunition – it had 12 compartments each holding 10 rounds. Getting ready for battle was a complicated business – all very well in the safety of the training field but an unnecessary hazard on the battlefield. Having landed, the paratrooper had first to take off his overall, remove his equipment, put on his overall again and then put his equipment on over the top – quite a performance with the enemy shooting at him.

Campaign cuff-title 'Kreta'
Post-Crete, on the special orders of Adolf Hitler, those personnel of all the three armed services who had taken part in the battle were awarded a white Armelband (cuff-title) with gold-yellow edging and lettering KRETA with two palms (actually acanthus leaves). Instituted from 29 September 1942, it was to be worn one centimetre above the turn-back cuff on the left forearm of all types of uniform, and there was no distinction between officers and other ranks. The criteria for the award were:

a   for troops (including glider crews) who had made a parachute descent or a glider-borne landing on Crete between 20-27 May 1941.
b   for crews of recce aircraft, fighters, bombers, dive-

bombers and long-range day fighters who had taken part in operations over Crete or Cretan waters before 27 May 1941.

c   for naval personnel who had been on active service off Crete on 19 May 1941. [2]

The parachute

The first German parachute was the RZ1, made of silk panels forming a 28ft diameter canopy (area 648sq ft). It was attached by the suspension lines to a pair of short straps which joined together to form a single support strap attached to the back of the harness, giving the impression that the user was hanging by a single cord! It was obsolescent at the start of the war and a replacement – the RZ16 parachute – was introduced in 1940, only to be replaced again by the RZ20 the following year. This was the parachute first used in Crete, and it would remain in service for the rest of the war. It still had a buckled harness, but there was an improved release buckle which made being dragged along the ground less likely, although still possible – hence the need for the gravity knife as already explained. The German parachute held the paratrooper in a face-forward position in the air, and it was mandatory that one landed with a forward roll (just the way to sustain an injury as one couldn't choose the ground one would be rolling on). The parachute harness was very tight fitting, which meant that nothing more could be carried under the smock other than a machine carbine or a pistol, because the parachute opened with such a jerk that any solid objects under the harness would have caused the wearer injury. This also meant that the majority of the arms and additional equipment had to be dropped separately in a special container, so the first task on landing safely was to locate the requisite container – not always easy and, as will be seen in the battle for Crete, not finding containers could and did have disastrous consequences.

The aircraft

The paratroopers and glider-borne troops used only one type of aircraft and one type of glider for their operations in Greece and Crete. This was the odd-looking – as if it were made out of sheets of corrugated iron – but reliable transport aircraft, the Junkers Ju52. The glider was the DFS230.

The three-engined 'Tante Ju' (Auntie Ju), as the Junkers Ju52 was affectionately called by all who flew in her, was an ideal machine for parachuting. It had begun life as a civilian airliner, under the clever subterfuge employed by Germany to circumnavigate the Versailles Treaty which did not allow the building of warplanes. Instead, Lufthansa used aeroplanes that were designed to become the bombers and supply planes of the Luftwaffe, as their airliners and transports; indeed, the Ju52 became the mainstay of Lufthansa. In its military role it could carry 13 paratroops, or 18 air-transported troops or 10,000lb of freight out to a maximum distance of 700 miles. As a glider tug it could pull two DFS230s, although for safety reasons one only was normally towed.

The DFS230 was another of Germany's subterfuges, being designed in 1932 by the Deutsche Forschungsanwalt für Segelflug (DFS – German Gliding Development Office) as a glider for high-altitude meteorological work. With its one-ton payload, it caught the attention of senior Luftwaffe officers who asked for a military version. This was produced in 1937, making it probably the first military glider in the world. Towing speed was about 100-120mph and landing speed around 40mph. The normal load was the pilot and nine men, all sitting in a line down the fuselage, the pilot and the first five passengers faced forwards, the rest faced to the rear. Passengers sat on a bench with their rifles/carbines clamped beside them. The front passenger could fire a machine gun through a hole in the fabric on the right-hand side (later models had a proper defensive MG mounted in the top of the fuselage).

Strength and equipment tables

An historical survey of the Cretan operation, written by Generalmajor Conrad Seibt, was included in the war diaries of the C-in-C and Armed Forces Commander, Southeast, and was translated and published by the Historical Section of the HQ US Army, Europe. It gives the following details of paratroop units and air transport formations:

Air Transport formations

Wing staff – 7 x Ju52
Group staff – 5 x Ju52
Group – four squadrons, each with 12 x Ju52 and 15 x DFS230
Corps transport squadron – 12 x Ju52
Corps recce squadron – 3 x Bf109, 3 x Bf110, 3 x Do17, 1 x Ju52, and 3 x Fi153

Paratroop units

HQ and Sig pl – 95 all ranks
Bicycle pl and Engr pl – 120 all ranks
Battalion HQ and Sig pl – 70 all ranks (50 only in airdrop)
Company – 195 all ranks (156 only in airdrop)
- Equipment – 1 x pistol per man, 1 x SMG per NCO, 1 x carbine per man (below NCO rank), 22 x LMG, 3 x lt a/tk guns, 3 x lt mortars, 18 x trucks, 1 x car, 3 x motorcycles

Heavy Coy – 200 all ranks (135 only in airdrop)
- Equipment – as for above per man plus: 8 x Hy MG, 8 x medium mortars, 2 x lt arty guns, 20 x trucks, 4 x cars, 12 x motorcycles

13th Coy – as above per man plus: 9 x 100mm rocket mortars, 6 x LMG
Truck Column (arrived later) – 30 x trucks
Arty Bn HQ and Sig pl – 80 all ranks
Battery – 4 x lt arty pieces (model 02) or 4 x mtn guns(model 36)
Armd Bn HQ and Sig pl – 70 all ranks

Coy – same as 14th Coy
AA Bn HQ and Sig pl – 90 all ranks
Coy – 12 x Mtn AA guns (model 38) or in airdrop 9 x guns
Engr Bn – as for para inf bn but without heavy coy

Junkers Ju52/3mg4e

Height	14ft 10in
Length	62ft
Wingspan	95ft 10in
Empty weight	14,325lb
Max weight	24,320lb
Max speed	171mph at 900m
Troop transport cruising speed	130mph max
Service ceiling	5,900m
Range with auxiliary tanks	1,300km

Gotha DFS230

Height	9ft
Length	37ft
Wingspan	72ft
Empty weight	1,900lb
Max weight	4,620lb
Max towing speed	100mph
Glider capacity	8 troops 2,720lb

Fallschirmjäger operations in Greece, April 1941

On 26 April 1941, in order to stop British and Commonwealth forces from escaping from Greece via the Peloponnese, it was decided to launch an airborne operation aimed at capturing a vitally important bridge in the Corinth Isthmus. The operation was undertaken by two battalions of the FJR2, reinforced by one parachute engineer platoon and one parachute medical company. On 25 April more than 400 Ju52s for troop carrying and glider towing, together with numerous gliders, were transferred from the Plovdiv area of Bulgaria to the former

British airfield at Larissa. H-hour for the airdrop was 0700hrs 26 April. Sebastian Krug, who now lives in Bietigheim, was a member of the assault force. He writes:

'On 25 April we were moved with the Ju52s to Larissa and slept under the aircraft on that same night. The next day came the order to put on our parachutes and get ready to make a drop near the Corinth Canal. As we were flying low over the mountains at about 1,500m, we came into a very heavy hailstorm and could hardly see our noses in front of us. We lost contact with the Ju52 to our right and discovered later that it had crashed into a high mountain. He must have been flying too low. All but two of our chaps were killed in the crash. They must have been standing at the doorway waiting to jump and were thrown out into the deep snow just before the crash. They made their way down through the snow to a low-lying village and further on with a donkey until they met up with other German troops. The people in the village treated them very well.

'Flying on to the canal we met up with some heavy anti-aircraft fire. We landed on very stony and uneven ground which resulted in very heavy casualties. Our battalion landed on the north side of the canal and our job was to try to stop the enemy coming from the south and to take them prisoner if possible. Well, we soon had so many prisoners that we didn't know what to do with them! A short time later we all jumped as there was a very loud bang. Looking over we saw that the bridge had been blown up and fallen into the canal; some soldiers and a war reporter were killed. Our company had to build a temporary bridge at the mouth of the canal. On the 29th a tank division relieved us and we had time to take a rest and to take care of the dead and wounded. After this action we stayed for a short time on the canal at a place called Lautraki. We had to capture some caiques with their crews to transport our heavy equipment to the Peloponnese, also to take the mountain troops to Crete. On 15 May, we were transferred to the airfield at Megara.'

During this action Hauptmann Gerhart Schirmer, then commanding the 6./2FJR had to take command of the battalion when the CO was badly injured while landing. Schirmer pursued the enemy relentlessly, taking prisoner 72 officers, 1,200 British soldiers as well as 9,000 Greek troops, including the commander-in-chief of the Greek Army on the Peloponnese. He would later win a Knight's Cross in Crete for capturing Hill 296.

Had this operation taken place just a few days earlier, then it would have been even more successful, since greater numbers of British troops would have been captured and thus prevented from reaching their ports of embarkation. By the time the isthmus was seized, most of the British had escaped. This was the only operation undertaken in Greece by the airborne troops, but the rest of them were now on their way, having left by rail from their training area in northern Germany on 2 May. The thousand-mile train journey took them nearly two weeks, via Austria, Hungary, Romania and into Salonika. From there they moved by lorry to the Aegean coast. They were taken to bivouac areas close to half a dozen of the airfields/airstrips in Attica. Here they waited, while their commanders assembled in Athens for briefing on Operation 'Merkur'.

One of those making this long trip was 20-year old Gottfried Emrich, who now lives in Northeim. He had been called up on 1 April 1939, to serve in the Reichsarbeitsdienst, the state labour service, in which all able-bodied citizens had to serve – he was in Building Battalion 4/103 repairing roads and bridges, to the rear of the Eighth Army during the Polish campaign.

'From 18 November until 12 February 1940, I went back to my civilian occupation as a surveyor, but was then called up for my army service. I went as a volunteer to the training school for Fallschirmjäger in Braunschweig (Brunswick) and eventually joined the 4th Company of the new FJR3 on 1 August. After very tough training the regiment got ready to take part in the

invasion of England, but that was postponed. On 24 April 1941, we were sent to Wolfenbuettel to get ready for another major action – we all had to complete a Last Will and Testament and were not allowed to write to our families or to anyone else. Then on 2 May, we were loaded onto a train and spent the next five days on the move first to Dresden, then Prague, then Budapest and on to a place called Arad in Romania. From there we went in our own transport over some very bad roads to Nikopol in Bulgaria. For security reasons we were dressed in our everyday uniforms; our jumping smocks had been hidden, along with other special equipment. When we were driving through Sofia some people threw stones at us, but they didn't do any damage. We were in Greece now, on our way to Larissa and we saw a lot of knocked-out British tanks, also many enemy graves. Most of the damage had been done by the Luftwaffe. On 17 May we made our way to Tagoda, a little cove where we found a number of tents that had been left behind by the British, also cases of weapons, heavy machine guns, anti-tank guns, all painted in an extraordinary colour. I was a trained communications man, but they gave me the job as No 2 on an MG. Also with us were mountain troops. By the way, in our platoon was the old heavyweight boxing champion of the world, Max Schmeling, who was also a paratrooper.

'On 17 May we had our first orders about the coming battle for Crete.'

Hitler's War Directive No 28

After Yugoslavia had capitulated on 17 April the Wehrmacht was able to turn its full attention to Greece. Three days later, the Greek armies on the Albanian front surrendered, leaving their left flank exposed and this meant that the rest of their forces, together with their British allies, had no alternative but to withdraw from the positions they held at Thermopylae. On 24 April the Greek Government formally surrendered, leaving the British to begin the difficult evacuation of their forces, many of whom were taken to Crete rather than be subjected to the longer and thus more hazardous journey to Alexandria. The British still occupied the important harbour at Suda Bay and had garrisoned the island. Hitler, however, had made up his mind by then to take Crete, both as a stepping stone to Egypt and, perhaps more importantly, to protect his Balkan flank as he prepared to attack Russia.

The Führer's Headquarters, therefore, issued Directive No 28 Operation 'Merkur' on 25 April 1941, which began:

> '1. *As a base for air warfare against Great Britain in the Eastern Mediterranean we must prepare to occupy the island of Crete. For the purpose of planning, it will be assumed that the whole Greek mainland including the Peloponnese is in the hands of the Axis powers.*'

The directive goes on to say that command of the operation will be given to C-in-C Luftwaffe and that he will, therefore, be employing primarily airborne and air forces stationed in the Mediterranean area. As far as the army was concerned, they were to make available, in Greece, suitable reinforcements for the airborne troops, to include a mixed armoured detachment, which could be moved to Crete by sea. The Kriegsmarine would have the task of ensuring sea communications, which must be secured as soon as the occupation began and, as far as necessary, the provision of troopships. C-in-C Navy was to liaise with the Italian Navy as necessary.

C-in-C Luftwaffe was to designate the assembly area and to use 'all means' to transport the airborne troops and 22nd (Luftlande) Division which was under his command. As events would dictate, the 22nd Division would not be available for Operation 'Merkur', as it was considered too difficult to extract it from guarding the Romanian oilfields. In its place, it was proposed to use 5 Gebirgs (Mountain) Division and despite some opposition, this was agreed. The necessary space for freight lorries was to be put at the disposal of the Chief of Wehrmacht Transport by both High Commands of the Army and Air Force; however, it was essential that these transport movements did not entail any delay to the mounting of Operation 'Barbarossa' (the attack on Russia). As far as anti-aircraft protection for Greece and Crete was concerned, C-in-C Luftwaffe could bring up as many Twelfth Army AA units as needed, making the necessary arrangements for their relief and replacement with C-in-C Heer.

After Crete had been occupied, all or part of the airborne troops involved were to be made ready for new tasks, which meant that the army had to make arrangements to relieve them. Finally, in preparation of coastal defence (which was always a naval responsibility), C-in-C Kriegsmarine might if necessary draw upon guns captured by the Army.

Hitler closed his directive with a request that the C-in-Cs inform him of their plans and that the C-in-C Luftwaffe should inform him when his preparations were completed. The last sentence read, 'The order for the execution of the operation will be given by me only.'

5 Gebirgs Division

Before dealing with the outline planning details for the coming assault, it is necessary to look at the 'new players', namely 5 Gebirgs Division.

> 'To fight in the mountains was to go to war in a desert. Not the familiar horizontal wilderness of flat sand, but a vertical and equally arid desert, in which to gain the objective of a mountain peak just a handful of miles distant usually meant a steep descent into the valley and a time-consuming, exhausting ascent – and all the time under fire.'

That is how historian James Lucas begins his book *Hitler's Mountain Forces* in which he describes the mountain troops as being among Hitler's toughest. 5 Gebirgs Division had been formed under Generalmajor Julius 'Papa' Ringel in autumn 1940, from the 100th Gebirgs Infanterie Regiment of the 1st Gebirgs Division and elements of the 85th Infanterie Regiment of the 10th Infanterie Division. Like their commander, who was an Austrian Nazi from before the Anschluss[3], they were recruited from hardy Bavarian and Austrian mountain stock. They had seen action in the Balkans, helping to break the Metaxas Line, and taken part in the subsequent sweep through Greece, so they were suitably placed for this new operation. Their commander, Julius Ringel, who sported a 'full set' (moustache and beard) was born in 1889, had served in the Austrian Army from 1909 to 1938 and briefly commanded 3rd Gebirgs Division in 1940. He would go on to command LXIX Korps in 1944, and then, as a general of mountain troops (General der Gebirgstruppen), Korps Ringel, a miscellaneous collection of units, fighting against the Russians in southern Austria in 1945. An outstanding soldier, during his service he was awarded the Knight's Cross with Oakleaves.

The attack forces
Gen Alexander Loehr, commander of Luftflotte IV was in overall command of Operation 'Merkur' with the chain of command shown in Appendix 2.

The plan of attack
Initially there were two invasion plans. The first, submitted by Luftflotte IV, was for airborne landings on the western part of the island, between Maleme and Canea, followed by the seizure of the rest of the island by an eastern thrust from all air-landed troops. This plan had the advantage of allowing the Germans to concentrate their forces in a small area over which they could achieve total air superiority. The drawbacks were that it might mean extensive mountain fighting to 'winkle out' the enemy, and it also left him in possession of Heraklion and Rethymnon airfields.

The second plan, submitted by XI Fliegerkorps, proposed the simultaneous drop of paratroops onto seven locations – the most important being Maleme, Canea, Rethymnon and Heraklion. This proposal had the advantage (if successful) of putting the Germans in charge of all the major strategic locations on the island in one fell swoop. It would then be followed by 'mopping up', to take over the rest. Attractive though this sounded, it did have the major disadvantage of dispersing the available forces over a wide area and making it extremely difficult for the air forces to provide cover everywhere at the same time.

The final plan – the one that was accepted – was a compromise between the two. Some 15,000 troops were to be air-landed (by parachute and glider) in three groups, Gruppen West, Mitte (centre) and Ost (east), while 7,000 were to come in by sea. On *Null Tag* (the German equivalent of D-Day) the 7th Flieger Division would land in two waves: the first, in the morning, on Maleme airfield (Gruppe West) and near Canea (Gruppe Mitte); the second wave in the afternoon, near the airfields of Rethymnon (Gruppe Mitte) and Heraklion (Gruppe Ost). VII Fliegerkorps was to provide strong air support for all the landings. At H-Hour, the first groups of gliders, each containing one battalion of the Sturmregiment, would land near Maleme airfield, their task being to neutralise the ground defences and thus protect the paratroop drop which would follow them. Additional groups of gliders would arrive at roughly 15-minute intervals, to consolidate the gains. The combat group landing at Maleme would thus comprise the assault regiment, reinforced by parachute infantry, one battery para AA artillery and one para medical platoon. A similar drop would take place near Canea, where the glider-borne troops would land on the beaches. Commander 7th Flieger Division would establish his headquarters near Canea. At H+8 hours, the second wave would arrive – comprising only paratroopers without glider-borne support, they would drop over

Rethymnon and Heraklion. Each group would be one parachute combat team, including infantry, AA artillery, engineers and medical personnel.

The three groups were thus going to be some 10 to 75 miles apart and it was vital for them to establish communications as quickly as possible. Then, on *Null Tag*+1 the mountain troops were to be airlifted to the three airfields (Maleme, Rethymnon and Heraklion) which, meanwhile, would have been cleared of all enemy forces. The naval convoys would land at the same time and then open Suda Bay and the other smaller ports to shipping.

By any stretch of the imagination it was a daring plan, which did not allow much leeway for unforeseen problems – a typical plan, perhaps, for a force which was supremely confident of its abilities and fighting prowess.

Assembly

The assembly of all the units that were to take part in Operation 'Merkur' took place in just under two weeks – a remarkable achievement when viewed against the poor road and rail system that existed in Greece, the bomb damage to both, together with the difficult terrain. Lorries were in short supply, especially when one remembers that Twelfth Army transport had to bring supplies all the way from their bases in Romania, Bulgaria and Austria. Sea movement was equally fraught with difficulty due to a shortage of ships, low port capacities and, most importantly, the risk of interception by the Royal Navy. The provision of aviation fuel presented a major headache, because of the small size of the tanker fleet and their vulnerability. To quote from a German report, 'The shortage of gasoline gave rise to all the more anxiety because an adequate supply was essential for an operation in which aeroplanes were to play such an important role.' [4]

A four-day delay

The Quartermaster of Twelfth Army also stated in a report of

8 May, that traffic congestion, railway demolitions, makeshift road repairs and mined harbours in Greece were more of a hindrance during the assembly period than during the entire period of military operations which had preceded them. It was these logistical problems that led to the postponement of *Null Tag* from 16 to 20 May 1941. In addition, there were other problems that just had to be lived with, including the locations of the aircraft to support the operation. The dive-bombers and single-engined fighters were based on recent, hastily constructed airfields on the islands of Milos and Scarpanto was well as in the Peloponnese. Twin-engined aircraft had to fly in from Rhodes and other fields within a 200-mile radius of Crete. The bases for long-range bombers and reconnaissance aircraft were in Athens, Salonika and even as far away as Bulgaria. The troop carriers would be operating from a number of fields near Athens. ('Field' was probably an apt description – see later for the problems caused by the choking dust which was an unexpected hazard, causing delays and discomfort.)

The balance of the troops of 7th Flieger Division was moved by rail and truck, while the mountain troops were in Greece already. However, 'Papa' Ringel's doughty warriors had first to be given special training in airborne operations – for them going into battle from the air would be a new experience. All this activity did not pass unnoticed; indeed, there was some British bombing of the assembly areas for a few nights before the assault began, but it was largely ineffective. All this activity also jeopardised the security of the operation, as did reports from British agents in Greece. What the Germans did not know, of course, was that the British already knew much of the details, thanks to the work of the cryptanalysts at Bletchley Park.

What did the British know?

Ultra was the British codename given to the intelligence obtained from intercepting and deciphering highly secret communications which had been enciphered by the German

Enigma code machine, called the *Geheimschreiber*. It was employed by all three German armed services, also the SS, Abwehr and even the German State Railways, so it was used for a mass of top secret, secret and confidential information. At no time during the war did the Germans realise that their incredibly complicated code had been broken. Deciphering was done at the British Code and Cipher centre at Bletchley Park. The Germans were so confident that it couldn't be broken that they used it constantly, sending thousands and thousands of messages, providing the Allies with a constant stream of invaluable information. However, the Allies had to be careful not to give away the fact that they had broken the German codes, so Ultra information had to be kept to as small a circle of senior leaders as possible. The decision whether or not to take remedial action was always carefully considered – the invasion of Crete being no exception. On the plus side, the new Mediterranean key for Enigma had been broken just a few weeks before the German invasion of the Balkans in April 1941, so by the time Hitler issued Directive No 28, it was possible for the British to decode the entire plan for Operation 'Merkur' – but would they use this information to their best advantage, if by doing so they would give away the fact that they had broken the Germans' 'foolproof' system?

One of those 'in the know' was Capt Monty Woodhouse, now Lord Terrington, but then a 23-year-old staff officer, who would later be promoted full colonel and be awarded the DSO and OBE for his work when commanding the Allied Military Mission to the Greek Resistance. As a staff officer at the Expeditionary Force headquarters, he would be amazed by the depth and accuracy of the information they received – but they were never told *how* it had been received. 'We had the German Order of Battle every evening,' he wrote later, 'but we could not do anything about it, having virtually nothing to hit back with.' [5]

Although Gen Freyberg was not totally in the Ultra picture, he was given a vast amount of intelligence information which had been obtained from Bletchley Park, via Churchill and Wavell. Some idea as to its depth and coverage can be seen by the following summary of Ultra signals for air operations and related subjects, sent from the UK to Crete during the period 8-19 May 1941, which dealt with the German preparation to invade the island.

8 May

Report of recce made on behalf of XI Fliegerkorps, including photos of Kastelli aerodrome (western Crete) and also of the area south and south-east of Canea.

10 May

Report of additional aircraft and gliders arriving in Athens area for operations against Crete. Date for completion of move by 14 May was well within original orders for ending preparations by 17 May.

12 May

Elements of ZG26 (Luftwaffe) to prepare for attacks on Crete airfields on 14 May.

13 May

    a At least 10 transport Gruppen involved in the movement referred to in the 10 May report. Main airfields are: Topolia (45 miles NNW of Athens), and Tangara; others are Dadion, Elefsis, Megara, Corinth and Mycene.

    b Dive-bombers and fighter-bombers in readiness in Corinth area.

    c Dive-bombers also based at Argos and Maloi (Peloponnese).

14 May

    a Antikithera to be occupied by Germans and equipped with AA defences.

b If recce fails to reveal shipping targets on 14 May, Ju88 dive-bomber Group I LG will attack Suda Bay.

c In future, the word "Colorado" will be used instead of Crete in all messages in this series.

d This signal dealt with the organisation, strength and armament of German Parachute troops. The most important details were:

Para Regts consist of 1,600-1,800 men.

Para Bns consist of 550.

Para Coys consist of 120.

They are armed with MGs, Tommy guns and rifles. Air-landing troops will have supporting weapons including AA and A/tk guns, 81mm mortars and 75mm infantry guns. Ju52s might carry light tanks up to 3 tons.

16 May

a On 16 May attacks by heavy fighters on British aircraft at Heraklion aerodrome intended, also transfer to Scarpanto (Karapathos) of about 20 x Ju87 to close Kasos Strait.

b Further information confirms the postponement of Day One for the Colorado operation. 19 May now seems earliest date.

17 May

Photo-recce of aerodromes in Colorado also Suda Bay and tented camp eight miles west of Canea being carried out in strength today. Aircraft dispersed around aerodromes of particular importance.

19 May

a 0800hrs conference of OC Luftwaffe units will take place at Elefsis Aerodrome. Discussions concern Colorado Operation, particularly Maleme, Canea, Rethymnon and Heraklion. Sorties by all units in spite of this conference. Single-engined fighters from Maloi, in strength of about one flight at a time, will repeatedly attack aircraft on Maleme aerodrome on 19th. Dive-bombers on Scarpanto also expected to operate probably on shipping. It appears today that Monday may be "Day Minus One".

b   Dive-bombers probably from Scarpanto and Maloi to operate against shipping targets from dawn, 19 May. Recce of whole of Colorado to be carried out and particular attention paid to aircraft dispersed in olive groves or vicinity.'

On 13 May, the following summary of information was also sent to Gen Freyberg:

'The island of Crete will be captured by XI Fliegerkorps and the 7th Air Division, and the operation will be under the control of XI Fliegerkorps. All preparations, including the assembly of transport aircraft, fighter aircraft, and dive-bomber aircraft, as well as troops to be carried both by air and sea transport, will be in co-operation with Admiral South-East, and will ensure the protection of German and Italian transport vessels (about 12 ships) by Italian light naval forces. These troops will come under command of XI Fliegerkorps immediately on their landing in Crete. A sharp attack by bomber and heavy fighter units to deal with the Allied air forces on the ground, as well as with their AA defences and military camps will precede the operation. The following operations will be carried out as from Day One. Firstly, the 7th Flieger Division will make a parachute landing and seize Maleme, Heraklion and Rethymnon. Secondly, dive-bombers and fighters (about 100 aircraft) will move by air to Maleme and Heraklion. Thirdly, air-landing of XI Fliegerkorps, including corps HQ and army elements placed under its command, probably including 22nd Division. Fourthly, arrival of sea-borne contingent consisting of AA

batteries as well as more troops and supplies. In addition Twelfth Army will allot three mountain regiments as instructed. Further elements consisting of motorcyclists, armoured units, anti-tank units and anti-aircraft units will also be allotted. Depending upon the intelligence which is now awaited, also as the result of air recce, the aerodrome at Kastelli, SE of Heraklion and the district west of Canea will be specially dealt with, in which case separate instructions will be included in detailed operation orders. Transport aircraft – about 600 – will be assembled on the aerodromes in the Athens area. The first sortie will probably carry parachute troops only. Further sorties will be concerned with the transport of the air landing contingent, equipment and supplies, and will probably include aircraft towing gliders.

'With a view to providing fighter protection for the operations, the possibility of establishing a fighter base on Scarpanto will be examined. The Quartermaster General's Branch will ensure that adequate fuel supplies for the whole operation are available in the Athens area in good time and an Italian tanker will be arriving in Piraeus before 17 May. This tanker will probably also be available to transport fuel supplies to Crete. In assembling supplies and equipment for the invading force it will be borne in mind that it will consist of some 30-35,000 men of which some 12,000 will be the parachute landing contingent and 10,000 will be transported by sea. The strength of the long-range bomber and heavy fighter force which will prepare for the invasion by attacking before Day One will be approximately 150 long-range bombers and 100 heavy fighters. Orders have been issued that Suda Bay is not to be mined, nor will Cretan aerodromes be destroyed, so as not to interfere with the operations intended. Plottings prepared from air photographs of Crete on 1/10,000 scale will be issued to units participating in the operation.' [6]

The use and the non-use of this amazing amount of intelligence will be dealt with again in the conclusions to this

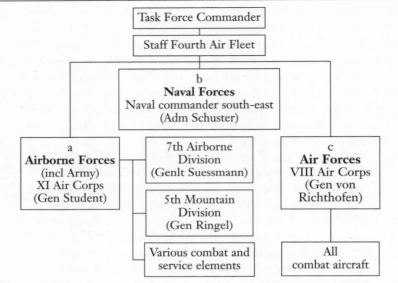

KEY

a Consisted of 10 air transport groups with a total of approximately 600 troop carriers and 100 gliders; one reconnaissance squadron; the reinforced 7th Airborne Division (one assault and three parachute regiments); 5th Mountain Division (incl one regiment of 6th Mountain Division); several AA, engineer and medical battalions forming corps troops. Total strength = 25,000 approx.

b Admiral Karlgeorg Schuster had no German naval units under his command. Instead, there were 63 motor caiques and seven freighters, each with a 300ton capacity, to form two convoys, to be escorted by Italian destroyers and motor torpedo boats. The transport vessels had been captured during the Greek campaign and were assembled at the port of Piraeus. The caiques would carry one battalion of 6th Mountain Division, the service elements and such equipment of the 7th Airborne Division which could not be airlifted; together with the pack animals and equipment of 5th Mountain Division, as well as rations and ammunition. The cargo vessels were loaded with tanks, anti-aircraft and antitank guns, heavy equipment, ammunition, rations and other supplies. In addition under command were: one naval patrol group and one air-sea rescue squadron; one bombardment group which was to lay mines in the Suez Canal area (the assistance of additional bombardment groups from X Fliegerkorps based on Sicily had also been promised to Luftflotte IV.

c Consisted of two medium bomber wings, one dive-bomber wing, two fighter wings (one single-engined, one twin-engined) with 150 planes each, and two reconnaissance groups

Full details of the German forces employed in the assault are given in Appendix B.

book. However, the fact that such information was available to Gen Freyberg was well illustrated by Lord Terrington, in his Foreword to a fascinating little book entitled *Crete 1941 Eyewitnessed* by Costas Hadjipateras and Maria S. Fafalios. In it he tells how he came into the story of Freyberg's dilemma, on the morning of 20 May 1941, when he was sent with a message to the general who was at his villa on the outskirts of Canea. After he had delivered the message, Gen Freyberg kindly invited him to stay to breakfast:

> *'We sat on the small veranda of his house, just the two of us. It must have been about seven o'clock when I happened to look up and saw the blue sky full of German aircraft and gliders. Some of the gliders were already detached and floating downwards. Hundreds of parachutes were dropping from the aircraft. The General continued quietly eating his breakfast. What should I do? It seemed impolite, not to say insubordinate, to interrupt the general's breakfast. On the other hand, the sight was extraordinary. Eventually, very respectfully, I drew the general's attention to it. He looked up and said, "H'mph." Then he looked at his watch and added, "They're dead on time!" He seemed mildly surprised at German punctuality. Then he went on with his breakfast.'*

As Lord Terrington comments, the general clearly knew that the assault was coming, 'Ultra' had already told him so, but of course his breakfast guest did not know this and Freyberg's apparently mild reaction to such a traumatic and important event must have been very puzzling to the young officer and raised all sorts of questions. However, as he says:

> *'One can only speculate on the answers to these questions. All I know is that after finishing my breakfast with the general, I left his villa about 8 o'clock and went back to my olive tree on the way to Maleme. Within 48 hours the battle had turned*

decisively against us. After that, there remained only the long march across the Levka Mountains to Chora Sphakion on the south coast. On the night of 30 May I was taken off from there by the Royal Navy. The battle for Crete was over.' [7]

As already mentioned, on 17 May, Gottfried Emrich and his comrades in FJR3, were getting their initial briefings on the coming battle and he recalls how,

'We saw many aerial photographs which showed exactly where we were going to drop − it was to be near the old prison in the Ayia valley [to the south-west of Canea, it was known in the battle as "Prison Valley" because of the low, white buildings of Ayia gaol]. We took the prison as the marker for our landing. Behind it was a big vineyard and we were told to go there after landing and meet some chaps from the Geheimdienst [espionage agents]. Our 1st Battalion under Hauptmann Freiherr von der Heydte would start from Topolia airfield, while the other two battalions would be using the Dadis and Tangara airfields. We all must try to land as near the prison as possible, because to the north on the high ground there was a Greek Army unit not far from Galatas and towards Perivolia.'

Notes

1. James Lucas: *Storming Eagles*.
2. B. L. Davis: *Uniforms and Insignia of the Luftwaffe, Vol 2*.
3. The Anschluss (connection) was the invasion of Austria by the Germans which was completed on 13 March 1938 and joined the two countries together.
4. As quoted in 'The German Campaigns in the Balkans Spring 1941' contained in *WWII German Military Studies Vol 13*.
5. As quoted in Ronald Lewin *Ultra Goes to War*.
6. 1745/13/5/41 GMT. Source: Public Record Office, Kew.
7. Lord Terrington's reminiscences are included here with his kind permission.

Softening up the Island

Early days in Crete for the Military Mission

We left Capt Michael Forrester having arrived safely at Kastelli at dawn on 30 April; from there he had gone to Canea, where members of the mission were assembling:

'Here I learned that, thanks to the magnificent efforts of the Royal Navy, the evacuation of our forces from Greece had proceeded relatively smoothly and units of the Australian and New Zealand Divisions were quickly re-forming under Gen Freyberg who had been appointed Force Commander. He and his staff were established in a quarry on the Akrotiri peninsula above Canea in the headquarters he had inherited. Nevertheless, his units were without their artillery and infantry support weapons; there were also a number of units, not required for the defence of Crete and awaiting evacuation, whose lack of defined purpose led to a sense of apathy.

'I then reported to Col Salisbury-Jones, who told me that the King of Greece, Sir Michael Palairet, the British Minister in Athens, and Maj-Gen Heywood, Head of our Mission, had all safely arrived in the island and that he was in close touch with Gen Freyberg. The not inconsiderable number of officers in the Intelligence Branch of the Mission, who had all been carefully selected for their appointments, were now allocated to strengthen the intelligence network between Force Headquarters and the sectors. Col Salisbury-Jones gave me responsibility for determining the needs of the Greek Army units and for ensuring that these were met, as far as possible, bearing in mind

the general shortage of weapons and ammunition. This task was somewhat simplified following Gen Freyberg's decision to reorganise these units into eight regiments, deployed within the chain of command, with two regiments in each Sector (see Appendix 1 for details). Here it is important to remember that the Cretan Division had been moved to the mainland to take part in the fighting against the Italians.

'*During the second week in May, I was invited by Prince Peter to join him and Paddy Leigh-Fermor, one of the Mission intelligence officers, in a cottage on the coast at Ayios Nicholias, a few miles west of Canea and across the bay from the 7th General Hospital. Here we would meet at the end of the day for a swim – Prince Peter was a keen snorkeller – and a good dinner cooked by our charming elderly Cretan named Marcos, over which we would exchange our experiences and discuss the likely trend of events. It was about this time that I remember hearing that the German invasion, airborne and possibly seaborne, could be expected on 18, 19 or 20 May. I was not able to ascertain the authenticity of this information, nor did I know how widely it had been circulated, though in the light of subsequent history the source was, no doubt, Ultra.*

'*On 18 May, I left in a 15cwt truck to deliver ammunition which had suddenly become available for the Greek regiments in the eastern half of the island. I called on Maj John Ford of the Welch Regiment who was at Rethymnon with the 4th and 5th Regiments, leaving them their share. Then on to hand over the remainder to the 3rd and 7th Regiments at Heraklion where Paddy Leigh-Fermor had already taken up his intelligence role. That evening Paddy and I met for dinner in the main hotel, where I had decided to stay the night. A most vivid recollection on waking early is of a Henschel reconnaissance aircraft flying slowly up the main street at roof-top level. There was something sinister and foreboding that the aircraft could operate with such impunity. Later I learned that Brig Chappel had issued orders that, until the invasion had started, no enemy aircraft were to be engaged from the ground – a policy which paid off in that, due to lack of information about ground dispositions, the Germans incurred very heavy casualties on 20 May.*

'On return to the cottage at about 1800hrs – it was now the 19th – I found Marcos on his own, Prince Peter having left that morning. I heard later that he had joined the King and others at Periviola. So that left Marcos, Albert Hursey and myself; in the absence of any further information I decided to stay the night there.'

The air raids increase

The weeks that immediately preceded the invasion became more and more difficult for the defenders, as the tempo of air raids increased. On 1 May, three weeks of even heavier, sustained bombing began, as the Germans started systematically to 'soften up' their major target areas: Maleme, Rethymnon and Heraklion aerodromes, Canea and Suda Bay. However, these raids, unpleasant as they were, did not deter the garrison or the newly arrived troops from Greece, from improving their defences. Rex Hey, the Ordnance Corps vehicle fitter we met in Chapter 3, continues his account of the days on Crete prior to the invasion:

'We often had aircraft carriers and other ships in the bay [Suda Bay] and, of course, the crews had shore leave ... we chatted to them in the town and were always intrigued at their reaction to air raids ... There was an absolute panic to get back to the ship. We never quite understood this, as we were terrified if we were caught by a raid starting whilst crossing the bay by boat. It was obvious that the aircraft carrier would be a prime target so one would have thought they would have been more than happy on shore.

'We had managed to find a new workshop and billets – the workshop was a disused olive oil factory, quite spacious, giving us all the room we required. Our billets were in a disused

school which was on the outskirts of Canea. So the whole set-up was first class except for the fact that our beds – consisting of the usual straw palliasses – were infested with fleas. It seems a petty thing to complain about, but there must have been literally millions of them. And it wasn't the complaint of just one or two men. It soon became an impossible situation and we tried everything, with full army support, to get rid of them, but without any success. One flea is enough, but in these numbers it was terrible, sleep was out of the question. Eventually the whole building was fumigated, which fortunately had the desired effect.

'The workshop was actually by the side of the sea – a delightful situation with the crystal clear water of the Aegean lapping the rocky beach a few yards away. We settled in happily here, with no problems except the air raids ... The air attacks continued, indeed, increased, and we would immediately take cover although the attacks were never (at that time) directly on the workshop for some reason. In the open area of the factory somebody had half-buried a huge steel pipe – it must have been around three feet in diameter, probably a sewer pipe. To us this was the ideal air raid shelter and when the bombing started we would immediately take cover – as per instructions – in this huge steel pipe. We learnt some time later that it was the worst possible place to shelter, as the straight pipe, open at both ends, would be deadly if bombs were to burst anywhere near it, as the blast was likely to kill everybody in the thing.

'We had started to hear most unpleasant rumours about the about the situation in Greece – Australian and New Zealand troops had been sent to Greece to hold back the Germans who, as ever, were driving forward under cover of overwhelming air support. Once again the air support for the Allies was literally non-existent. Apparently the Luftwaffe had destroyed the port of Piraeus, the major port in Greece, on one moonlit night, as ever, without opposition. It rapidly

became obvious that there was no way to hold Greece and the Allies must get out (again) as quickly as possible. The battered and exhausted troops began to arrive in Crete, some with arms, but mostly without. Once again valuable equipment had been abandoned ... Some troops arrived in destroyers or other Royal Navy vessels, but many arrived in a miscellany of small boats. The first time we really knew of this evacuation (except by previous rumour) was when they began to arrive. Incredibly their morale was ridiculously high. This was not a beaten army. There was no admission of defeat, but a sense of real bitterness that once again they had been let down by the War Office of both London and the Middle East (which in the books I read after the war was commonly known as the "Muddle East"!).

'The air attacks started to increase in intensity. The strafing and bombing was almost continuous – the Junkers Ju88 and Messerschmitts became our daily companions (I could say hourly). Life became really hectic. The Germans had airbases on Rhodes which was a comparatively short distance away – as were the Greek mainland airfields. We continued to work but spent a great deal of time in the shelters. I can assure the reader I was no hero during these attacks, but we had an Irish Corporal of the Ulster Volunteers who would not, under any circumstances, come out of the shelters. Ironically, as so often is the case, under normal circumstances, before the raids, he was a bastard – a most sadistic man.

'The air raids continued to build up and, for the first time, bombs were dropped on Canea, but strangely not the workshop. The civilian population, who up to that time had been very pro-British, suddenly began blaming the attacks on us – this shouldn't be misinterpreted, as it was just the fear of incessant air raids. During the battle of Crete and after, the Cretans left no doubt of their allegiance to the Allies. A very touching memory of mine during one of the air raids was when we came upon a little Cretan boy of about eight or nine. He was

wandering quite unconcernedly down the street. We went to him and told him he must take cover, he must not walk around while there was an air raid in progress or he would get hurt. He looked at me and showed me a medallion he had around his neck (of the Blessed Virgin) and said most politely, "Thank you, but it's quite all right, nothing can happen to me while I'm wearing this." Real true faith, but just for luck we managed to persuade him to take cover. I often wonder if his faith was justified in the days that were still to come.

'I suppose it should have been very clear that there was a reason for this increase in intensity of the air raids. Almost from dawn to dusk we were literally pinned down. There had never been any official suggestion to us of an attack on Crete, except for the rumours that after Greece we were to be next.'

Problems for the RAF, too

LAC Colin France, whom we met in Chapter 2, had been one of the many escaping from Greece, although he had come by air:

'At dawn on or about 22 April, four Blenheims from No 30 Squadron, carrying about 45 airmen, left Eleusis aerodrome for Maleme in Crete. In our aircraft about 11 of us were huddled together in the nose of the aircraft, hoping against hope that we would meet no enemy aircraft during our flight. I wasn't sure at the time whether I was one of the lucky or unlucky passengers. Occasionally, as we flew over the Mediterranean, the aircraft seemed to fly a little faster and we searched the sky to see whether there were any enemy aircraft about – luck was with us and we continued on our flight to Crete without incident. I had only the clothing I stood up in, later I was to be issued with Army clothing, complete with gaiters which later I was going to find very useful.

'Maleme, I believe, was originally used by the Fleet Air Arm, a couple of Brewster Buffaloes [1] were parked at the edge of the airfield but were unserviceable. A number of naval

personnel were employed on various jobs about the camp. We were a mixed bunch, comprising FAA staff, No 30 Sqn and No 33 Sqn airmen. The unit was renamed the Hurricane Unit. As the CO, Sqn Ldr Pattle had been shot down over Piraeus, a new one, Sqn Ldr Howell, was appointed [see Chapter 3 for the story of his arrival in the squadron]. We were rarely bombed during our first couple weeks on Crete, but the very day that some heavy coastal guns were sited in a position that overlooked the 'drome, over came some Ju88s. The time was approximately 2000hrs and I was chatting to members of the Yorks and Lancs who were manning the Bofors guns which had been placed around the airfield. As the wailing of the siren faded away, down came the bombers.

'The gunners were soon loading the Bofors and firing as fast as they could. Each one of the flight of six aircraft came machine gunning along the coast and near to where the coastal guns were situated. One of them dived on the gun emplacement where we had been talking, his machine guns firing at the same time ... The gunners opened fire, firing some rounds before he passed overhead – they missed – he was soon followed by another who dropped four bombs, the nearest exploding about five yards away to our right. As the gun post was getting a little too hot for me I left and started walking along the road to the camp, just in time to get strafed by an aircraft diving on the road. I made for the ditch and, after being the subject of some near misses from tracer shells which fell and ricocheted about a foot away, finally moved on to find my tent in the darkness. During the daytime we had been working feverishly on the building of pens on the airfield to protect the aircraft from damage, but all our work proved to be in vain. By 19 May, we had only one Hurricane remaining undamaged and it left for Egypt early that morning.'

During their 27 days flying from Crete, No 30 Squadron spent much of their time escorting convoys as was explained by Wg

Cdr John Jarvis DFC, AFC, who was then serving in the squadron:

> 'On Crete we spent most of our time escorting convoys – and I think I am right in saying that we never lost a ship. Escorting the Navy with fighter Blenheims was not funny, we looked too much like Ju88s. Despite approaching the convoy into the sun, line astern, undercarriage-down, at 1,000 feet ahead of the convoy, furiously firing off the colour of the day, they still plastered us. And the sight of a cruiser such as HMS Carlisle letting rip with all its guns was not a pretty sight if you were the wrong side of the barrel. It became quite dangerous ... we had one more go when the Fleet Air Arm, who had a couple of Fulmars there, said they would lead us out to a big convoy which had eight destroyers as escort, saying, "They never shoot at us."
>
> 'They did, and the Fulmars high-tailed it for home and were never seen again.
>
> 'In another incident, Flt Sgt Innes-Smith, flying a Blenheim, having established his identity with the convoy he was protecting, was turning to intercept an incoming Dornier Do17 onto which he had been "vectored". As he was closing to attack he was hit and nearly shot down by RN AA fire. Fortunately he just managed to crash-land back at Maleme!' [2]

Cannibalising and patching up

During their 27 days' flying from Crete the squadron flew over 100 operational sorties each of about three hours' duration and achieved this with a steadily dwindling number of aircraft and virtually no spares; it was a matter of cannibalisation and patching. Sqn Ldr G. H. Hartup recalled those days:

> 'Food was scarce, facilities negligible and spares non-existent. Day in, day out, masses of military personnel were arriving (presumably mostly evacuated from Greece) and whilst this build-up was going on the Germans were doing a continuous

run of "Line-Overlaps" – they must have photographed every grapevine between Maleme and Canea! For the first and only time I ever remember I lost all sense of time and date. We did – had to do – amazing and unorthodox things to keep those old Blenheims flying. For instance, we had an aircraft grounded for over-oiling, a known problem with the Mercury engine and always recurring in the bottom cylinders; we became desperate to rectify this. We knew that, tucked away at the far side of the aerodrome on the sea boundary, was a lone Gladiator left behind by 80 Squadron. It was generally accepted that this aircraft was seriously unserviceable and unflyable. I knew that Blenheims and Gladiators both had Mercury engines, though I was not sure whether they were of different marks. We did a recce and satisfied ourselves that the cylinders at least were identical. So we "borrowed" the two bottom cylinders from the Gladiator and fitted them in their respective positions on the Blenheim's engine and refitted those from the Blenheim onto the Gladiator, ensuring that the work was done neatly and thoroughly! We had no permission from anyone to do this, and we worked happily on the principle that exchange was no robbery. We then had to file up the valves with a hard file to try to get some compression to provide enough power. It worked, and without a word to anyone we ensured that one more tired-out Blenheim went home to roost in Aboukir with no problems. And then sadly, the decision was taken that all the Blenheims were to be flown off. So long as they could fly they were taken back to Egypt – to a glorious retirement I hoped – but I was not too confident!'

Wg Cdr Jarvis was one of the Hurricane pilots and he had the doubtful distinction of having been evacuated from Crete twice as he recalled:

'The first time was when the Blenheims were withdrawn due to

the proximity of the Bf109s and Bf110s which were fatal to the fighter Blenheim. Then in Egypt, I and three others were clobbered to take four Hurricanes to Crete. All very exciting as I had never seen inside a Hurricane cockpit before, and my first landing in the desert was in a dust-storm. We made it back to Maleme all right, but the aircraft due to pick us up went unserviceable and we were stranded without the proverbial toothbrush. It was a very hairy four days, on one of which Bob Davidson and I were strolling along the beach at Maleme when we picked up a German fighter pilot. He was armed and we were not, but he surrendered and we took him back to the "Mess" whilst awaiting an escort. He was a typical Hitler Youth type, blond and arrogant, who told us he didn't mind being a prisoner because his friends would rescue him in a few days' time. He was right. We were evacuated on the last Sunderland to leave at 0100, when the invasion started at 0400.'

A Sunderland to the rescue

One of the most amazing rescues from Greece to Crete was made by a Sunderland flying boat of No 228 Squadron. That squadron, and its sister squadron No 230, evacuated more than 200 people in five days, one of them having to take off blind through the dense smoke of a bombed ammunition ship and a burning troopship, The pilot of Sunderland T9048, Flt Lt Henry Lamond (now Wg Cdr retired) confirmed to me that his aircraft had rescued an incredible 72 men in one trip from Kalamata to Crete on top of the 10-man crew, so there were 82 in total in the Sunderland, crammed into every inch of space in the aircraft. Henry Lamond told me:

'In the morning of 25 April I had found a party of RAF on the coast at a place called Githeon. It was so mountainous they were more or less just following the beach! I picked up 52 of them. In the afternoon, instead of going back to pick up the rest, I was ordered to fly to Kalamata (on the other side of the

mountains from Githeon) because other Sunderlands had picked up both RAF and Army personnel there. It turned out to be the end of the line as most of the Army finished up there and they couldn't go anywhere else because of the mountains and the lack of roads. I was low on fuel but reckoned I could pick up more than 70 – all Army. I ordered the crew to pack them in from the nose back to the end of the step which they did so effectively that I can assure you that not a single extra man could have been loaded ... Anyway, 72 plus 10 in the crew, a total of 82 on the aircraft was possibly a record number of people carried by air at that time. The aircraft handled normally but was a bit heavy for the landing.'

'We had made camp in a disused brewery,' one of the rescued wrote later, 'when we heard the good news that some men might be evacuated from a nearby bay by Sunderland. A rota was drawn up and my name came up on the fourth list. I remember the Sunderland failed to become airborne after a five-mile run and we were requested to move forward, then another five miles at full throttle before eventually reaching enough height to claim we were airborne, despite the larger waves still lapping the hull! Eventually we landed at Suda Bay, Crete.'

Sadly there was to be a tragic sequel to this record-breaking flight. That evening, plans were made for the Sunderland to prepare for another operational trip before first light the following day, Henry Lamond and his crew being ordered back to Kalamata to deliver an important message to the senior army officer still in Greece. They took off successfully without a flare path, and at Kalamata harbour attempted a landing in calm sea conditions using the aircraft's landing lights. Here they must have struck some floating obstacle and T9048 crashed and broke up, only four members of the crew surviving – Lamond, first pilot Plt Off Sean Briscoe, second pilot Bill Goldfinch and Sgt Davis. All were injured. Briscoe was taken to a nursing home and later evacuated safely with another RAF party, but the other three went to a military hospital and were later made prisoners of war. Bill Goldfinch ended up in Colditz and was one of the POWs involved in the making of a glider in which it was planned to make a daring escape over the rooftops. It was never put to the test, but a replica made for a TV programme in the late 1990s flew perfectly. Henry Lamond commented to me when he recalled that last flight, 'It was a suicidal trip and I will spare you the details, but I crashed the Sunderland on attempting the landing. I delivered the message but it had been through the ocean, so I hope it could be read – the most expensive message of the war I should think.'

Finally, to close this miscellany of RAF recollections from the period, I have chosen an extract from the Operations Record Book of a No 112 Squadron detachment, which was kindly sent to me by David Musther, who joined the squadron later. On Crete they were flying some obsolescent old Gloster Gladiators as their record tells:

'Somewhere about 10 May, towards the evening, five Bf110s came over. Owing to insufficient warning only one Gladiator managed to take off. Plt Off Bowker immediately attacked and put up an extremely creditable performance, getting in one very good burst at a Bf110, almost certainly severely damaging it if not destroying it (it was later confirmed as a "kill"). He then took effective evasive action by coming low over the aerodrome, where the enemy was disinclined to face our AA defences. It may be added that for two or three days after this action, which took place in full view of the aerodrome, our stock in the view of the Army went up to an extraordinary height, only to relapse again to its normal rock bottom level after two or three days during which nothing of note happened. However, three days later a much larger formation came over – again Bf110s. On this occasion five Gladiators were up piloted by Flg Off Reeves, Flg Off Hutton, Plt Off Westenra, Plt Off Bowker and Sgt Bain. Plt Off Westenra put up a remarkable display

against six Bf110s. He got in several good bursts and eventually landed his aircraft safely with four main spars shot through, large areas of fabric missing and numerous bullet holes in other parts of the aircraft. All deserve great credit for the fearless way in which they attacked superior numbers of more formidable aircraft, and for the skill with which they extricated themselves from difficult positions when they could no longer do damage to the enemy. Plt Off Westenra's action also took place near the aerodrome and was a great tonic to those of us who were on the ground.

'Somewhere about 14 May, the enemy carried out his first bombing attack on Canea. Little damage was done, the enemy on this occasion obviously avoiding bombing the town itself. Nevertheless, most of us spent the greater part of the night in shelters and it was obvious that if we were to continue as an effective operational unit, pilots and crews had to have a decent night's sleep; we moved under canvas at the aerodrome the next day. As later events were to show, as a measure of ensuring a quiet night this was not altogether successful. The next event of importance was the arrival of two Hurricanes for the squadron. Although we had been longing for re-equipment, this was not how we had hoped it would take place. Of our total numbers, only three pilots had ever flown a Hurricane and of these only Flt Lt Fry had any real experience. Heraklion was hardly the best spot to choose for operational training! Nevertheless, most of the pilots got off solo in intervals between attacks, and some carried out patrols. Flt Lt Fry attacked a formation of about 50 Bf110s and it is hoped destroyed the one on which he expended his ammunition before he himself was shot down. He jumped with his parachute and landed little the worse except for a bad bruise on his chest caused by a collision with his own tailplane!

'These low-flying attacks by Bf110s now became frequent. On 18 May they became really intense. Bombs were dropped, the aerodrome rendered unserviceable and the two Hurricanes

and a Gladiator up to intercept were ordered to land at Rethymnon. During the night of 18/19 May it became obvious that we could no longer operate under existing conditions of air inferiority, so orders were given for all serviceable aircraft to fly to Egypt at dawn on the 19th. Flg Off Dennant and Plt Off Westenra left from Rethymnon in Gladiators, Flg Off Costello and Sgt Bain in Hurricanes. The "serviceable" Gladiators were also due to leave Heraklion, but the enemy attack started before they had got off the ground. As a result, a proper formation could not be made up, one Gladiator getting off before the others. However, all eventually reached the Western Desert safely. The Heraklion air party consisted of Flg Off D. H. V. Smith, Sgt Weir and Sgt Bates. They subsequently reached Heliopolis and were glad to avail themselves of the fortnight's leave which they were offered.'

It is of interest to note that Gerald Westenra survived the war and died aged 81 in 1999. A New Zealander, he had transferred from the RNZAF to the RAF when he arrived in England in 1940. He was officially credited with nine 'kills' although several more were likely, and won the DFC and Bar. It is said that he was also responsible for the fearsome shark's teeth motif which was put on the front of the American Curtiss Tomahawk aircraft, with which his squadron was re-equipped after Crete.

Plt Off Bowker, who was among those wounded and captured when the Germans took Crete, managed to escape by walking out of the German hospital where he was being held on 27 May and rejoined a party of British troops, who escaped on board the cruiser HMS *Orion*. In total, the RAF losses over Crete were some 38 aircraft, but of course the Germans were to lose many times that number.

Gaining air superiority

As far as the Luftwaffe was concerned, it was the task of the 119 Bf109s which made up II and III/JG77 and I(J)/LG2, who would cover the air assault on 20 May, to gain air superiority over the battlefield. Operations began in earnest on 14 May, but the fighters' part was never to be very large, in view of the pitifully small number of aircraft the RAF had to oppose them. Once all the RAF fighters had either been destroyed or forced to evacuate to Egypt, the Germans could start making the intended landing areas as safe as possible for the Fallschirmjäger and Gebirgsjäger who were to follow in defenceless transport planes and gliders. Many strafing sorties were flown – as we have read in the accounts of those on the receiving end on the ground. Losses of aircraft from AA fire were heavier in this period than in the brief aerial war, as the British and Commonwealth AA guns were both well sited and well dug in. Not only on land were the Luftwaffe heavily involved; indeed the Messerschmitt Bf109E-4s achieved some of their most notable successes of the war against ships of the Royal Navy. They would, for example, seriously damage the battleship HMS *Warspite* and sink the cruiser HMS *Fiji* on 22 May, but these were but a fraction of the vessels which the Royal Navy would lose during the battle for Crete.

British naval plans

Adm Cunningham's part in the coming German assault on Crete would be to plan a defence that would prevent enemy seaborne landings, and to do this no matter what would be thrown against his ships from the air where the Luftwaffe reigned supreme, or from the sea where the hesitant Italians might still make trouble. He had decided to form four separate forces, whose main task would be to carry out nightly sweeps of the enemy sea approaches to Crete, but making sure that they withdrew from the most dangerous areas before first light. In outline terms these four forces were as follows – but, of course, due to the complexity of operations once battle was joined, there would be some 'spontaneous intermixing' of these forces. The breakdown shown is as it was at first light on 20 May:

FORCE 'A'

OC: Rear-Adm H. M. Rawlings
Location: c100 miles to the west of Crete
Units: two battleships, *Warspite* and *Valiant*, and five destroyers, *Napier*, *Hereward*, *Decoy*, *Hero* and *Hotspur*
Main task: to protect against the possible appearance of heavy units of the Italian fleet

FORCE 'B'

OC: Capt H. A. Rowley
Location: further to the north sweeping the area between Cape Matapan and Sapienza Island. At first light on 20 May it was on passage to rendezvous with Force 'A'
Units: two cruisers, *Gloucester* and *Fiji*, and two destroyers, *Greyhound* and *Griffin*
Main task: covering the north-western approaches

FORCE 'C'

OC: Rear-Adm E. L. S. King
Location: south of the Kasos Strait
Units: two cruisers, *Naiad* and *Perth*, and four destroyers, *Kandahar*, *Kingston*, *Nubian* and *Juno*
Main task: sweep the area eastwards – Kasos to Leros – and deal with any landings at Heraklion and Sitia

FORCE 'D'

OC: Rear-Adm L. G. Glennie
Location: just west of the Antikithera Channel
Units: three cruisers, *Dido*, *Orion* and *Ajax*, and four destroyers, *Isis*, *Kimberley*, *Imperial* and *Janus*
Main task: to prevent landings west of Rethymnon
First VC awarded

During this preliminary phase, the first VC of the campaign would be awarded – it was also the first VC of the war to be awarded to the Mediterranean Fleet. It was won by PO A. E. Sephton, the director gunlayer on the AA cruiser HMS *Coventry* which was part of Force 'C'. His citation reads:

> *'For valour and fortitude in action against the enemy on 18 May 1941. Petty Officer Alfred Edward Sephton was Director Layer when* HMS Coventry *was attacked by aircraft, whose fire grievously wounded him. In mortal pain and faint from loss of blood he stood fast doing his duty without fault until the enemy was driven off. Thereafter until his death his valiant and cheerful spirit gave heart to the wounded. His high example inspired his shipmates and will live in their memory.'*

As was so often the case in World War 2 the citation benefits from further comment. John Laffin explains how Adm Cunningham had personally written that Sephton's brave action in staying at his key post 'may well have saved the *Coventry* and the *Abdiel*'. The latter was a British hospital ship which *Coventry* had gone to assist when it was attacked by seven Stukas, which then transferred their attentions to *Coventry* raking it with machine gun bullets, one of which struck Sephton in the back. Refusing help he continued to direct the fire of his guns until the attackers were driven off. He died the following day. [3]

Arthur John Stevens, the Fleet Air Arm fitter on HMS *Gloucester*, whom we met in Chapter 2, remembers taking part in those pre-invasion sweeps:

> *'Our job was, from what I can remember as a lower deck member, to keep at bay any attempt by the Germans to make a seaborne landing on Crete. And listening on the radio or the ship's tannoy, we did hear Winston Churchill at that period*

*speaking to the nation that Crete had to be held at all costs ...
We had a fairly easy day on the Monday (19 May), but we
were at alert – at action stations – that evening, from what we
thought was likely to be sea craft or submarines. So we were
on our toes all the time. But come Tuesday morning we were
sweeping on the southern part of Crete, to the west, with a
view of stopping any caiques, as they called them, Greek
caiques loaded with German troops. We understood they were
attempting to land Fallschirmjäger from the air to take Crete,
because they, the Germans, had been trying for months to take
over Malta, because it was a stepping stone. But they knew they
couldn't get Malta, so they attempted to take over Crete instead
... I think on the Tuesday morning we were under early attack
from dive-bombers Ju87s and 88s ... and that went on all day
with near misses. I was at action stations continually with the
exception of just a head down in the after galley flat. None of us,
I think, at that stage got any kip, real kip. Snatching food – eats
and tea – in between different attacks from the air.'*

The Kiwis settle in

Ed McAra, the New Zealand mortar platoon commander, and
his men had already had their first taste of action in Greece, so
knew what to expect. As he had been forced to leave his
mortars in Greece, he was without a job, so he had been loaned
to A Company as they were very short of platoon commanders.
He wrote home on 9 May about his new appointment:

*'Here I am installed in my temporary job a mile further back
from the beach, holding a ridge from which one looks backwards
to the purple shadowed sea, blue-green in the sun, with its thin
line of white tossing into view above the sandhills; and the little
village next to HQ Coy toy-like in the distance. Looking inland,
there are hazily-blue mountains, still snow-patched, upon the
left; with a confusion of semi-cultivated gullies and olive groves
to the immediate front; rising to another line of hills similarly*

patterned with vineyards, barley fields and bushy plantations. To the right is a shingly riverbed that gives one a queer yen for South Canterbury, with a low ridge beyond and then a blue arm of the bay, backed by high barren ground poking determinedly out to sea. The colours are mainly drab olive green, the richer yellow-green of the vines against interlacing stone walls and the sun-blenched pink and white of half-hidden villages. A difficult type of country to hold against the type of attack we are expecting and I did a lot of thoughtful prowling around believe me, before we finally decided where and how to site our posts.

'Sgt Murphy is one of those tough, restless souls who can never fit into a peaceful world. Fought first for the Republicans in Spain, then changed to Franco's side just to vary the monotony – a humorous, indomitable fellow whom nothing seemed able to ruffle. Coming over to Greece with the advance party he was in charge of the AA guns and we all heard how, when the ship was dive-bombed and the boys were made keen to let fly, old "Spud" stood calmly on the open deck, a mug of tea in one hand, a huge sandwich in the other, counselling between mouthfuls, "Hold it boys, hold it." When the plane was within 300yds he gave the word and had the satisfaction of seeing the bomber making off, low over the water, pouring out smoke and every indication of failing engines. An expert on explosives, he'll discuss for hours the charms and excitement of stalking tanks. One wonders where in this ideal world Peter Fraser [4] visualises, places can be found for men of Murphy's type – the sort of men who would be the life and soul of a Sunday School picnic, yet the despair of a Sunday School teacher! Sometimes human qualities, whatever they lead to, seem of infinitely more worth than commonly accepted ethical values. The more one thinks of it all, the more certain it seems that the true mainspring of life is adventure; the glad acceptance of the inherent risk and the willingness to gamble one's life. Hard work is not the key to success, despite the moralist. Life, Fate, God – call it what you may – demands something more of a man than dutiful application before the great prizes are dispensed –

something that just won't go into words! Where, either in His Life or His words did Christ preach safety! Yet what looks more than a normal Christian congregation?!

'Well dear girl, I must cease these meanderings and get on with a list of kit deficiencies that has to go in tonight, but don't worry about us over here, in what I hear the BBC calls the "last impregnable fortress of Greece" – I wouldn't exactly go so far as that, but we're about ready now to give him a damned good go for it, particularly as he is not likely to bring tanks. Though I don't really see why he can't just ignore us and go through Turkey and Palestine – certainly there's no monotony in this war! Hug our little man for me and buy him something for his birthday from Daddy.'

This wasn't McAra's last letter home; he wrote again on the 11th, when they were still busy improving their positions:

'. . . the platoon is busy wiring the exit of a nasty little tree-filled gully on our front. Behind the wire I'm putting a small pit for two men with a tommy-gun and a box of grenades, with half a dozen riflemen in pits 100yds further back to cover their withdrawal if the pressure becomes too great. My own little HQ, with the reserve section of 10 men, is only five minutes in rear and we will be in boots and all as soon as the balloon goes up. The rest of the platoon frontage is more easily covered by fire and as far as I can see, it's just in this one corner we'll be likely to strike real trouble.

'Last night was full moon and the countryside looking seaward from my "bivvy" beneath the stone wall, lay mysterious and still in the hazy light; trees and grasses unstirring; the ridges folding down into the shadowed gullies, the valleys opening upon the cultivated levels by the sea. The only sounds were the "toot-toot" of some night bird and the crunch of a sentry's boots on the stones, and the long sighs of the distant surf breaking around the bay. In many ways this existence is pure

Jeffery Farnol,[5] yet always – and unreal almost in its imminence – is the threat of sudden invasion from the skies. We have no desire to repeat the experience of one company of New Zealanders guarding an aerodrome in Greece, who woke up one morning, as the Irishman says, to find themselves dead men – overwhelmed by parachuting troops before they knew what was upon them. One hears amazing stories of the fatalism of these fellows – one lot were dropped on a drome with orders to destroy all the planes on the ground. Spraying the drome with their tommy-guns as they descended, the first to land were out of their harness and lobbing grenades into our planes before you could say "knife"; then calmly walked away to be shot down by troops coming in. The machine gunners and artillery tell bewildering accounts of the way in which platoons followed platoons over fire-swept ground; melting away one after the other and always replaced without hesitation. ...

'Have just returned from a trip round our position with a Tommy artillery officer who is bringing in some 3in guns today – welcome as the flowers in May! Our defences are slowly but surely thickening and we're beginning to feel once more as we did after Dunkirk, that soon the blighter will have left it too late. The morning is warm and glorious, the countryside with its myriad olive trees and lush greenness not so very unlike parts of Surrey. It is pleasant to hear the North Country accents as the gunners busy themselves preparing their gunpits. The Empire has returned to its old "splendid isolation", but ours is one family that won't split! A battery of 75s somewhere down on the flats is doing a ranging shoot on the beach, the flat reports drifting to the ear long after the spray of the bursts has subsided.'

This was to be the last letter that Ed McAra would write home, as he would be killed in the first day of fighting on Hill 107 at Maleme, leaving only his wonderfully descriptive, lyrical letters as a reminder of this part of his young life. A note penned on the last sheet reads, 'Killed on 20 May after the first day of fighting, while showing another officer round, who was taking over his duty – something that is usually told by word of mouth, but Ed did that little bit extra and so was killed.'

Allan Jackson, another Kiwi, from Mount Maunganui was a gunner in Greece, but the regiment had to leave its guns behind when it was evacuated by the Royal Navy on 27 April and became, as he calls it, 'infantillery'! One of the main things that dominated his first few days was food – or the lack of it, as he recorded in his diary:

'29.4.41 – Set off on a 10-mile march. Packs seem extra heavy and it was very hot. Arrived at divisional camp, given another small snack and then went to sleep. In the morning down to the sea. The water was beautiful. Returned to camp to find we were to become infantillery, fitted out with rifles. England all over again. The days are fine and everything seems very peaceful. We heard Lord Haw-Haw on the radio calling Crete, "The Island of Doomed Men!" According to earlier broadcasts we were to be wiped out in Greece.

'2.5.41 – No rations so we picked some broad beans and field peas. But things have improved somewhat as we sent to gunners to forage around the distant village. In the meantime the YMCA truck arrived with chocolate and biscuits. Then the boys returned from the village with loaves of bread, jam and eggs. We decided to go into Suda ourselves – had roast mutton, three eggs and a glass of wine. It's either feast or famine!

'3.5.41 – A heavy air raid on the harbour, 24 dive-bombers attacked the shipping. This was to become a daily occurrence and eventually prevented any more supplies coming during the day. A prelude to the coming attack – we are busy on the old pastime of digging holes. The fine weather ended, strong winds and rain making things unpleasant. My section now had two guns as well as rifles. We are to be a mobile force.

'12.5.41 – We have acquired two 75mm Italian guns

made in Germany in 1906. Now we should be able to thrash the Germans!! So now I'm back with Jack Cooper and some of our troop – much happier.

'13.5.41 – At 5.30am Jerry came over and dropped a bomb 100yds away. That was the start. Then Suda Bay got its daily ration. Later, about 9.00pm there was a very heavy raid on Maleme airfield. The bombing is increasing in tempo. Softening up. No planes of ours "extinct as the Moa" is how the RAF is now ... Jack and I went through the hospital grounds for a swim. Over came Jerry and bombed right across the ground. We were behind some rocks with shrapnel bouncing everywhere. We weren't hit, but on the way back saw the body of an RAMC orderly and the hospital was slightly damaged. From then on it was our turn. He bombed and machine gunned all areas hour by hour day by day. The planes had a sort of screamer on them. Even if they run out of ammunition they continue diving. We had nothing with which we could retaliate. The olive trees concealed us somewhat. There was an observation plane that came over regularly. If he saw us he would wave and we knew that in an hour the area would be strafed again. The wonder was that more did not get hit. We would have a lookout. He would yell, "Aircraft!" and we would dive into our trenches. I dug mine into the side of a bank and felt fairly safe except for bombs. After they had gone you could see every tree marked by bullets.'

Heraklion is garrisoned

When it became evident that the entire island must be defended, part of the garrison moved over to Heraklion. One of these was John C. 'Syd' Croft who had rejoined D Troop of 234th Medium Battery, RA, after being parted from them for some 20 days or so, some days after the main body had arrived in Crete from Greece. So he had been missing when the casualty lists were made up and was therefore posted as 'Missing, believed Prisoner of War' – and, as he put it, 'that was the unhappy telegram my parents sadly received. However, I was able to send a brief card home, but that went by the slow Army Post Office of that time, which took six or seven weeks because all mail had to go by boat round the Cape.' John would be posted missing again after Crete, and again when his regiment was captured at the fall of Tobruk! Fortunately neither was true and by the time they were back at El Alamein, he was able to send airgraphs which were much quicker, getting back to the UK in about 10 days. But back to Crete:

'The camp we were in was between the Suda Bay area and Canea. Some members of the unit, who had arrived before me, were able to get into Canea. However, I was still very tired and footsore and just wanted to rest. Meanwhile, 234th Battery was gradually taking shape, and we were soon rearmed with Italian field guns captured in Libya and brought over to Crete. C Troop was allocated five 100mm howitzers and D four 75mm guns. On 10 May, transport collected us and we were taken to our "new" guns. There was also 400 rounds of ammunition per gun. We went down to Suda Bay and embarked on a light tank landing craft. At dusk we set sail for Heraklion on the eastern part of the island. At that time I must confess I had very little knowledge of the island and, along with the other chaps, had little idea where we were going. It was also my first introduction to a tank landing craft, and our night jaunt along the northern coast was not a particularly pleasant one, bumping along in a rather unsettled sea and being frequently drenched in spray. And out in that darkness one imagined all kind of things. Would we be discovered and attacked by one of those fast torpedo boats that the Germans and Italians had? We were not at all happy and I have never been the best of sailors! But at long last, dawn found us arriving at Heraklion and we were on solid land again. There were trucks waiting to meet us and the guns were soon hitched up and we moved off to our new gun positions which had already been reconnoitred for us.

'It was now 11 May and at long last we had limited equipment – spades, a few more rifles, slightly improved rations, signalling equipment, etc. As there was some air activity we quickly set to work digging gun positions, a command post, slit trenches and rifle posts around the gun positions. The Italian guns were some 50 to 80 years old, and there were no range tables, etc to accompany them. However, they did have dial sights and they were graduated in millimetres. So, as soon as possible, steps were take to calibrate the guns by working out the relationships between elevation and range – this was done by firing out to sea. However, there was another problem and that was to find out how the fuses on the Italian ammunition worked. Those difficult problems were overcome by the command post staff and gunlayers, and before long they had produced simple but workable tables.

'It was, of course, well known now that an airborne attack on Crete was expected. We appeared to be fairly well prepared in our gun position, which was about three or four miles east of Heraklion. [6] On one occasion I had to take a message to what I believe was brigade HQ. It was about a mile or two behind us, towards the town. It was in quite a substantial cave in an inland cliffside and everything there certainly appeared calm and well-organised. Our guns were part of a perimeter defending Heraklion aerodrome and harbour, and we were facing north-eastwards towards the aerodrome with the possibility of sweeping the beaches to the north and the area beyond the two hills known as the "Two Charlies" and which were to the south-east of our position. C Troop soon followed us onto the perimeter and dug in facing west towards the town. A Troop from the 64th also joined us in the perimeter and they faced east. Meanwhile, about a hundred yards away on our right flank, a 3.7in HAA gun had just arrived, manned by the Marines of 234th HAA Bty, RA. This was quite a different unit to ourselves; we shared the same number, no more. There were probably Bofors LAA units in the perimeter as well, but I cannot remember seeing or hearing their easily identified sound. And so now all the gunners in our sector *were set and ready. Besides us there was a brigade of British infantry – I believe they included a battalion each of the Leicesters, the York and Lancs and the Black Watch. There was also an Australian battalion who occupied the "Two Charlies" and where we had OPs. There were also several Greek units who were based in and around the town. The brigadier (Brig Chappel) also had about eight light tanks available. I now understand that the Germans thought we only had some 400 men in the area. If that was so, then the airborne troops charged to take Heraklion and its airport had a nasty surprise coming to them. Obviously the heavy raids we were receiving were leading to something. But what would follow, we were not sure and we could only wait and hope for the best. I believe it is true to say that we certainly expected airborne troops to attack the aerodrome and seaborne troops to attack the harbour and make landings of the beaches to our north.'*

Tanks arrive

John Croft has remembered the composition of the Heraklion garrison reasonably well as Appendix 1 will show. At over 8,000 men, the garrison would certainly give the Germans a shock, despite its lack of satisfactory weaponry. True, the British had received some tanks – in total there were just six heavy and 16 light tanks on the whole of the island, the heavy Infantry tanks being the obsolescent Matilda Mk IIs which had done well against the light Italian tanks, but were heavy, cumbersome and had only a 2pdr gun as their main armament. To make matters worse, they had been rejected by the desert army because they had mechanical faults which had not been repaired before their dispatch. They were manned by RTR crewmen from B Squadron, 7RTR. The Light Mk VIs, which belonged to C Squadron of the 3rd Hussars (commanded by Maj Gilbert Peck, later killed in action at El Alamein), were also 'battered ancient hulks' to quote the words of one 3rd Hussars officer (Lt Roy Farran – later to become an early member of the SAS), although they had been 'hastily repaired' in base workshops. The radios were not fitted and the water-cooling attachments for the .5in and .303in Vickers machine guns, which were the main and secondary armament of the light tanks, were not available. This would lead to many stoppages in action when the guns overheated.

According to the 3rd Hussars' War Diary, they were loaded at Alexandria on to two ships – the tanks on the *Logician* and the lorries (30 15cwt trucks) on to the *Dalesman*. They were at sea on 12/13 May, had a reasonably stress-free voyage with other vessels, the convoy escort being a "Dido" class cruiser, an AA cruiser, four destroyers and a corvette – stress-free that is apart from being tailed by a submarine and attacked twice by aircraft, one of which they shot down! Problems really began while the unloading was taking place during an air raid in Suda Bay, when the *Dalesman* was hit by a bomb in the hold aft of the funnel. She immediately started to fill with water and had to be beached. All the 3rd Hussars vehicles were forward but some of their equipment was aft (including the radios). The tanks were unloaded on 15 May, the tank crewmen working as stevedores to get them ashore on lighters. They then had to be divided among the various garrisons (see Appendix 1). More about the tanks later; however, mention must be made here of the medical officer who accompanied the squadron – Capt Tom Somerville, who had volunteered to rejoin the army aged over 50, having won an MC and Bar during World War 1, been awarded an OBE for services rendered in North Russia in 1919, then a DSO at Buq Buq in 1940 (where he was originally cited for the VC for attending to wounded tank crewmen whilst under continuous heavy enemy fire). He would sadly not leave Crete alive.

More late arrivals

While most people know that, in addition to the British troops sent to garrison the island or evacuated from Greece, there were also plenty of Australian and New Zealand soldiers fighting alongside, I wonder how many know that there were also the survivors of some 2,000 Palestinians, mostly Jews, of the Jewish Pioneer Corps who had been serving with the BEF in Greece. Although mostly non-combatants employed as port service troops at Piraeus Harbour, No 604 Company Auxiliary Military Pioneer Corps (AMPC) had been sent to northern Greece in support of the Australian brigade defending Mount Olympus, where they were engaged in some savage battles with German Panzer forces. The Jewish pioneers fought side by side with the Australians, attempting desperately to block the Tempe Gorge, but were finally overwhelmed by combined attacked from Stukas and German mountain troops.

At the last minute the survivors were withdrawn to Kalamata, where they waited to be evacuated by the Royal Navy. Most of them, having low military priorities, were captured and spent the rest of the war as POWs, under constant threat of being exposed to Nazi brutality in the concentration camps. However, on 21 April, two AMPC companies at Piraeus were told to evacuate and boarded the vessel *Pankeriaton*, which left harbour with 400 troops on board. Soon after leaving port, they were attacked by Stukas, which blasted the helpless ship for six hours, killing and wounding some 25 Palestinians. Morale received a huge boost when two of the Stukas were shot down by Jewish gunners manning Lewis guns. After seven traumatic days at sea, the ship reached Milos where they went ashore. They found a derelict radio station and from it they tried to make contact with the British HQ on Crete. Then the water ran out and the exhausted men were soon at their last gasp. Fortunately, two RN destroyers arrived in the nick of time and took them off, bringing them to Crete on 1 May. Their exploits in the subsequent battle will be told in a later chapter. [7]

Another late arrival was Lt-Col (Retd) Andrew Brown MBE, of the Argylls, who was then the battalion intelligence sergeant. The Argylls travelled from Alexandria to Crete on 17/18 May.

'The ship had been scheduled to leave at midnight, but owing to the air raid and hold-up in loading, eventually left at 0100hrs. Only the main essential stores had been loaded because of the time factor. As a German attack on Crete was imminent there was a possibility the landing might be opposed. The landing craft were loaded accordingly: two companies and Carriers to lead the assault. This was where our Assault Landing Training earlier in the year would prove beneficial.

'The voyage over was uneventful although a little uncomfortable for me, as prior to departure I had yet another carbuncle lanced on my neck – very painful. The ship arrived at 2330hrs on 18 May and was not scheduled to sail until 0400hrs on the 19th, which gave plenty of time for unloading. Unfortunately, however, a breakdown occurred in the gear for lowering the landing craft into the water, causing the loss of an hour, and later the motor landing craft had several breakdowns, with the result that when the ship sailed for Alexandria, large supplies of petrol were still on board and miscellaneous baggage which included the cigarette rations for 10 days.

'The landing was unopposed, and after disembarking we walked about five miles and lay down in a field for a sleep. I shall never forget waking up, surrounded by green fields and hearing the noise of farm animals including a cockerel signalling dawn – such a difference from the desert.

'The role of the battalion was to guard the Messara Plain as it was a most suitable area for airborne landings. I was with Bn HQ in a village called Ay Deka. During the day the CO placed the companies in various positions to withstand any attempt by the Germans to land in the very large plain – approximately 20 miles long by 10 miles wide. On 20 May, my intelligence section and I were given the task of climbing a high hill adjoining our camp area and keeping our binoculars trained over this area, to quickly spot any landings. We were *assured the German airborne forces were expected, but no one knew where. The CO, Lt-Col Anderson, travelled to Heraklion that day to see Brigadier 14th Brigade. Whilst he was there, the area was subjected to intense bombing and towards late afternoon 200 troop-carrying planes flew in from the north and the first 2,000 parachutists dropped from a height of 300 feet.'*

Bombed!

Gunner Cole of the Northumberland Hussars and his companions had a lucky escape from the German bombing on their final 'softening up' on the day before the invasion began. He had just been relieved from look-out duty, gone to his billet with some others for a wash and shave, followed by breakfast, and was just preparing to return to his post, when the air raid alert sounded.

'We went outside to investigate and met the sergeant-major coming out of the HQ, yelling and shouting to us to get back inside pronto and keep under cover. Then, within seconds the peaceful serenity of the area was shattered and turned into a hell-hole! First the fighter escort came in strafing every building, cannon shells were ricocheting all over the house – how the bloody things missed us I'll never know – all you could do was to sit on your pack, hang onto your tin hat and pray! This went on for what seemed like hours but must have only been a few minutes, then suddenly all went dead calm so we got up for a look round, but not for long as the bombers came in, diving very low, firing their cannons, then they released their bombs.

'All of a sudden, there was a terrific "Whoomph" and a flash, then the whole of the house seemed to cave in. I was sitting on my pack, holding onto my tin helmet with both hands. I must have blacked out for a moment as I remembered something very heavy falling on my head. I knew my eyes were open but I

couldn't see a damned thing. I rubbed my hand over my eyes and mouth, tasting something sweet, then my vision cleared and I saw it was blood. Fortunately, on further inspection I discovered it was only a slight nose-bleed. By then the room had cleared somewhat and I saw what had hit me – a roof beam, which had fallen, fortunately hitting the top of the door, which broke off the last four feet, then the rest had landed on my tin hat, denting it and finishing up on my knees. I removed the offending beam and stood up, dusting myself down, then I saw what remained of our billet – all the roof was gone and most of the walls were down with just the corners standing. Charlie Brown was inspecting his chest, which I thought was streaming with blood; however, after a little cleaning up we discovered that it was only superficial pinpricks – the fool had been standing behind a window which had shattered into tiny fragments when the bomb exploded only a few yards away and his torso from neck to waist was embedded with dozens of tiny glass slivers. Then I received a shock, the door behind which I had taken cover had a huge hole in it about head height and at the other side of the room there was a large scar on the wall, while on the floor lay the jagged nose cap of the bomb!

'We counted up and found we were one man short, it was Lampton Stoker, so we searched the other rooms and the kitchen, negative. We stood there aghast, everyone's eyes anxiously glancing around the room, when, just then the huge pile of stones in the corner moved and a tin hat and a pair of arms burst out of the top of the pile and there was Lampton, buried up to his neck and grinning like a Cheshire Cat! One of the lads said, "Christ, Lampton! Why didn't you come up sooner? You had us all worried sick." In reply he smiled, and said, "Well, I was all right where I was. I was well protected by stones, I could breathe OK and as far as I knew those bastards could have still been strafing hell out of us, so I thought I was safer right here!" With that we carefully lifted the stones away, fearing the worst. However, he stepped out

with nothing worse than a few grazes on his legs and several bruises on his body.'

Despite the almost continuous daily bombing, there was no drop in the morale of the garrison, as evidenced by a signal sent to Gen Wavell by the Commander of the Cretan Garrison, who wrote with confidence:

'Have completed plan for the defence of Crete and have just returned from final tour of defences. I feel greatly encouraged by my visit. Everywhere all ranks are fit and morale is high. All defences have been extended and positions wired as much as possible. We have 45 field guns emplaced, with adequate ammunition dumped. Two infantry tanks are at each aerodrome. Carriers and transport still being unloaded and delivered. 2nd Leicesters have arrived and will make Heraklion stronger. I do not wish to be over-confident, but I feel that at least we will give an excellent account. With help of Royal Navy, I trust Crete will be held.'

Notes

1. The Brewster Buffalo was a single-seat fighter, the first monoplane to equip a squadron of the US Navy. Portly lines and high weight gave it a relatively poor performance and limited manoeuvrability. The Fleet Air Arm had a small number in 805 and 885 Squadrons.
2. From a fascinating little pamphlet entitled *30 Squadron RAF – the time in Greece and Crete, 1940-1941*, compiled as a supplement to the 30 Sqn RAF Association Newsletter 2/87, thanks to the hard work of the late AVM David Dick. The association has kindly allowed me to quote from it.
3. John Laffin: *British VCs of World War II – a study in heroism*; Sutton Publishing, 1997

4. The Right Honourable Peter Fraser, MP, Prime Minister of New Zealand.

5. Jeffery Farnol (1878-1952) was an English writer of popular historical romances.

6. John Croft was not the only one to feel confident: Gen Freyberg, replying to an enquiry from Churchill on 5 May said, 'Many thanks for your cable. Cannot understand nervousness. I am not in the least anxious about an airborne attack.' However, he does go on to say that a combination of seaborne and airborne attack would be different, especially if it came before he received the rest of his guns and other equipment. Nevertheless, 'When we get our equipment and transport, and with a few extra fighter aircraft, it should be possible to hold Crete.'

7. I am grateful to my friend Lt-Col David Eshel for this fascinating snippet.

6

Invasion!

Red shines the sun, stand by, it may not smile for us tomorrow.
Start up the motors, let them have it full.
Get going now, lift off against the foe
There's no way back, Comrade, no way back.
Dark clouds ahead, far to the West.
Come then, say nothing – come!

Engines athunder, in thoughts alone,
In thoughts of dear ones left at home.
Now lads it's time to jump
And we are floating to the foe
Quick we are landing now.
There's no way back, Comrade, no way back.
Dark clouds ahead, far to the West.
Come then, say nothing – come!

We are but few yet our blood is wild!
Dread neither foe nor death.
One thing we know – for Germany in need – we care!
We fight, we win, we die
To arms, to arms!
There's no way back, Comrade, no way back.
Dark clouds ahead, far to the West.
Come then, say nothing – come!'
The Song of the Fallschirmjäger

Landing at Maleme

Helmut Wenzel wrote a graphic account of jumping on 20 May 1941, near Maleme aerodrome.

'Crete appears in the distance. We stand and hook up the static lines of our parachutes, check each other out and prepare for the drop. I realise we are flying at 550ft; this means it will take some time to float down, thus increasing the risk of being hit in the air! No sooner has this thought crossed my mind, when the clacking noise of bullets and little holes in the aircraft tell us that we are already under fire. Events reel off very rapidly as we approach the drop zone. The chap behind me is hit and curls up on the floor, probably dead. There is no time to see to him – we have to get out and jump! Heaving out my bicycle first, I jump ahead of my men, holding my camera with one hand, as it will not fit inside my jumping smock any more, my gasmask taking its place.'

'As I float down, bullets whistle past me and I hear the crackling noise of small-arms fire. The enemy is putting up a hot reception for us and, looking down, I can see we are dropping right onto enemy positions.

'Infantrymen stand upright firing at us with all they have! I wrench at the shoulder straps of my parachute harness to free my pistol inside. Seconds before I touch the ground, a bullet hits me! It enters my jumping smock near my right armpit and exits somewhere near the neck. Fortunately, I am not too badly wounded. The bullet has torn my braces, jumping smock, binocular straps and damaged the strap of my Leica camera, but there is no time to look at anything. Damned dogs – wait till I get you!'

Helmut's immediate reaction must have been typical of many of the Fallschirmjäger; indeed, many of them considered it to be totally against the rules of war that those on the ground should actually be allowed to shoot at them while they were dangling helplessly from their parachutes – very unsporting!

'*After that first shock, the landing in a vineyard was surprisingly soft, but a mere 25yds in front of a British position. Immediately after landing, I open fire with my pistol, hitting two of the Tommies, the others taking cover – which gives me a chance to free myself from my harness. Moments later, machine gun fire rips my haversack and canteen to smithereens – so much so that the enemy thinks I must be dead because they stop shooting at me, leaving me with a chance to get to better cover. Where is my section? I have to rally my men! In desperation I shout, "Third Section over to me!"*

'*Immediately I receive a hail of bullets from the nearby enemy positions. This time I'm hit in the head, more severely than I was a year ago at Eben Emael on the Albert Canal. I receive a terrific blow to my head and nearly black out as the bullet penetrates my helmet and damages my skull. Red dots and rings appear before my eyes and I have to use all my will-power to stop myself blacking out.*

'*Some of my comrades hear me calling and four of them come crawling over to me. They are Obergefreiter Engel and Groefeld, and Gefreiter Primke and Mospack. Groefeld gives me first aid and I camouflage my dressing with dirt. We form a defensive circle and are under heavy small-arms fire for most of the time. One bullet rips my jumping boot and cuts the lace. They try to close in on us, but our hand grenades keep them at bay and they don't know exactly how many of us there are. The worst problem – we cannot get hold of our supply containers which have ammunition, rifles and automatic weapons. One does drop quite close, but when we get to it we find that it contains the B and L short-wave wireless set and, luckily for us, one rifle and one machine pistol, which is something because until now we have fought with hand grenades and pistols only. One of the Gefreiter in his frustration smashes the wireless set. Our Stukas, bombers and fighters circle and watch throughout the day, but differentiate friend from foe! The British use our captured flag markings* [1] *and weapons against us. There is no front line! The heat is unbearable and our clothing totally unsuitable. We chew on vine leaves, which taste very bitter, an unfavourable substitute for that precious commodity which we are denied – water!*

'Our spirits remain high and at no time do we think of surrender. Gefreiter Mospack puts up a particularly brave fight. We remain in this position for the rest of the day, as I watch with growing concern the enemy AA hammer away at our aircraft overhead. But it is impossible for us to get to that battery and silence it. Towards evening, however, our aircraft finally pinpoint the battery and destroy it – my first moment of joy on Crete! All day long I have been struggling to remain conscious – I have lost a lot of blood and am physically very weak. My chest wound has not been bandaged – nor seen to all day, and is now emitting a pungent stink. My right arm is getting progressively weaker and, as night falls, it is time to move on, to avoid capture. Cautiously we begin to move towards Maleme airfield. My pistol at the ready, I lead our small section. Suddenly, in front of me to the right, I hear rustling noises and then more noises to the left. Everyone freezes, listening with every fibre of our beings, blinded by the blackness of the night and our own terror. It must have been a Tommy approaching and passing us in the next row of vines – Damned close! Too close for comfort!

'Within seconds flares light up the sky behind us, from the very place we have just been. The silence of the night is broken by a wild outburst of small-arms fire. The enemy must have been firing at each other – lucky we moved on! Onwards we go – crawling through the thick undergrowth, over rocks and stones – expecting to meet the enemy at any moment. My efforts to get to the village of Maleme seemed to have misfired as we emerge on the slopes to the west of the airfield. After crawling for over a mile we arrive at a gorge. I am too exhausted to go on and in grave danger of losing consciousness. Groefeld and Mospack set off in the direction of a wadi and return eventually without water – totally exhausted. For the

first time I have the opportunity to examine my wounds. My vest and shirt are soaked with sweat and blood and my arm feels dead. Groefeld and Mospack put a field dressing on me and remove my bullet-riddled haversack – my camera has survived! We immediately take up defensive positions for the night – Groefeld and Mospack covering the left, Engel ahead and myself to the right.'

The big picture

Let us leave Helmut Wenzel and his companions, holed up in the darkness, somewhere on the Maleme battlefield and look quickly at the bigger picture. Operation 'Merkur' had begun at dawn on 20 May with a series of concentrated air attacks on the known British defensive positions by the Dornier Do17 bombers of KG2, the Heinkel He111s of II/KG26, the Messerschmitt Bf109s of JG77, the Messerschmitt Bf110s of ZG26 and, of course, the Stukas of StG2. This air bombardment had been swiftly followed by the first wave of the glider-borne elite of Sturmregiment 1, followed by the paratroopers of the 7th Fallschirmjäger Division. Meindel's elite assault troopers had been the first to arrive – he was seriously wounded in the chest within an hour of landing – three companies landing at Maleme, a fourth south of Canea and a fifth on the Akrotiri peninsula, while the low-altitude bombing and machine gunning of the defenders positions went on ceaselessly in order to keep them pinned down. At Maleme, some 40-50 gliders took part, the majority crash-landing in the bed of a gully to the west of the airfield, out of the direct line of fire of the defenders. They managed to capture the high ground to the west, which overlooked the airfield. In the Canea area, similar surprise tactics also made for some initial success. Gun crews were killed or driven underground by the continual bombing and machine gunning, so some of the gliders were able to land almost undetected. However, this was not always the case and at least one glider which crash-landed on some rough ground just outside the town was savagely dealt with, the garrison troops holding their fire until the Germans had climbed out, then opening up at point-blank range and killing them all. The garrison troops were then able to salvage SMGs, ammunition, hand grenades, etc from the glider. Many brave deeds were performed by the garrison, two of which are recounted in a small pamphlet issued later by the Admiralty. One concerned Capt (now Lt-Col Retd) A. L. ('Bill') Laxton, whom I mentioned in an earlier chapter. When a party of parachutists had secured a footing in a gun position, he made a determined effort to get within grenade range, but was wounded in the head and back and in both legs. Nevertheless he remained in observation and signalled back the numbers and position of the enemy, thereby enabling the gun position to be completely cleared and recaptured. He was awarded the Military Cross for his bravery. This is how he recalled the action after the war:

'I was at our HQ building in Canea when it started. Our Signal Company was there basically to provide communications, and we were not essentially front-line fighting troops. However, our work of setting up the communications system was 90% completed by then and we were standing by to await developments. We anticipated the need for repairs to be made and fresh lines to be set up, but later that morning there came an urgent call for troops to help clear out the enemy from an AA gunsite a little south of Canea, towards the mountains. I gathered a team of available men from around the HQ, and we set out in a truck toward the area indicated. We circled around the site and found no opposition until we were just a field away from it. We left the truck, and as we cautiously approached a sandbagged emplacement we were met by a British soldier in a highly emotional state, pointing at the emplacement, almost sobbing, "Oh My God ... Oh My God." I fired a few shots at the emplacement and presumably they found their mark because a

German suddenly bolted out of the emplacement and ran across the field away from us and to the left. He was about 400 yards away and, as he ran, I fired two more shots at him and saw him fall forwards, whether to take cover or because he was hit I couldn't judge. I spread out my men and we advanced carefully across the field towards the AA gunsite. When we got there I found some others from our unit under Sgt Potts. They were in a small wooden hut on the edge of an olive grove and that was the gun site. Potts pointed to a dug-out about 200 yards across the grove which he said was still manned by Germans. A young German soldier lay at the side of the hut, dead, with a bullet hole in the centre of his forehead.

'I led my troops to the left looking for a way to approach the dug-out from a flank. I jumped over a low wall into another trench, only to find myself standing on a heap of bodies – bodies of British soldiers. I was closer to the enemy dug-out from here and as I calculated my next move, a voice came from beside my feet. It was a quiet voice, almost apologetic, absurdly so under the circumstances. It said, "Excuse me sir, some of us are still alive." All I could do was to reassure the man that I would send help as soon as I could. Looking over the edge of the trench I saw about a dozen German soldiers in single file heading across the olive grove into a cornfield. I had left my rifle in the hut and carried only my pistol and a hand grenade, but I did try a couple of long range shots at them as they went. I then jumped out of the trench and made a dash for one of the olive trees nearer to the enemy dug-out. As I ran there was a burst of automatic gunfire from the right front and I was hit in both legs. There was no pain, just a sharp "tap" and my left leg went numb. My right knee had been shattered, the bullet passing right through and the left leg had a bullet through the upper thigh, grazing the sciatic nerve as I afterwards learned. I had dropped to the ground when I was hit and lay there uncertain what to do next. I thought perhaps I would try to ease myself forward to within grenade range of the dug-out, *but when I moved there came a single shot from the same direction, giving me a flesh wound, so I lay still. After a while I tried again and this time another shot came over my right shoulder and ripped across my back.*

'I realised that I must be more exposed and unable to move; however, I could still see where they had gone. Moving very cautiously I slipped my whistle out of my pocket and signalled to my men in Morse code, "I have a message." At once the reply came back and I sent a message indicating where I had seen the German soldiers entering the cornfield and had the message acknowledged. I remained in observation, not anxious to move, hoping that whoever had fired at me would assume that his last shot had killed me. After what must have been a long time, I saw our troops advancing across the olive grove towards the cornfield and as they came I grabbed a branch of the olive tree and hoisted myself to my feet. To my alarm one of them dropped on one knee and raised his rifle at me! I called out, "No, don't shoot!" A companion beside him put a restraining hand on his shoulder, but he still seemed unconvinced. Without lowering his rifle he shouted, "What the hell are you doing there?" All I could think of saying was, "Wounded!" and to my great relief he got to his feet and moved on with his group. I found that my numb left leg could bear weight and I could hobble on my right, so I was able to make my way back to the hut where I had left Sgt Potts. There was a German automatic weapon lying on the ground as I came in and I picked it up. I think it must have given me a sense of security to have some kind of a weapon in my hand even though it wasn't loaded and I wasn't familiar with that type of weapon. In the hut, I lay with my back to the wall facing the opening holding the useless weapon in my lap. Some time later, Potts appeared with Bailey, my MOA (batman) and a bottle of rum. After a time the bottle was empty and I felt no pain; darkness had descended and a jeep arrived to take me to a casualty clearing station up in the hills. I was there for

*two nights and on the first night we heard a steady barrage of
gunfire out to sea and someone told us that a seaborne invasion
had been beaten back by the Navy.'*

It would take Bill some painful days and nights before he
eventually managed to escape from Crete in a small fishing
boat, reach Alexandria and then begin three long months of
recuperation in various hospitals.

On the Akrotiri peninsula it was an even worse story for the
attackers. The air support failed to arrive, some of the gliders
unhooked over the sea and dropped into the water, while
others crashed on landing. It was a complete shambles and
there were many casualties and many others were taken
prisoner.

About 15 minutes after the gliders, the parachutists arrived.
At Maleme some came down just to the south and east of the
airfield. They were swiftly dealt with and practically wiped out.
Those landing to the west were protected by the fire of the
glider troops, and so managed to rally and form a sizeable force
which, by early afternoon, had killed or wounded all the
defenders on the western edge of the airfield.

The second wave

Once the Fallschirmjäger had been dropped, their troop-
carrying aircraft returned to Greece to collect their payloads
for the second phase. Taking stock of the returning 'Tante Jus'
it must have been very clear that not everything had gone
according to plan. Everyone was taken aback by the strength of
the defenders, and consequently casualties had been much
heavier in some areas than anticipated. Back at the airfields in
Greece there was an unexpected hazard – dust! The runways
had become so churned up that the pilots could hardly see to
land for the thick, cloying dust, which covered everything.
There were also further delays while the aircraft had to be
refuelled using hand pumps – the Fallschirmjäger being forced

to carry out much of this work burdened with their heavy jump suits. And the Greek people were playing their part too – disrupting the civilian telephone links on which the Germans depended for co-ordinating the flights between airstrips. This caused considerable delay to the second wave and also meant that the drops were spread, as this quote from the official battle report of the XI Fliegerkorps illustrates:

'The formations started in incorrect tactical sequence and arrived over their target areas between 1600hrs and 1900hrs not closed up but in successive formations and at the most by squadrons. The bulk of the forces had to land without fighter protection. Moreover, in the end the force delivered was some 600 men less than had been intended.'

This 'staggering' enabled the defenders to kill many of the enemy before they had even reached the ground. But we move on too quickly. Going back to Maleme, Gottfried Emrich, a paratrooper in FJR3, was airborne and heading for Prison Valley:

'We flew at 0530 and this was the formation – transport Ju52s flying low, then fighter Bf109s and 110s for security (and they were firing red recognition flares), the para gliders flying much higher. My division commander was in one of the gliders with his staff which crashed for some unknown reason.[2] We flew over the high mountains of Crete, the pilots getting ready so that we were able to land somewhere near the spot that we had marked, the old prison and the road between Alikianou and Canea. We had seen from the aerial photos that the high ground was strongly held by the enemy, so by landing in the trees we would get good cover, but it would be difficult to find our heavy weapons' containers.

'We were to jump from a height of about 650ft. As we got closer to our drop point we hooked onto the rail, then we

jumped one after the other. A short while after jumping, the parachute opened with a jerk and we hung there like helpless worms. I found it difficult to orientate myself because I had spun round a couple of times while I was descending, but then I made out the prison – our landing marker. There were other paras beneath me, and because the weather was so hot we were all coming down slowly. I landed on both feet without doing the usual forwards roll, in the vineyard, with just a few scratches from the vines. On one side there was a drainage ditch and a stone water tank; on the other, a goat tied to a post. Above me were other Fallschirmjäger dropping, the planes coming over in groups of three. The pilots had to be careful not to hit the people dropped by the earlier aircraft. There was machine gunfire all round, and you could hear the screams of those who had been hit while coming down.

'By now it was now about 0730 ... I had landed some 200 yards south of the prison, and the only weapon I had was my pistol. Now I had to find the container with my machine gun and other equipment. I kept meeting comrades, some of whom were wounded or injured, but I couldn't find my box, so I took another one with an MG and ammunition in it and ran to the prison along the road Canea-Alikianu. I went along the ditch towards Canea and it gave me good cover. On the way I saw my first dead comrade – it was a really bloody sight. This first day of action must have been the hottest and our clothes didn't help matters. All over the place were discarded gasmasks and steel helmets. We were all getting very thirsty, but couldn't find water. We did find some oranges and ate them unpeeled, then an old lady gave us some wine – but with the heat you can quickly get drunk!

'On a small lane off the main road to Galatas, where there is now a war memorial, was our primary rendezvous point, behind a high wall. At that time we had two heavy machine guns and six machine gunners, so they all had plenty to carry. We also had a distance calculator and medical orderlies. Many comrades were now joining us behind the high wall. We

planned to attack and take an enemy strongpoint in a cemetery on the high ground. The ground around was burnt black from previous air attacks. We needed a donkey and cart to carry all our ammunition. Prisoners (Greeks) were sent to the rear. We left the main road, turned right and walked until we reached a small river (the Gladiso). There wasn't much water in it and what there was, was red with blood – it looked as though the wounded had been cleaning their wounds in it.

'We began the offensive from field positions off the road from the prison to Canea. We took heavy casualties, mostly from our own aircraft who were dropping their bombs right in front of us. All over the place you could see dead and wounded Fallschirmjäger, some still hanging from their parachutes … Although we had identification flags (swastikas) and also flare pistols, our aircraft couldn't identify us because the Tommies had looted some of these flags, and we had no radio contact with our planes. The advance, therefore, didn't go too well. We found tins of fruit and sweet condensed milk in a trench we overran, but nothing for our thirst. The enemy gave us a lot of trouble despite their desperate situation. There were snipers in the olive groves from a special British unit, also Australians and New Zealanders.

'We got the order that we must take the high ground behind us, set up a defensive position with our two heavy machine guns and hold it. So we moved into the thick olive groves. From the little village of Potistiria we could oversee the terraced ground down to the prison (see map). The Greek Second Army had held this area before we took it. We were, therefore, able to enlarge existing trenches and we dug others, so that we could cover the ground more effectively, one of our MGs covering towards the prison and over to the little village of Marmia, the other towards the cemetery on the high ground called Galatas, where the Englanders were – about 2,000 yards away from us. In the evening, with the help of the

setting sun we could see our enemy. Just before it started to get really dark, some transport planes came to bring us supplies, but most of them landed in enemy lines. The prison was now in our hands and we used it as an HQ and a POW camp. We mounted a guard of two men on duty all the night, staring into the darkness. There had been a lot of bloodshed and you could hear the crying and shouting of the wounded and dying – it was one of the worst nights of my life.'

On the receiving end

From these accounts I think one can gather that all had not gone 'according to plan' as far as the invaders were concerned, but what was it like on the receiving end?

'On 20 May, there was heavy bombing of all our anti-aircraft guns and I guessed that the real attack was about to begin. I went up to an observation post on a hill with my glasses, and watched the parachutists landing about three miles away. They came in three waves – of about 30 machines each and it was a marvellous sight to see the air filled with their parachutists.'

That is how New Zealander Lt-Col Jack McNaught described the first moments of the airborne assault. Jack was 43 years old when he was asked to go to war with the 22nd Battalion (he had served under-age in World War 1 and would go on to serve with the 25th Battalion, be wounded in Libya, recover and serve with the 32nd before returning to New Zealand in 1942). He had been put in charge of a number of units who were running the harbour at Suda Bay, and had some 1,000 men, including New Zealand and Australian engineers, plus some Cypriots and the Palestinians mentioned in the last chapter. They had already faced numerous air raids, including the dive-bombing and machine gunning of the dock area. He had decided that it would be better to work at night, despite it being slower, because at least they could operate unmolested.

He continues:

> *'In addition, there were a number of gliders. The big machines carrying parachutists were led in by bombers at about 300ft, and these bombers circled round continually outside the area where the parachutists were landing and gradually increased the size of the circle. Our AA fire had, of course, largely been put out of action. I was ordered to prepare a defensive ring round Suda – but most of my men weren't infantry and not much used to fighting. I got them all rifles and ammunition. There were also some 200 marines, but at 1600hrs I had a ring from the general who wanted me to send 150 men to Area HQ to go out and clean up some enemy who had landed by glider between Canea and Suda. I sent out 50 marines and three carriers, who did the job at the expense of just one of our men killed. I went up at 1700hrs to see how they were getting along. Saw several dead and seven or eight gliders, but our men were still mopping up. In the evening more parachutes were dropped – mostly containing supplies I think. I had five hours good sleep, which was all the well as I was to get very little for the next six or seven days, or even 10 days.'*

Colin France, RAF, was considerably nearer the first action: he was at Maleme aerodrome. He was due on duty at 0800hrs on the 20th and was having his breakfast when the air-raid alarm sounded, so he nipped into a slit-trench close by. He comments that he wasn't certain whether it was the dining tent that was the target for the dive-bombers and ground-strafing fighters, or the crowd of ex-diners who streamed out, breakfast forgotten:

> *'After a while I decided that the first aid post, which was situated a few feet from the top of Kavkazia Hill (107) was a safer refuge, and so, along with others, I made my way dodging a hail of bullets as best I could. The first aid post was,*

in reality, a cave with its entrance suitably hidden and protected by a high stone wall. A view outside from inside the cave was not possible, neither could one see inside the cave from the outside. At that time the noise outside was deafening – the constant rat-a-tat of machine guns, the bomb explosions, the cries and the never-ending roar of aircraft engines above us.

'*Inside the cave was the Unit Medical Officer, Dr Cullen, and LAC Darch, a medical orderly. A flight lieutenant, a corporal and a couple of airmen made up our numbers. We had been inside for less than 20 minutes, when LAC Greenhalgh crawled in. We could get nothing out of him. Later we discovered that a bomb had exploded in the slit-trench where he had been sheltering, killing some of its occupants; as a result of the explosion poor old Greenhalgh was stone deaf. He was soon followed by another airman who stumbled across the entrance. His clothes were muddy and tattered, down his right side we could see where chunks of his flesh had been torn from his body by shrapnel. He explained that he was also in a slit-trench which had received a direct hit, killing three airmen. While his injuries were being attended to, he dropped his own bombshell, inasmuch as he told us that paratroops were landing all around us and a number of gliders were crash-landing around the camp. The news caused a deadly silence for a while and then everybody began talking at once. The flight lieutenant was the first to leave to join the forces higher up the hill, closely followed by the doctor and LAC Darch. Later a corporal, another orderly and myself left, but in the ensuing excitement the corporal shot himself in the foot and was lowered back into the cave.*

'*Once on top of the cave and sheltered by some shrubs, I surveyed the landscape which included our tented camp. I had just made myself comfortable in what I thought was a favourable position when I saw a man about 100 or more yards away, wearing what appeared to be Air Force blue trousers. I let him pass thinking he was an airman. A few seconds later he was followed by another, similarly dressed but also wearing the Swastika flag draped over his back. As he turned to face my direction I fired and increased the enemy casualties by one (permanently I hoped). My first shot of the war – but now I imagined many guns were trained on my position and a few shots did come within a few feet of my hiding place which made me feel uncomfortable. I decided to return to the cave to ask for advice. I slid down into the entrance and had scarcely recovered my breath, when a hand grenade exploded on the outside wall and a guttural voice commanded that we come outside with our hands up. Outside were six paratroops, all armed to the teeth who searched us and then questioned us about some big guns. We informed them that we were airmen and could tell them nothing. We were later marched down the hill to the tents where we were told to discard our helmets and sit down.*

'After what seemed to be an hour, during which time we were informed that for us the war was over, more prisoners joined us and some of us scrounged some German cigarettes. I noticed my friend Ginger and went over to him to ascertain how he had been caught. Instead of getting a reply from him, we were ordered to stand up – about 30 prisoners in all. We were then ordered to about turn, with our backs to the Germans. Each prisoner I'm sure said a prayer, I know I did. We had heard that the paratroops took no prisoners. We fully expected to be shot where we stood. Instead it was a great relief to hear the German officer shout "March!" instead of "Fire!" We were then separated into groups of nine or more, with three Germans behind us as an escort. We were ordered to put our hands up and shout "Don't shoot!" as we clambered to the top of Kavkazia Hill. When we reached the summit, a number of shots were fired at us by our comrades on the other side of the hill. Ginger Hutchinson who was a couple of feet to the right and slightly behind me, crumpled up. Two of us went to his assistance and noticed his intestines oozing from a small hole in his stomach. We tried to bandage him but were ordered

to carry on with the march.

'Meanwhile we were more than half-way over the top and nearing a position held by a mixture of Marines, New Zealanders and other troops. Someone shouted to us to get down and as we did so we heard yells and a fusillade of shots whistled around us. I crawled on my stomach to the NZ position on the far side of the hill and on looking around I noticed a number of airmen and soldiers with fixed bayonets rushing to us from our right. Our three escort were lying prone on the ground.'

Colin France was again with friends, and a free man – but sadly, as we shall see later, not for long.

'Most of us were given Canadian Ross rifles with 10 rounds of ammunition and told to join others in forward positions overlooking the airfield. Two New Zealanders and myself were told to keep a sharp look-out for a sniper who was, as our officer informed us, taking odd potshots at the machine guns covering the airfield, with a certain amount of success. We fired at various targets and I think we must have deterred him as we had no more complaints from the machine gunners. We noticed a few Fallschirmjäger still swinging from their parachute harness in the trees. Perhaps they were dead – we made sure. One of the few British tanks was making its way along the far end of the airfield but it stopped and the soldiers who had been using it to shield themselves from the Germans, soon ran for more secure cover. Throughout this period we were subject to bombing, strafing and not a little shelling. One of the reasons for this, I think, was a truck which had been abandoned nearby and was a popular target for demolition. This made our position very precarious as their aim was by no means good.

'At dusk we withdrew, mainly because we were out of ammunition for our .300 rifles. [3] I was reallocated to help the stretcher-bearers and I experienced that night the trials of a front line medical orderly, as we half-stumbled up hill and down dale

for what seemed miles. It was not until 0200hrs the following morning that we managed some welcome sleep. The night was bitterly cold, much more for us as we had no overcoats or blankets to wrap around us. At about 0400hrs we were awakened by cries for help, which upon investigation proved to come from two Germans, brothers from Essen. One of them was badly wounded in the chest and hand. As a result of the assistance given by the MO, the other brother would have done anything for us. As we were now at the receiving end of some bombing and strafing, the brothers laid out some crosses cut from parachutes and thereafter we were left in peace. Some of our comrades thought that the crosses were pointing to positions the Germans wanted to attack.

'By now the front line was only a few yards away and we could hear the mortar shells whistling over our heads, the staccato crack of machine guns and the shouts of many voices. Hungry and thirsty, the only water we had was from a tin of potatoes – the potatoes we ate raw. Then came midday and our forces withdrew again, leaving our party in no man's land. Two hours later the enemy forces advanced and we were prisoners again. A Luger pistol which I had captured while in the front line on Kavkazia Hill was hastily buried in the roots of an olive tree for possible future use. We were soon marched back to Maleme where we were put to work bringing in wounded paratroops.'

Kiwi Allan Jackson recalled that first morning thus:

'At 0800hrs over came the planes. For a solid hour they flew back and forth, sideways and crossways non-stop. We cowered in our trenches. Then suddenly it was dead quiet. We got out of our trenches – surprisingly again no one was hurt physically, but nerves not so good. Then someone pointed and coming up the valley were scores and scores of gliders, flying at a few hundred feet and so quietly – no sound at all. For a few moments we watched in amazement. Then out came the

parachutists, hundreds of them. Then it was all hands firing with whatever we had, which wasn't much, but they lost heavily. Then a box, something like a coffin, floated down near us. We were not sure whether it was some sort of bomb. Nothing happened so we went over and opened it. A Spandau machine gun, ammunition, hand grenades and Mausers. A gift from the Gods! Things were really hectic and those first waves of Germans suffered terribly. As the box came down so did seven Germans. They were dead before they hit the ground. There were three separate waves that came over. All suffered big losses. If only we had been better equipped.'

Capt Michael Forrester of the Military Mission was shaving in the cottage in which he had been staying, on the coast at Ayios Nicholias, a few miles west of Canea, on the morning of the 20th, when there seemed to be,

'. . . even more Luftwaffe activity, strafing and bombing, than on previous mornings; then, shortly before eight o'clock, I heard the concentrated drone of aircraft and there, over the sea approaching the coast, was a huge concentration of transport aircraft which positively darkened the sky. Soon German Fallschirmjäger were dropping all around; especially visible to us were those landing on the tents and marquees of the 7th General Hospital, despite huge red crosses marking the area; and every now and then, the odd rifle shot whistled over the cottage. Hursey and I had rifles, and at first we concentrated on our own safety and then, after one or two abortive attempts, succeeded in crossing the main coast road where we joined men of the Composite Battalion of the newly constituted 10th New Zealand Brigade under Col Kippenberger. Here we were viewed with great suspicion and it took a while to convince our new-found friends that we were genuine "Brits" and not enemy agents.

'That evening we made our way to New Zealand Divisional Headquarters where I reported to Lt-Col Gentry,

the GSO1, who enabled me to get through on the telephone to Col Salisbury-Jones at Creforce HQ. Having explained my circumstances and asked for instructions, Col Salisbury-Jones said, "Make contact with the nearest Greek units and do what you can to assist them," adding, "but don't get too involved." Accordingly Col Gentry arranged for us to be escorted to Col Kippenberger's HQ, which had the 6th Greek Regiment under command. It was during my first meeting with Karl Kippenberger that I realised I was in the presence of a very exceptional man – an impression that was to be reinforced during the next few days and again, years later, when I read his book Infantry Brigadier. *There is a short passage in this which does much to reflect the nature of the man. In a letter to a friend in New Zealand, written as a battalion commander before embarking for Greece prior to their first action, he said, "We have not wasted our time. We are ready. My men will do their whole duty." I was soon to realise, too, that those New Zealanders with whom I was to spend the next few days were a very special breed of men.'*

The respect was mutual and certainly with good reason. More than one historian commented that Michael Forrester's exploits in Crete in 1941 had 'impressed even the New Zealanders and become part of the legend of the battle for Crete'.

Roy Farran, then a 20-year-old officer commanding three light tanks of the 3rd The King's Own Hussars, recalled his actions on that fateful morning:

'One May morning, when we were breakfasting around the tanks in our olive grove, the sky suddenly became filled with German aircraft. Enemy planes raked our position, flying at tree top level, and we saw clouds of parachutes opening above us. There was complete chaos everywhere as we were taken by surprise. I mounted my tank and without waiting for orders from my superiors, drove off in the direction in which most

parachutes seemed to be falling.

'On the outskirts of Galatas, I encountered Greek soldiers in khaki who begged for ammunition for their rifles. They were already in action. I encountered one Greek who was stalking a German in the ditch on the roadside. I helped him and opened fire on another party of Germans on the edge of the trees. Galatas itself seemed firmly in the hands of the New Zealanders, so I returned along the road to Canea. All the time we were being strafed from the air. A New Zealander called me from the upper window of a building telling me that the tented hospital nearby had been attacked from both the air and the ground. I came across a party of Germans with several Allied prisoners and a captured truck on the edge of the road, and I opened fire. Some of the prisoners escaped when the German Fallschirmjäger scattered. My gunner shot one German down from a tree. My machine guns, lacking a cooling system, were red hot and I drove for the remains of the hospital looking for water to cool them. I found a severely wounded New Zealander in a hut and gave him a drink while the crew worked on our guns. Then we returned to our base in the olive grove where order had been restored, although one tank had been knocked out by an anti-tank rifle.' [4]

Lt Farran was ordered to support the New Zealanders around Galatas. The German Fallschirmjäger were advancing from the area of the prison at Agye, having captured the area around the cemetery, but the Kiwis were still holding the high ground. Farran reported to the battalion commander, who after he had first excused himself while he shot a sniper out of a tree, then ordered the tanks to attack across a field of grain towards the cemetery. Farran commented:

'We did this and despite mortar fire landing close to our tanks, drove the Germans back, crushing a machine gun under our

*tracks. Alone in my tank at one stage in the battle, I threw a
track. We repaired the caterpillar track under fire, but were
sheltered by cut-banks in the road. It was at that awful
moment that we saw what appeared to be a German in a
greatcoat approaching from the position that had been firing
at us. We opened fire only to discover that it was a woman in
a long grey dress, wounded and screaming to heaven as if
begging for mercy. She was not killed, although probably
wounded again by us or the Germans or both.'*

Ken Dawson was a member of the Northumberland Hussars
who were acting as infantrymen, defending the approaches to
the Akrotiri peninsula equipped with 'Ross and Remington
rimfire cartridge rifles and one anti-tank rifle.' Ken was
manning a road-block on the approach road and had a
grandstand view of the invasion, as he recalled:

*'. . . suddenly we heard a swishing noise and above our heads
appeared a glider. As it came over, the sides dropped and there,
sitting astride a central seat, were about 10 troops. In
retrospect, with the gun we should have killed all of them there
and then, but it all happened so quickly and so unexpectedly –
the nearby olive grove hiding our view of them until the last
minute. This particular glider, however, landed immediately
in front of our position on the road-block, about 50yds away.
We had taken out some stones in the wall which gave us cover
from an attack from that direction. We opened fire the
moment the glider landed. The occupants didn't have much
chance to return fire; some were killed, others wounded, until
eventually the survivors put up a white flag. Later, when it
was safe, the survivors were rounded up and taken to our
headquarters. We were amazed to see how well they were
armed and equipped. The folding bicycle in the glider had been
hit by an anti-tank rifle bullet, so it was in a bit of a mess. In
a short while the dead turned black and were hideously swollen*

in the very hot sun – not a pretty sight! I was told that about 10 gliders had landed on the peninsula; one near us burst into flames on landing, while others broke up when they hit large boulders which were everywhere about.

'. . . I put my head over the wall to fire once too often and the next thing I knew I was flat on my back! My helmet came off somehow and there was a neat hole through the front and a gaping, jagged one of about three to four inches in diameter at the back! My head was numb and I found that I had a cut about an inch long just above my right ear. Sometime later my head throbbed terribly and I was in a lot of pain and was taken to the first aid post. Later, after dark, I was transferred to the hospital in Canea with concussion and have been partially deaf ever since.'

Ken would spend the night of the 20th in hospital, then be sent to Suda Bay for evacuation. However, while waiting the pain began to subside, so he decided to make his own way back to his regiment and was safely reunited with his pals, his rifle and his kit!

The second wave: Rethymnon and Heraklion

Despite the problems of visibility at the take-off airfields in Greece, the second wave of paratroops were embarked and subsequently dropped at Rethymnon and Heraklion. One of these was Sebastian Krug, whom we met earlier in the drop on the Corinth Canal. He had been waiting at the Megara airstrip and recalls:

'Our battalion was to be part of the second wave to jump near Rethymnon, to take the airfield and the town. The first wave, which had dropped near Canea and Maleme, had trouble and many of the aircraft did not come back. Of those that did, many were damaged. About 1430hrs we started to get on board, but because of the damaged aircraft we couldn't all find places, and I was left in Greece. Thinking about it later, I realised that this was my lucky day, as we lost all our officers

and NCOs (140 out of 156 who landed now lie in the cemetery at Maleme). I was eventually one of the third wave and they dropped us west of Heraklion, where we met stiff resistance from Australian and New Zealand troops, also Greek soldiers and Cretan civilians. In the dark we couldn't tell friend from enemy. Our password was "Hermann Goering"; when you made the challenge you said, "Hermann," and the person you challenged had to reply, "Goering." However, many of the Englanders could speak some German, so they had no trouble with such a simple challenge – then it was being taken prisoner or being killed!

'As we flew in to our drop zone, the first man to jump was standing in the doorway and got shot in the foot, so he had to stay on the plane and return to base. When we reached the ground, in the dark we were unable to find our Waffenbehälter (weapons box), so had to make the best of it with pistols, machine-pistols and hand grenades. We even had difficulty finding each other in the dark. All around Heraklion was a very high wall with not many entrances. From the top of the wall, the defenders could see for miles, consequently we were easy targets.'

Felix Gaerte, another paratrooper who was landed at Rethymnon, writes:

'On 20 May we were woken by the noise of the transport planes flying over our tents … we were supposed to be at the airstrip at 1300hrs, to take the middle part of the island. On arrival we could see that some of the transport planes were already in a bad state having returned from taking the first wave, and that every time a plane took off or landed there was an enormous cloud of dust. The crew didn't say much before take-off, just got on with planning the new flight. As you can imagine, tension was very high as we climbed on board. We were sweating heavily because of the weight of all our gear – our uniforms, for instance, were made of wool (the same as we

had worn last in Norway in the winter) also we had our parachute, full bread bag (rations), pistol, grenades, knee-pads, lifebelt, etc. ... I started to sing the song "Wohlauf, Kameraden, auf's Pferd" (Good health comrades – on your horse!) and they all sang with me.

'We sat in the aircraft in two rows looking at each other. As we sat down, it started to move, then took off and climbed. The first one to jump would be Lt Laun, second Sgt Franz Knaeble, then me as number three, and so on, including Dr Rusch the assistant doctor. We flew at about 600-900ft over the sea, followed by two "watchdogs" (fighter cover) ... About half-way over we could see a squadron of skiffs and sailing boats with German soldiers on board. They waved up at us. The ships were escorted by two Italian warships, the sailors also waved to us and we waved back but they couldn't see us waving as the windows in the plane were very small. The sad fate of these "Filzlausgeschwaders" [Crab Squadrons] as they were called by the Army, was not known until after the fighting, many of these soldiers being drowned, killed or wounded and lying in the water for many days in their yellow lifejackets off the coast of Rethymnon.

'After flying for about three hours we reached the north coast of Crete. We could now peacefully observe the scenery as our plane turned to the west and then westwards along the coast. Everything looked very peaceful at first. It was a very mountainous area and at the back of the mountains, the sea; you could see snow on the tops of the mountains. [5] After we had been flying along the coast for a few miles, all hell broke loose, and there were crashes and bangs all round us. We could see that we were in the middle of heavy enemy fire and that our cabin had taken hits – we must have been down to between 300-600ft and the motors were cut. We were relieved to hear the jump master give the order to get ready – we had to pass it one to another as we could not hear above the noise from outside. All 12 of us stood up, put our hooks on the rail and Lt

Laun went to the door ready to jump. But he waited in vain as the doorway was under heavy fire, so he came back inside. After a while we received the order to jump, but were still not sure as we hadn't received the green light from the crew. We were told that it had been hit and broken so we jumped. In the air it was quiet, despite bullets flying by. They say you don't hear the one that hits so I ignored them. Below me I saw a trench with enemy soldiers in it, so I threw my hand grenades at them.

'Over Rethymnon town, some two miles away, I could see – and hear the deafening noise of – the Stukas diving and dropping their bombs. I had a very soft landing in a vineyard, close to my friend Cpl Kurt Martin. We got rid of our parachutes as quickly as possible. The first thing we looked for was our weapons box as we were under rifle and machine gunfire, but no luck. So we started to make towards our company commander and on the way found a weapons box containing rifles, ammunition and an MG, so I hung them on my shoulders and crawled towards a ditch, where I could see Lt Laun, Dr Rusch and Cpl Kurt Martin. They had also collected weapons, and Dr Rusch was looking after Kurt who had been badly wounded – shot in the chest many times, so he would not live much longer. Lt Laun was hit in the legs and had difficulty in standing. I made up my mind to defend the place where we were – it was about half a mile from the coast, in a hilly vineyard area ... In the next half an hour we made contact with more of our company, there must have been six or eight. In the sky behind us I could see the wonderful sight of hundreds more Fallschirmjäger landing. But as we watched we could see many of them were getting hit and then hanging dead from their harness. They were from FJR2. Some of the aeroplanes were shot down, crashing to earth and exploding. The same happened to one of the fighters which had protected us on the way down; he came down in a cloud of smoke.

'Most of the paras who landed around Rethymnon went through a similar ordeal, especially on the day we jumped. There

were many casualties, because the enemy was well dug in and waiting for us. We had been told that the enemy was not very strong and would give us little resistance – they were wrong.'

Bdr John Croft, who was part of the Heraklion garrison, remembers that 20 May had started very quietly, several men actually going down for a bathe in the early afternoon. A failure of communications with the other end of the island meant that no one knew about the enemy landings at Canea and Maleme. The daily 'blitz' was particularly heavy that day, the ground shaking constantly with the heavy bombing and clouds of dust everywhere. But then:

'. . . everything seemed to stop – the bombers went away and it became most eerily quiet – nothing appeared to move, all was still. The dust settled around us. It was just as though the end of the world had arrived. Instinctively I knew, as did all my comrades, that this was the moment that we had all dreaded for the last two weeks or so. It wasn't as if we were all armed. We had possibly one rifle between three men and we certainly hadn't got a Lewis light machine gun anywhere in the troop … And then, at first in the far distance, then nearer and nearer, there came the heavy drone of another kind of aeroplane – much heavier and far slower than the bombers and fighters which had been terrorising us over the last few days. At that moment, my fear was disturbed by one of the gunners who was running around the outlying slit-trenches, calling all the men to the gun pits, the command post and the rifle pits. Only just in time were we able to take post.

'The large Junkers Ju52s were now overhead and those with rifles were firing continuous volleys of shots. Where all the ammunition came from I can't imagine – men must have been collecting masses of it whenever the opportunity arose. And then swarms of parachutists were silently floating down towards us. There seemed to be hundreds of them. Those of us with rifles now changed our targets from the planes to the falling figures.

Sketch Map of Crete 1941

Above: Sketch map of Crete, 1941.

Below: British troops embarking at Alexandria on their way to Crete, 14 November 1940. Note the Westland Walrus light seaplane on its catapult. This was the type of aircraft which Arthur John Stevens looked after on board HMS *Gloucester*.
IWM — E1143

Right: Cold Steel. In the fierce hand-to-hand fighting which took place between the invaders and the defenders, the long British sword bayonet (1913 pattern) as seen here was a formidable weapon. *IWM*

Below: The garrison assembles. British troops disembarking in Crete towards the end of 1940. Note the interesting mixture of headgear — steel helmets, sola topees and forage caps. *IWM — E1166*

Above: A splendid mixture of uniforms among these Greek servicemen in Crete, plus a Cretan civilian for good measure. *IWM – E1174*

Below: Soon after unloading, this Royal Signals truck is giving a party of local Cretans a lift into town! *IWM — E1177*

Above: The Bishop of Canea blessing a column of Bren carriers on their way through the outskirts of Canea. The original caption read: 'light tanks and bren carriers' but the former seem to be submerged in people! *IWM — E1199*

Below: Teamwork. Greek and British soldiers combine to move a large artillery gun from the jetty in Suda Bay. *IWM — E1164*

Above: The difficult terrain in Greece can well be seen in this shot of tortuous mountain roads along which soldiers and civilians alike had to withdraw. *IWM — E2523*

Below: British troops resting during the withdrawal in Greece. They all wear the prewar pattern webbing, and their anti-gas respirators in the 'ready' position on their chests. Rifles are the .303in Short Lee Enfield. *IWM — E2520*

Right: Withdrawing in Greece. British troops have a quick 'wash and brush up', shave and rest their aching feet, during their long march to the embarkation ports. *IWM — E2751*

Below: Heavy artillery moving through a town in Greece during the withdrawal. *IWM — E2530*

Left: Escape from Greece. Exhausted British troops on board one of the Royal Navy vessels which rescued them from the beaches.
IWM — E2763

Left: Their first glimpse of Crete. British soldiers and sailors scan the shoreline of Suda Bay as they sail in.
IWM — E1155

Above: New Zealand Maoris perform their unmistakable 'Haka'. This originally was a dance before battle to instil courage and fight into the dancers and terror into any of the enemy who might see it. *IWM — E3261E*

Right: The inevitable result when AA cover was lacking — a stricken vessel in Suda Bay after a dive-bombing raid. *IWM — E3137E*

Above and below: Shot down in flames. Two graphic photographs taken of the skies over Crete showing a Ju52 crashing in flames while others still drop their loads of Fallschirmjäger. These pictures were taken over Heraklion aerodrome. *IWM — A4144 and A4145*

Above: A crashed glider, which belonged to the Sturmregiment, with some of its occupants lying dead beside the fuselage. *IWM — E3064E*

Below: This Fallschirmjäger has come down in an olive grove; note his parachute still hanging from a tree. *B. L. Davis Collection*

Above: The Royal Tigers in action. This painting by the late Terence Cuneo depicts the German Fallschirmjäger landing directly on top of positions near Heraklion, of the 2nd Battalion The Royal Leicestershire Regiment on 20 May 1941 and appears here by kind permission of the Trustees. *Royal Leicesters Museum*

Below: The follow-up force were to be the men of 5 Gebirgs Division, with their distinctive edelweiss badge which they wore on the left-hand side of their fieldcaps. *IWM — HU55009*

Above: Two recently dropped Fallschirmjäger look towards smoke rising near to Suda Bay. Note that one carries a slung rifle (Karabiner 98k), whilst the other hefts an MP38 Schmeisser sub-machine gun. *B. L. Davis Collection*

Below: First aid to the wounded. This temporary aid post, close to a crashed German aircraft, has been shaded from the sun by parachutes, underneath which a German prisoner has his wounds dressed. *IWM — E3135E*

Published in Canea
by Cretaforce
Editorial Office
Percival House
Canea
Telephone 460

CRETE NEWS

THE FIRST BRITISH PAPER PUBLISHED IN CRETE

THURSDAY
22
MAY 1941
Sunrise 5.18
Sunset 7.52

Vol 1 · No 3   CANEA, CRETE   Price 2 Drachmas — Free to troops

NAVY SMASHES NAZI SEA LANDING ATTEMPT

BIG CONVOY SUNK LAST NIGHT

THOUSANDS OF GERMAN REINFORCEMENTS DROWNED

German convoys packed with troops and heading for the coast of Crete were intercepted and sunk by the Royal Navy last night. The convoys, heading towards the island in the darkness at full speed, were picked out by searchlights. Whole broadsides were fired at them and ship after ship caught fire and sank. Ammunition vessels exploded. The red glow of burning vessels could be seen clearly from the island.

The Navy continued their hunt throughout the night. Thousands of German troops and great quantities of stores, including guns, ammunition and almost certainly tanks more went to the bottom.

No German ships reached the Crete shore at all.

VIGOROUS BRITISH COUNTER ATTACKS

AUSTRALIANS PRAISE GREEK ATTACK

SUCCESSFUL ACTION BY COMBINED FORCE

Greek and Cretan troops, fighting side by side with Australians, yesterday gained praise from an Australian Brigadier.

They took part in a counter attack which was completely successful, pushing strong parachute forces out of a position they had managed to seize.

After the attack the Brigadier sent in the following despatch:

"Greeks and Cretans did magnificently and our steps are proud to fight beside them."

THE EYES OF THE WORLD ARE ON US

IN GREECE ONCE MORE

Greek Humiliations

Crete News will continue publishing the 23th cut this State as long as the printing press remains undamaged. We cannot guarantee as prompt delivery as in earlier times. We print no news from the outside world because all radios were being used yesterday for the battle. Before the present in the outside world, the battle for Crete is the news.

Above: Held in a
street is this large
group of German
prisoners, some of
whom are wounded.
IWM — E3066E

Left: Front page
of *Crete News*
for 22 May.
IWM — E3133E

Right: Italian destroyers seen here in the Aegean. They are of the 'Navigatori' class, with a 1,628-ton displacement, so considerably larger than the 'Partenope' class which were guarding the convoys. *IWM — HU55011*

Below: HMS *Dido*. This cruiser was the flagship of Rear-Adm Glennie. It engaged the caique convoy on 21 May, some 18 miles north of Canea. Later, during the evacuation, it was hit by dive-bombers on its 'B' turret on 29 May. *IWM — FL5208*

Above: HMS *Nizam*, port broadside view. It took part in the bombardment of Scarpanto airfield on the night of 20/21 May, assisted with the landing of 'Layforce' on the night of 26/27 May and with the evacuation from Sphakia when it suffered minor damage only. *IWM — FL4196*

Below: Keeping watch for enemy aircraft. The gun crew of this multiple 'pom-pom' 2pdr AA gun mounting shade their eyes as they try to spot enemy aircraft coming out of the sun. The 'Chicago Piano', as it was called, was the major small-calibre British close-range AA weapon, with a range of some 6,800 yards and a rate of fire of 100rpm. *IWM — A474*

Above: HMS *Kipling* 'making smoke'. The destroyer was a member of Lord Louis Mountbatten's 5th Destroyer Flotilla and rescued survivors when the *Kelly* and *Kashmir* were sunk on 23 May. *IWM — FL14424*

Right: The debris of destroyed Junkers Ju52s have been swept off the runway so that more troops can be air lifted in. *S. Krug*

Above: This photograph dramatically illustrates how low the low-altitude drops really were! *B. L. Davis Collection*

Left: Comrades in arms greet one another and provide an excellent close-up of their personal arms and equipment. One has an MP 38 sub-machine gun, the other a rifle (98k), both have binoculars and numerous other items such as waterbottles, ammo bandoliers, etc. The British and Commonwealth troops were most impressed by the lavish scale of both weapons and personal equipment carried by the Fallschirmjäger. *B. L. Davis Collection*

Above: Pursuit. Fallschirmjäger pressing on into the foothills as they push the British and Commonwealth troops back towards Sphakia. *B. L. Davis Collection*

Below: The little fishing village of Sphakia, from where the major portion of those troops rescued from Crete were evacuated by the Royal Navy. The beach was so small that most arrivals had to remain on the high cliffs until being called down to embark. *Bob Sollars*

Above: A convoy of evacuated troops leaving Suda Bay for Alexandria; the closest ship is the destroyer HMS *Nubian*. This was one of the early convoys taking non-essential troops off the island. Later, on 26 May, HMS Nubian had her stern blown off, but was still able to steam at 20kt and reached Alexandria safely. *IWM — AX53A*

Left: Safe arrival in Egypt. Troops are packed solid on the deck of this warship, newly arrived at, as the original caption says (for security reasons), 'an Egyptian port'! *IWM — E3363*

Right: ANZAC troops bring a stretcher case off the ship at Alexandria harbour.
IWM — E3284

Below: A souvenir from Crete. This soldier has one of the Nazi ground-to-air recognition flags as his souvenir of Crete.
IWM — E3370

Above: This Australian soldier made an incredible single-handed journey in a small boat with a ragged, rotting sail, from Crete to just west of Mersa Matruh. 10 miles off the coast, the boat literally fell to pieces and he had to swim, using his two-gallon water tin to help him stay afloat. He had been machine-gunned by enemy aircraft, guided himself by means of a pocket knife stuck in a bottle cork (when the sun made a long shadow he knew it was pointing south!), and had eaten only some chocolate dropped by a British plane. *IWM — E3771*

Below: While the destroyer HMS *Kimberley* was *en route* to Tobruk in November 1941, it sighted this small rowing boat drifting, so it stopped to investigate. It was full of soldiers who had been hiding in Crete ever since the Germans had captured the island, then escaped in this small rowing boat. They had navigated using just a map torn from an atlas and a sixpenny compass! *IWM — E3711E*

Above: After the battle there was time for the Fallschirmjäger and mountain troops to relax, while they waited for fresh orders. By the end of July a large German garrison was on the island and had taken over control. *IWM — HU29708*

Below: This was the first graveyard for the fallen of I and II/MG Bataillon at Rethymnon. Later, all were moved to a main German cemetery (see Postscript). *E. Schrer*

Left: Two German officers in tropical uniform inspect the damage in a rubble-strewn street in Canea, 14 June 1941. *IWM — HU66983*

Below: Typical guerrilla group of SOE (Special Operations Executive) and Cretan partisans who roamed the mountains of Crete during the occupation. *IWM — HU66036*

Above: This evocative photograph of two female partisans typifies the determined spirit of the entire population to resist the Germans. *Hellenic Army General Staff Military History Directorate*

Left: Partisan leader Kapetan Manoli Bandooras, from Asites near Heraklion, was the most important and powerful of the Cretan guerrilla leaders. Of peasant stock, he was almost illiterate, yet he had a very forceful personality and wielded immense influence. Fearless, headstrong and domineering, he was prone to rash acts. *IWM — HU66051*

Above: One of the most famous guerrillas was George Psychoundakis, 'The Cretan Runner' — seen here on the left with a bearded compatriot. His wartime autobiography *The Cretan Runner* was translated by Patrick Leigh-Fermor who also wrote the introduction. George Psychoundakis was awarded a BEM for his part in the Cretan Resistance. *Hellenic Army General Staff Military History Directorate*

Above: Before returning to New Zealand, 100 officers and men of the New Zealand Expeditionary Force under commander Lt-Gen Freyberg VC revisited Crete for a memorial service on 22 October 1945. They spent three days there and were given a wonderful welcome by the Cretans. This photograph shows Gen Freyberg laying a wreath at the NZ memorial. *IWM — NA26434*

Above: The tranquil Suda Bay War Cemetery contains 1,509 World War 2 graves, together with some 46 others from World War 1 and the Consular cemetery. *Either War Graves Commission or C. Buist*

Above: The emblem of the UKCVA. *C. Buist*

Above: Anniversary poster produced by Mr Bob Sollars on the occasion of the 58th anniversary of the Battle of Crete. *Bob Sollars*

Above: Men of 5 Gebirgs Division waiting to embark on the Ju52s that will take them to Crete. *Alexander Turnbull Library — DA01313*

Below: Suda Bay, Crete. Note the RN vessels in the fine anchorage, the two Greek Gendarmerie and the British AA team with their World War 1 vintage Lewis gun on its Ack-Ack mounting. *IWM — E1189*

Above: A waterbottle or some kind of water container was a vital necessity during the hot, difficult withdrawal over the mountains to Sphakia. Here a New Zealand officer, using straps, lanyards, etc lowers his into a well so that it can be filled with the precious liquid. *Alexander Turnbull Library — DA08185*

Below: Once they had captured Maleme aerodrome, the Germans brought in light AA defence, such as this 2cm Flak 30. Introduced in 1935, it had a maximum effective ceiling of 7,200ft and a rate of fire of 120rpm. *Alexander Turnbull Library — DA11983*

SOLDIERS

OF THE

ROYAL BRITISH ARMY, NAVY, AIR FORCE!

There are **MANY OF YOU STILL HIDING** in the mountains, valleys and villages.

You have to **PRESENT** yourself **AT ONCE TO THE GERMAN TROOPS.**

Every **OPPOSITION** will be completely **USELESS!**

Every **ATTEMPT TO-FLEE** will be in **VAIN.**

The **COMMING WINTER** will force you to leave the mountains.

Only soldiers, who **PRESENT** themselves **AT ONCE.** will be sure of a **HONOURABLE AND SOLDIERLIKE CAPTIVITY OF WAR.** On the contrary who is met in civil-cothes will be treated as a spy.

THE COMMANDER OF KRETA

Above: Poster displayed in Crete after the German occupation to try to get escaped POWs or others to surrender. *Alexander Turnbull Library — DA10726*

A German Fallschirmjäger, wearing his knee-length jumping smock; this one is made of camouflaged material, but the majority of those worn in Crete were plain olive-green. In its capacious pockets would be clips of ammunition, message pad, maps, mapcase and compass. *Alexander Turnbull Library — DA12631*

Above: Medics of 5 Field Ambulance attending to a German casualty in an olive grove somewhere in Crete. *Alexander Turnbull Library — DA09598*

There was no time to think about the horror of it all. We instinctively knew that it was them or us. And it was the invaders who must be killed. We shot them in the air! We shot them as they landed around us! One lay dead right in front of our command post. Most of them didn't stand a chance. About a hundred or so yards away we had the satisfaction of seeing one of the Ju52s crash, disgorging bodies all around, many of them burnt and charred in the fire that followed. Just a few yards away, another parachutist was hanging from his parachute which had been entangled in a tree. He pointed his machine-pistol towards us but too late. Someone on the ground had watched him come down, taken careful aim and shot him first. The shot hit one of the grenades strung around his waist and that was another one who would cause us no further trouble.'

One of the major British infantry units in the Heraklion garrison was the 2nd Royal Leicesters, who had arrived on the 14th, only six days before the German invasion, to become the mobile reserve for 14th Infantry Brigade, who were defending Heraklion and its airfield. Their history records that the 'clean sea air of Crete was like a tonic to the troops, who but a few days before had been undergoing the hot Khamsin and the dust of the desert'. Despite daily strafing from the Luftwaffe, they had got themselves firmly ensconced by the morning of 20 May, although the company commanders still had quite a number of reconnaissances to make, as they had to be able to go 'parachute-hunting' anywhere at a moment's notice. There were the normal morning 'hates' then things quietened down, and the CO (Lt-Col Cox) decided to have a bath at the only hotel still equipped.

'At 1545hrs a single reconnaissance plane circled slowly overhead. Ten minutes later the news came that the Australians were warmly entertaining parachutists at Canae. The Adjutant at once despatched Pte Blythe on his motorcycle to fetch

the CO. Blythe had an exciting trip. As he reached the main road he was machine gunned by a Bf110 strafing the road. His cycle was hit and he hurried on foot. He reached the CO, who dressed rapidly, only to find that his truck was missing. However, he commandeered another one to take him part of the way and ran the remainder. By this time an intense air attack was in progress. The sky was filled with hostility. Heinkels, Dorniers and Ju88s abounded. Fortunately the battalion position was not yet on the enemy map and only Bf110 machine gunning was directed at it ... By 1720hrs the attack died down, though there were a number of planes still circling overhead.

'Suddenly, looking out to sea, there was a host of little flashes of light, like the twinkling of stars. It was the sunlight on the "blisters" of the Ju52 parachute aircraft. Soon this long snake of troop carriers could clearly be seen, flying low over the sea, past the little rocky island in the bay. One stream of aircraft headed straight up West Wadi. Quite suddenly, the sky seemed filled with parachutes, many of brilliant colours. Battalion HQ was busy counting the plane-loads. The planes were flying in "Vics", the outside two dropped 13-15 parachutists and the centre one supplies on coloured 'chutes. It was a thrilling, exciting spectacle, quite outclassing the prewar Hendon air display and Cobham's air circus. Five troop-carriers were brought down in flames by the Bofors. Two were claimed by the battalion's AA LMGs. The air was filled with bullets and many parachutists died or were wounded on their journey to earth. One plane went on its way with a parachutist entangled on its wing. Meanwhile, the company commanders had been busy spotting the dropping zones. By 1815hrs the Carrier Platoon (on foot) and C Company under Capt Carden, had gone like hounds unleashed, to the "Buttercup Field", Porus area; A Company went to the Porus-West Wadi area; and B Company to Opps Wadi as local protection for Brigade HQ. This left only Battalion HQ and D Company. At 1830hrs these were ordered back within the perimeter to fill a gap between West Wadi and

the York and Lancaster Regiment. The carriers had an early success as a crowd of parachutists descended on top of them. As Capt Bryan said, "It was plain slaughter for them, poor chaps!" Having, in the interim, been parted from A Company, the carriers then joined C Company. This company became involved with and fought alongside 2/4 Australian Battalion. The Australians were lately out of the withdrawal from Greece and were only two companies strong. They were very short of weapons and had been lent two of the Battalion's six mortars and crews.

'C Company and the carriers kept hard at it with considerable success. They finally rejoined Battalion reserve early next morning. A Company had a good hunt too, and estimated 150 enemy killed. However, 2Lt Young, who had played rugby football for Scotland, was twice wounded, the second time fatally. While Capt Nicholls, the Company Commander, was wrestling with a German, his batman fired and killed the German but the bullet in transit wounded Spike Nicholls in the hand. The MO (Capt McLeod) duly amputated his little finger, which was ceremoniously buried by Maj Serjeantson. Nicholls was awarded the Military Cross for his gallantry and leadership. The Brigade Commander reported that the dash and determination of A Company was instrumental in clearing the inner perimeter of the enemy. L Cpl Sydney Markham received the Military Medal for the way he led his section on 20 May and again on the 25th.' [6]

Rethymnon

The Rethymnon garrison was mainly composed of Australian units of which the 2/1st and 2/11th Infantry Battalions, 2nd AIF, formed the nucleus of the force detailed to hold the airfield (see Appendix 1 for full details). This force also included both other Aussies (infantry, artillery, engineers and machine guns) and some improvised Greek battalions. There were also two Matilda Mk II tanks, under the command of Lt

George Simpson, detached from B Sqn 7RTR, which had arrived on 17/18 May, having been driven by road from Suda Bay after the original plan to bring them by naval lighter had to be abandoned due to rough weather. The two tanks were originally to be dug in on the airfield, but the CO of 2/1st Infantry, Lt-Col Ian Campbell, disagreed and got permission to keep them in a mobile role, concealing them in an olive grove along the Wadi Pigl which was to the immediate south-west of the airfield. Paul Handel writes:

'At approximately 1615hrs the first troop-carrying aircraft arrived, dropping paratroops who landed along the coast near the airfield. Some nine aircraft were brought down by small-arms fire. There was a concerted effort by the German paratroops to capture a hill (Hill "A") which directly overlooked the eastern end of the airfield. At about 1715hrs, Campbell ordered the two tanks to go round to the east of the hill to support an attack. Due to terraces in the vicinity, it was impossible for the tanks to go far off the road. One of the Matildas bellied on the edge of a ditch on the north side of the airfield, and the second Matilda fell into a wadi, a drop of eight to ten feet. Lt Simpson dismounted from his tank, but was killed by a burst of machine gunfire. With nowhere to go, the remaining crews apparently stayed with their immobile machines, unable to provide any support to the battle. The Germans had occupied the hill by 2200hrs and captured the two tank crews. During a night action, C Company of the 2/1st Battalion recaptured the airfield which had been briefly held by the Germans. A dawn attack by both Australian battalions, the 2/1st against Hill "A" and 2/11th against Hill "B" (which was to the west of the airfield) had mixed results. 2/1st Battalion was forced to withdraw due to lack of support by the Greek battalions, but the 2/11th cleared the Germans off Hill "B". Later on the morning of 21 May, Hill "A" was captured and this and subsequent actions during the day netted the Australians about 140 prisoners of war.' [7]

The seaborne operation

Felix Gaerte says that he saw part of the amphibious portion of the operation from the window of the Ju52 in which he was travelling to Crete. This must have been very early on in their voyage, as the first wave – which was aiming for Suda Bay – had an anticipated landfall during daylight hours of 21 or 22 May, and when Gaerte saw them it was still only the afternoon of the 20th. As will be told in detail later, they would be intercepted and mainly sunk by British cruisers and destroyers on the night of 20/21 May, while transporting some 6,300 troops – mainly from Ringel's 5 Gebirgs Division – in two improvised flotillas each of some 30 plus shallow draught Greek barges (caiques) and escorted by Italian warships. The second flotilla, which was originally designated for the support of Gruppe Ost and Gruppe Mitte or would be redirected to Gruppe West on the 22nd, would suffer a similar fate although their losses would be smaller.

Another possibility is that Felix Gaerte actually saw caiques belonging to one of the other formations that was involved in the initial phase of the seaborne operation, namely units of the 5th Panzer Division, which had also allocated a tank company (5/Pz Regiment 31) and their Motorcycle Battalion (Kradschützenbataillon 55) in direct support of 5 Gebirgs Division. The tank company [8] contained both PzKpfw IIIs and IVs – so had they managed to arrive in Crete in time to support the assault, then they could have had a considerable impact on the battles for the island, as they were much more formidable than the obsolete British AFVs. The initial actions of the infantry element of this division involved the island of Kithera, which 2/Schützen Regiment 13, under Capt Graf von Schmettow, would invade on 14 May, then moving on to the neighbouring island of Antikithera which they were due to take on the 19th. The operation began on the 13th, the battalion moving from Sparta to Githeon, where they boarded fishing boats for the journey to Salion off Kithera. This was achieved without any interference, and on the 18th a company moved on to Kithera, then finally on to Antikithera. One member of the company explained how they had been allocated a motor sailing vessel with a Greek crew; they had four sergeants, seven other ranks, five Greek crew and a cargo of food and equipment. One of the NCOs recalled:

'When we were about half-way to Kithera, we noticed on the horizon to the east, aeroplanes and warships. We could also see a lot of smoke and AA fire – there must have been some hard fighting going on. All of a sudden one of the English ships saw us and came full steam ahead towards us with its guns pointing directly at us. The first shot was short, and there was a fountain of water near us. Then the second shot hit us and there was a splintering of wood. We could now see that the ship was an English destroyer. Some of our men were blown overboard and the rest jumped when the boat caught fire. They were still machine gunning us in the water, but fortunately it was stormy with high waves and these saved some of our lives. Then about 100 yards from us we saw some rocks stretching out into the sea, but to our dismay, the Englander started shooting at the rocks so we couldn't reach them safely. Then all of a sudden it stopped shooting at us, and at the same time there was a big flame from the destroyer – it had received a direct hit from one of our fighter-bombers. After a while it sank and I can truly say this action saved our lives, as we were then able to reach the rocks. We huddled together to keep ourselves warm in the night, as it was very cold. On the next day, before sunrise, we saw one of our planes – it was a Dornier. To make sure that he had seen us we all shouted and waved with all that we could find, because he had first just flown over our heads. However, after a while a boat came to fetch us, so we swam to it and our comrades pulled us on board.'

The Schützen Regiment 13 would remain on the islands until 31 May, when success on Crete was guaranteed; however, Kradschützenbataillon 55, which was committed to Operation 'Merkur', was loaded onto other fishing boats at Megara and Milos and set out for Crete. As already mentioned, this convoy was also partly destroyed by British warships. The rest reached the port of Piraeus, then marched to the landing fields at Lamia and Topolia where they were loaded onto Ju52s and flew to Crete, where the motorcycle companies would take part in operations.

Strange Infantrymen

Fighting with the New Zealanders, both on the airfield perimeter and on Hill 107, were all manner of *ad hoc* infantry, none more strange than the Jewish pioneers from 604 Company, AMPC. Among them was a former German-born Jew from Palestine, tall, fair-haired, a store-keeper from Hamburg known as 'Dutch' Holland (not his real name) who found himself fighting for his life in the camp, caught in the middle of the German assault. Racing for a nearby stone hut which appeared empty, he dived inside and found himself facing a frightened German paratrooper brandishing his Schmeisser. Holland threw himself at the startled German, grabbed his gun and shot him at point-blank range. He then continued to fire at passing enemy, keeping them at bay on his own until a party of Kiwis joined him. Soon afterwards, however, a large party of Germans stormed the building and the defenders had no choice but to surrender. Holland, who spoke fluent German, was able to ask for water and the paras soon became quite friendly with the new 'friend' not realising that he was Jewish!

Not far away another drama was taking place on Hill 107. Three men, including a short German Jew called Hess, had slipped through the German positions at last light and were hiding in the shrubs on the hillside. Hess, who was the most experienced, was leading. Bodies of both Germans and British were sprawled along the sand track, but no live Germans could be seen. To their right, in the fading light, the men could make out the forward platoon positions of 21st NZ Battalion, in front of which there were two gliders. Near them, a Kiwi was dragging an injured man up the hill; then suddenly, the entire slope came under withering fire from German paras located in the village of Vlakheronissa in the valley below. Pin-pointing some of the German paras advancing up the hill, Hess and one of the others started sniping to keep the enemy at bay until the Kiwi and his injured companion had reached safety. Next dawn, the Germans mounted a heavy attack to capture the hill. Fighting desperately, Hess and the others soon realised that their chances of survival were fading rapidly. Hess was very worried about his identity, because once captured he was in danger of being executed as a German alien (this had been announced over Berlin radio some weeks before the Greek campaign began). So he burned his paybook and, using the fieldcraft skills he had learned leading fighting patrols across no man's land during the Great War, he managed to get away unscathed. But his luck did not last and he was killed a few days later fighting in the street in the village of Xamoudhokhori, while trying to escape to the southern coast. In all some 300 Palestinian Jews managed to do just this and were safely evacuated to Alexandria.

And a last word from a paratrooper

Before summarising Day One let us return to Helmut Wenzel, who dropped at Maleme and was soon wounded. We left him with his companions Primke, Groefeld, Mospack and Engel, having taken up a defensive position for the night, but he soon decided not to stay there:

> 'Minutes had passed when we heard somebody moving up the gorge towards us. Our request for the password was answered by a hail of bullets. Engel, immediately to my right, received a fatal head wound. A careless moment and he died without so much as uttering a word. I heard the metallic click as his helmet hit his rifle.

'Then all hell was let loose. About half a mile away to the west we could hear our machine guns and small-arms fire picking up. I decided to make a daring dash to our positions, asking my men who would volunteer to come along? They all said I must be mad to take such an unnecessary risk. But I insisted on going, and told those who wished to stay to take up a defensive position again. As the fire died down I made a run for it down the gorge in a westerly direction, crossing a wide open plain. Immediately the fire picked up again and I could see some of the enemy standing up firing wildly at me – but missing! It was like hare shooting! Suddenly I fell headfirst into a wadi and, somersaulting back on my feet again, I saw, less than 15 yards away, a British Tommy, who at my sudden appearance, jumped behind a tree pointing his rifle ready to shoot. Like greased lightning I took cover behind the next olive tree, pointing my pistol at him. But neither of us fired. After seconds of cautiously watching each other, he decided to make a dash in the opposite direction while I raced down the wadi (nearly 50yds wide). I recognised in the darkness a few British who seem to be retreating from their position. I managed to get to the edge of the wadi without being hit and swung myself out of it. Immediately a fusillade of bullets from the German position forced me to take cover again. It took quite some time to make them understand who I was and my reunion with them was more than exciting! Meanwhile, Primke and Mospack also arrived – splendid fellows: well done!

'I gave my comrades a precise description of the territory ahead and the whereabouts of the British. We decided on an immediate return to the wadi to stage an attack. But I only got as far as the dried up riverbank before collapsing. I don't know how long I was unconscious but I woke up again as somebody dressed a wound to my head. I shall never forget that sight! A British soldier was bending over me with a big pair of scissors in his hands – cutting away my hair! All around me there were only English soldiers. Faintly I asked, "Am I a prisoner?" "No! No!"

came the quick answer from somewhere, "These are all our prisoners," and a little paratrooper appeared from nowhere wielding his pistol – once again I lost consciousness. On the arrival at Maleme airfield first aid post, I regained consciousness once more, when a German doctor told me, "Whoever attended to your wounds saved your life! We have no medical dressings left." He didn't even take my dressings off. To this day I should like to meet the English doctor who attended to my wounds on the early hours of 21 May 1941 on Hill 107 near Maleme airfield. I owe him a big "Thank you!"

'Lance Corporal Linde found my bullet-pierced jumping helmet again. On reading my name inside the torn helmet encrusted with blood and hair, he assumed I must be dead. He took it back with him to give to my wife as a last souvenir of me. Eventually, sometime later, he arrived a little embarrassed at my front door, not knowing how to explain to my wife the sad circumstances of his visit when she said, "Oh everything is alright. I received a card today from the hospital in Vienna from my husband, please do come in!" At this sudden good news tears ran over his face, as he handed over the battle-scarred jumping helmet to my wife. Never-failing comradeship among Fallschirmjäger! My wife now possesses two battle-scarred jumping helmets – one from Eben Emael, the other from Crete!'

Summary: End of Day One

When Gen Student and his staff of XI Fliegerkorps took stock that evening, the situation was far from satisfactory. Some 10,000 glider-borne troops and paratroops had been landed, but less than 6,000 remained effective, the rest being either killed or wounded.

- **Gruppe West** had managed to secure a foothold in the Maleme area, but had not yet taken the vital ground (Hill 107) nor cleared the defenders from the airfield, despite making a determined attack during the afternoon, which had been halted by a spirited counter-attack led by two tanks.

- **Gruppe Mitte** had failed both at Rethymnon and at Canea, the former situation bordering on the critical.
- **Gruppe Ost** was in no better state, having failed to take either Heraklion or its airfield.
- The leading flotilla of the seaborne reinforcements which was to have brought the mountain troops to Heraklion had been delayed.

Having weighed up the facts, Student rightly decided that the key to success lay in the west and that he would concentrate everything on the Maleme-Canea area. Accordingly 5 Gebirgs Division was ordered to switch to Maleme. As it turned out, Brig Hargest's 5th NZ Infantry Brigade did not make another counter-attack that night, despite having superior numbers. Whether they held off because they thought the situation was stable and that they should save their strength for the seaborne assault which was expected to come is not clear. However, they missed a golden opportunity to dislodge the German foothold. Lt Roy Farran recalled the incident thus:

> 'We next took part in a half-hearted counter-attack by night on the prison, supporting New Zealand infantry. My tank was damaged either by grenades or the barbed wire through which we crashed. When I met him after the war, Baron von der Heydte, leader of the German paratroops, told me that if that attack had been pushed home to the prison area, he doubted if his disorganised units could have resisted. As it was, they suffered heavily at the hands of the New Zealanders and small pockets of Greeks.' 9

Gen Freyberg was quite upbeat in his final signal to Cairo that evening:

> 'Today has been a hard one. We have been hard-pressed, but so far I believe we still hold the aerodromes at Rethymnon,

187

Heraklion and Maleme and the two harbours. The margin by which we hold them is slim, and it would be wrong of me to paint too optimistic a picture. Fighting has been heavy and we have killed large numbers of Germans. Communications are most difficult. The scale of air attacks on Canea has been severe. Everyone realises the vital issue and we will fight it out.'

Freyberg went on to say that they had captured a German operation order which contained 'very ambitious objectives which had all failed'. This was, of course, perfectly true at that moment and clearly accounts for the positive tenor of his report. However, had he, or his intermediate headquarters (Brig Hargest), been in better communications with those in action on Hill 107 or at the Maleme airfield, then remedial action might have been taken. As it was, Lt-Col Andrew VC, the CO of 22nd NZ Infantry Battalion, thinking that his three forward companies had been overwhelmed, would withdraw his other two during the night, leaving the hill practically undefended.

Nevertheless the situation in other areas was by no means as worrying. The Heraklion sector had seen major success, with at least a third of the 2,000-odd paratroops killed or captured, and many others wounded. The aerodrome was still in Allied hands, even though there were some small pockets of enemy within the perimeter that would have to be dealt with in the morning. The Germans had, however, penetrated into the town.

Notes
1. The paratroops had a recognition system using flags to indicate friendly positions. This was quickly spotted and made use of by the defenders which added to the chaos in this bitter, hand-to-hand fighting.
2. Generalmajor Suessmann and his staff had all been killed when the cable attached to their glider snapped shortly after take-off, while they were over the island of Aegina in the Saronic Gulf.

3. The normal calibre of British rifles during World War 2 was .303in. The .300in Ross was a Canadian manufactured rifle, 70,000 of which were sold to the UK by the USA in 1940 (some of which had been bought back in 1917 for training).

4. Roy Farran (later Maj, DSO, MC) was writing in the May 1991 edition of the *Parnassos Bulletin*.

5. My friend Werner Wagenknecht of Pelm told me that he had spoken after the war to two ex-Fallschirmjäger who had dropped over Crete, but had been swept by the high winds into the mountains and landed in the middle of a wilderness. They were finally found by Cretan mountain people, who locked them up in an old hut. During the night they killed their guards (they had been disarmed but their captors had overlooked their knives) and escaped. After wandering for days, they finally met up with some other German soldiers and survived.

6. *History of the Royal Leicesters*; Chapter VI The 2nd Battalion: The Battle of Crete.

7. Australian tank enthusiast Paul Handel wrote an article about these tanks in *Tracklink*, the magazine of the Friends of the Tank Museum, from which he has kindly allowed me to quote.

8. The tank company would eventually reach Crete and would remain there after the capture of the island and be known as 1./Panzer Abteilung Kreta. The tanks had to be loaded onto elderly wooden barges in Greece and then towed slowly across the 180 miles of sea – a hazardous undertaking!

9. Quoted from *Parnassos Bulletin*, May 1991.

7

The Battle Continues

Reinforcing Gruppe West

In line with his revised plan of action, Gen Student ordered his quite slender available reserves to be used to reinforce Gruppe West, some 300 Fallschirmjäger being dropped just to the north of Tavrontis on the morning of the 21st, then a further 250 just to the east of Maleme that afternoon. They were reinforcing success, because at about 0800hrs that morning a detachment of the Sturmregiment had captured Hill 107, led by Oberstarzt Dr Heinrich Neumann. Neumann, who was the Regimental Medical Officer of the 1st Fallschirmjäger Sturmregiment, and who had been awarded the Iron Cross First Class during the assault on 'Fortress Holland' in 1940, had taken over command of Maj Walter Koch's battalion (1st Bn), when Koch suffered a serious head wound in the battle for the hill. Some historians appear sceptical about the part he actually played, but nevertheless, he was awarded the Knight's Cross for this and subsequent actions during the fighting on Crete. Other officers of the Sturmregiment to win Knight's Crosses in the same engagement were Lt Josef Barmetler (OC C Kompanie), Capt Walter Gericke (CO of IV Bataillon) and Lt Horst Trebes (acting CO of III Bataillon on the death of its commander). In all, some 27 members of the Fallschirmjäger were awarded the coveted Knight's Cross for their bravery on Crete (see Appendix 3 for details).

With this, the most dominating feature in the immediate vicinity, now in their hands, it was possible for the German

Fallschirmjäger to gain control of the vital Maleme airfield. In the middle of the afternoon, following directly on after a prolonged and heavy air raid on the New Zealand positions to the east of the airstrip, the rest of the Fallschirmjäger reinforcements were dropped onto the airfield. This force comprised two companies of FJR1, plus an ad hoc third company made up of men from FJR2. Their arrival boosted the morale of the very tired remnants of the Sturmregiment, as did the arrival of more ammunition, which was brought in by a single Ju52 that, ignoring all the artillery and small-arms fire that constantly swept the airfield, landed, taxied down to the German-held end of the runway, unloaded the ammunition, took on board some of the most seriously wounded, and then calmly took off again!

It had been agreed that, as soon as possible, once the airfield was in German hands, a battalion of 5 Gebirgs Division would be flown in. In fact, the mountain troops did not wait until the airfield was completely safe, the first Ju52 containing the men of Gebirgsjägerregiment 100, arriving at about 1630hrs while artillery shells were still dropping on the runway. One can imagine the chaotic scene on the small strip, as the lumbering transport aircraft (which looked as though they were made out of sheets of corrugated iron), came slowly in among the wrecks of other aircraft which had been hit, many themselves being struck by fire as they landed and took off. Despite the heavy casualties which this operation incurred, it continued without pause, so that by evening some 650 mountain troops had been landed in the Maleme sector, complete with their commander, Oberst Willibald Utz. They were later joined by paratrooper Oberst Hermann Ramcke, who already had a reputation as a tough, uncompromising fighter, and who would later rise to the rank of General der Fallschirmjäger and be awarded the Oakleaves, Swords and Diamonds to his Knight's Cross. [1]

Ramcke was flown in to take command of Gruppe West, and swiftly exerted tight control over tired Fallschirmjäger and newly arrived mountain troops alike. To their surprise (and no doubt also to their great relief) they were not counter-attacked by the New Zealanders during the night of the 21st, although such an attack was originally planned to begin at 0100hrs 22 May. It was to have involved both the 20th and 28th NZ Infantry Battalions, but unfortunately the 20th Battalion did not arrive at the start line until gone 0300hrs, having been delayed by the late arrival of an Australian battalion, which had been sent from Rethymnon to relieve them. At first light the counter-attack was still over one and a half miles from the airfield perimeter and, as the light increased, so did the strength of the enemy opposition – especially because they were able to call on immediate close air support. Unfortunately, therefore, the attack ground to a halt. It was during this abortive counter-attack that 2Lt Charles Upham performed the first of many actions that would earn him the award of the Victoria Cross, when he eliminated an enemy machine gun nest single-handed – his account of this action being typically understated:

> 'There was TG (Tommy Gun) and pistol fire and plenty of grenades and a lot of bayonet work which you don't often get in war. The amount of MG fire was never equalled. Fortunately a lot of it was high and the tracer bullets enabled us to pick our way up and throw in grenades. We had heavy casualties but the Germans had heavier.'

It is true to say that this failure to deal with the German foothold at Maleme would have disastrous consequences for the defenders.

The Battle for Galatas

We left Capt Michael Forrester making contact with Col Karl Kippenberger's New Zealanders, who were close to where he had been staying just prior to the invasion. From there he was escorted by Brian Bassett, the acting brigade major, to the headquarters of the NZ Divisional Cavalry Regiment at Galatas. It was the divisional reconnaissance regiment, now minus its vehicles and fighting as infantry:

'The CO, *John Russell*, was a huge man who, like many others in the division, was a farmer. Having welcomed me warmly, he invited me to take command of the 6th Greek Regiment, which had been badly mauled in the airborne assault. There were about a hundred men including a junior officer. We were to form the reserve company of Russell Force; our task was to counter-attack as might be necessary, with the feature known as Pink Hill as the most likely objective. Pink Hill was on the south-western outskirts of the village, topped by a cluster of small houses; in enemy hands it could threaten the whole Galatas position.

'Throughout the 21st and for much of the 22nd, the main enemy activity was from the air. The Luftwaffe seldom let up and Galatas received its share of attacks from Messerschmitts and Stukas, all designed as much to undermine morale as to inflict casualties which, due to good discipline and deep slit-trenches, were relatively light. There was a memorable moment, I think on the 21st, when four Hurricanes flew over us in formation; their effect was dramatic: the New Zealanders jumped out of their trenches, cheered and waved enthusiastically, believing for a moment that the air battle was still to be fought. I used every opportunity to muster and organise the remnants of the 6th Greek Regiment, which stragglers continued to join. Briefings included the most likely course the counter-attack would take; during these, which were conducted through an English-speaking Greek officer, I noticed that villagers, men and women, were showing interest in joining the assembly. Recognising their character and determination, I did not discourage them from feeling that they could contribute to the defence of their village. Communication in action presented a challenge which I partially solved with the use of the whistle: one blast – stand to; two blasts – start moving forward; three blasts – deploy into tactical formation. I also suggested that when it came to charging the enemy, we would yell, *"Aiera!"*, the battle cry which I had heard the Evzones (an elite Greek infantry regiment) use to great effect on the Albanian front.

'At about 1800hrs on 22 May, Galatas came under heavy attack. In addition to bombing and strafing from the air, a ground attack was under way – mortar and machine gun fire was directed onto forward positions, and shortly I realised that Pink Hill had been captured, as fire was coming from there into our position, though it was not possible to assess in what strength the Germans were established. Without the benefit of any radio or telephone link with HQ Div Cav Regiment, I decided that the time had come for action and alerted my force with the whistle. Our route was up a shallow ravine which offered reasonable cover. We had not gone very far before I realised that we had been substantially reinforced by a considerable number of the inhabitants of Galatas – men and women – armed with old shotguns, garden tools, sticks, broom handles, some with kitchen knives strapped on to the end of them. I felt the excitement mounting as we gained momentum: with cries of "Aiera!" we topped the hill and charged across the open ground to surround the buildings, out of which came a platoon of Germans with their hands up. It could have been that our lack of supporting weapons had been more than compensated for by our extraordinary appearance and fearsome din!

'One of the prisoners was a large man, blond with a pink complexion. He was shouting abuse at his captors and ending every sentence with "Heil Hitler" – a thoroughly obstreperous character who was not easily quietened down. I noticed, too, that he was wounded in the left thigh and limped badly. Some 25 years later, when commanding 4th Division in Germany, I was staying at an hotel in Austria for the Rhine Army Ski Championships, when it struck me that there was something familiar about "mine host". He was a big man with a red face and greying hair, which had clearly once been fair. What was more, he walked with a limp. I engaged him in conversation on a number of occasions to learn that he was a fervent believer in the concept of the Greater Reich

*and that he had welcomed the annexation of Austria in 1938. He
also told me that he had fought as a paratrooper in the invasion of
Crete and had been wounded at Galatas, adding that he looked
forward to the day when Austria could again be incorporated into
a Greater Germany.'*

Michael Forrester would be awarded a Bar to his Military
Cross for his bravery that day – and for the high sense of
loyalty and devotion to duty which he had displayed both in
Greece and Crete. The last few lines of his citation, which was
recommended by Gen Freyberg personally, read:

'During the next few days, when the situation became difficult,
on his own initiative, he went forward and rallied the remnants
of a Greek battalion. He then organised a counter-attack and,
mainly by his personal example and disregard for danger, he
carried forward the Greek troops with him, drove back the
enemy, and momentarily restored a difficult situation.'

Tough hand-to-hand fighting

This short extract from the official New Zealand history of the
fighting during this period gives an indication of the ferocity
and hand-to-hand nature of the action:

*'At this stage Jim Tuhiwai came to me in some excitement
saying that there were many parachutists in the area who were
shooting our people up. I ran over to the mill race and saw a
German in the mouth of a filled-in well ... firing a tommy gun.
Told Tuhiwai to lie on the bank and shoot at him and calling to
another soldier to run out with me and we would rush the man
from the other side. We did that. As we got to him he crouched
down shamming dead. I told the Maori to bayonet him. As he
did so he turned his head away, not bearing the sight. Tuhiwai
had now joined us and we rushed out among the Germans
scattered every 15 or 20 yards ... One at about 15 yards instead*

of firing his tommy gun started to lie down to fire. I took a snap shot with a German Mauser. It grazed his behind and missed between his legs. My back hair lifted but the Maori got him (I had no bayonet). We rushed on ... Some tried to crawl away. A giant of a man jumped up with his hands up like a gorilla, shouting, "Hands Oop!" I said, "Shoot the bastard!" and the Maori shot him. That was because many others were firing at us and a Spandau from further off ... Suddenly bullets spluttered all around my feet.' [2]

Work for the prisoners

LAC Colin France had been captured on Hill 107 and found himself put to work the following day:

'. . . with other prisoners, removing crashed Ju52s, the three-engined troop carriers, from the runway. At times we were subject to shelling from the direction of Canea and from "enemy" planes, usually the Blenheims from Egypt who destroyed or damaged about 10 Ju52s whilst the artillery accounted for five more. We were glad to see the Germans running from the airfield; we even saw the humorous side of being bombed by our own planes.

'I noticed a number of Austrians landing with the Gebirgs Regiment, who wore the edelweiss as a cap badge. They did not believe in the Geneva Convention, as we were forced to unload the aircraft of arms and ammunition as soon as it landed. Needless to say we had many rests from this tiring job, much to the annoyance of our captors. I stayed on at the airfield with nothing to eat except what we could scrounge. I remember a time when our captors appeared to be pleased with us and we were given some of the hard tack biscuits they were eating, but none of the butter or margarine with which they had plastered the surface. I asked one of them for some margarine and he slapped me across the face sending me sprawling on the floor. He then informed me that German POWs did not get margarine and I was not getting any.

> '*I was sent with four others to load bombs, mostly British ones, onto a rubber dinghy, row out to sea and then to drop them over the side. Later I was sent on a burial detail and helped to dig graves for about 80 Germans, some of whom had been dead for five days, consequently we had no need to search for bodies, we smelled them out. When we had buried all the dead in our area, I managed to find a job after my own heart, in the German ration store, issuing food, drink and cigarettes to German units. It was situated at Trauronitis, about a mile of so away from the airfield at Maleme. Five men were chosen, three New Zealanders, another airman and myself.*'

Suda Bay

New Zealand gunner Allan A. Jackson, from Mount Maunganui, manning an ancient artillery piece (and a rifle) in the defence of Suda Bay, had spent 'quite a day!' on the 20th, when the parachutists had come in their hundreds and it had been 'all hands firing with whatever they could'.

He had bemoaned the fact that the defenders hadn't been better equipped. Next morning (the 21st) he recalls,

> '. . . *another six hundred paratroopers came down and were again harshly treated. Two of our gunners, Walsh and Jones, were killed – snipers. Unfortunately the airfield (Maleme) is now in Jerry's hands. He can fly in equipment and men. If only we had had our 25-pounders, we might have been able to hold the drome. In the meantime we had been using our two guns – no idea if they did any damage. During the night a German walked up the road. I heard Bdr Hill call out: "Halt! Who goes there?" A sort of guttural response then "Bang!" Hill was hit in the shoulder, but the German was killed. I took over Hill's place as Bdr on the gun.*'

Northumberland Hussar 'acting infantryman' Bill Siddle's hectic action began on the morning of the 21st when they were told that there were enemy ground troops near the village of Kounoupidhiana, and his section (Lt Arnold, one sergeant, one lance bombardier and 16 men) was ordered to make contact. Bill was allocated the gun 'rather a change from a file and spanner,' he comments, 'as I was the Battery gun fitter!' They moved out towards the beach and, as he recalled,

> *'the left hand of the section located some of the Germans having a wash! A hand grenade thrown down the cliff ended in three prisoners being taken. Further inland, the right hand of the section located a further three Germans. Hand grenades were exchanged but the Mills failed to explode.*
>
> *I watched the enemy grenade bobbing down the slope towards me, but about three feet away it hit a bump and rolled away to my right and below me. Sadly it hit L/Bdr Vivian in the chest – he would die of his wounds later in the day. The Germans were eventually sorted out, one taken prisoner, the other two shot by Lt Arnold and myself. Maps taken from them were all marked where they had to drop or land. Vivian was in a bad way, so we got a door from somewhere and the two prisoners had the job of carrying him up to the main road and so to hospital.'*

HM The King of Greece escapes

King George of Greece had been on the island ever since escaping from the mainland, being moved around between various 'safe houses', which ranged from the Bank of Greece in Suda, to the home of the famous archaeologist, Sir Arthur Evans, in Heraklion. However, when the German attack began in earnest it was quickly decided that he and his party, which included his brother, Crown Prince Paul, the Court Chamberlain, Col Levidis, and the Greek Prime Minister, Emmanuel Tsouderos, must be evacuated to Egypt. Protected by a platoon of 18th NZ Battalion infantry, led by 2Lt W. H. Ryan, they hastily began their journey across the mountains to the southern coast. The first leg was from a villa near Perivolia on 20 May, when the first wave of Fallschirmjäger was under half a mile away. Therefore they left in somewhat of a hurry, the escort with just their personal weapons, HM The King without some of his personal papers and medals. In addition, they had no means of communication, being without a radio set. [3] Nevertheless, they made reasonable progress and by that evening had reached Therisso. Here there was a telephone line still working and Col Jasper Blunt, the British Military Attaché who was also with the party, was able to arrange with the naval staff at Suda Bay to request a destroyer to be dispatched from Alexandria, to meet them at Agriarumeli on the south coast of Crete. Accordingly, on the night of 22/23 May, having eventually made contact with HMS *Decoy* and *Hero*, and after some tense moments as the captain of *Decoy* suspected an ambush, the VIPs were collected without further incident, after which the two destroyers rejoined Adm Rawlings' force and later brought the party safely to Alexandria. In his book *Crete, the battle and the resistance* Antony Beevor explains how the popular description of King George of the Hellenes escaping from Crete 'like Jesus Christ, on a donkey though wearing a tin hat' was not strictly accurate. Instead he was, 'In full service dress with medal ribbons, Sam Browne and highly polished riding boots, but without a steel helmet. He had ridden a mule for much of the way across the mountains. Rather embarrassingly, his mule attracted the amorous interest of another, which caused some alarm, since its abnormally pale coat risked catching the eye of a German pilot.'

Gen 'Sweat saves Blood' arrives

As one senior figure in the plot was leaving the stage, another was entering on the other side. This was the jaunty, bearded commander of 5 Gebirgs Division, Generalmajor Julius Ringel. He was one of the best soldiers from the old Austrian Army, a tactician who steadfastly believed in the maxim: 'Sweat saves Blood'. He arrived on the evening of the 22nd, to take command as he put it, 'over the entire combat forces employed in ground battles'. His account of the operation continues:

> *'Still during the evening, the units were organised, orders issued for the security and expansion of the bridgehead, units assigned to encircle the enemy south-wing with the objective to neutralise the enemy artillery.'*

This clearly would involve a large proportion of his force in expending much sweat, clearing out the southern foothills of the mountains, so as to eliminate the artillery which the air had failed to knock out. This would involve them using paths which were normally used only by animals, which threaded their way over seemingly unscalable peaks, the Gebirgsjäger loaded with everything they would need to fight with, in order to get around the flanks of the British and Commonwealth positions and attack their rear. It cannot have been easy for them, despite their mountain expertise, in their heavy uniforms and loaded down with gear. It would take them until D+5 to achieve this operation.

Ringel is positively euphoric about the successes which were achieved, commenting:

> *'The summarisation of the events of the first three days on Crete surpasses anything previously experienced as to momentum and dramatic heroism which was being accelerated from hour to hour. Uninterruptedly the motors of the German planes droned and thundered over the antique sea. They brought fighters and weapons, ammunition, food and medical supplies like a swarm of bees. Easy manoeuvrable fighters executed their loops high up in the skies. Twin-engined fighters attacked the observed enemy objectives, airfields and Flak batteries, substituting for the missing artillery. Again and again Fallschirmjäger jumped over the area, daring and death-defying, into enemy positions, unaffected by artillery fire,*

bombs or MG fire; Gebirgsjäger, hour after hour, climbed out of their transport planes, organised and unloaded calmly, received their orders unflinchingly and attacked sternly and steadfastly wherever they were ordered. An assault group made of steel, fire and men. Seemingly a chaos but yet order, determination and planning. The Battle on Crete, a unique, world-historical event, a daring play but yet thought through in minute detail.' [4]

Problems for the Germans at Rethymnon and Heraklion

Whilst Ringel's forces were increasing their hold on the west of the island, Gruppe Mitte at Rethymnon and Gruppe Ost near Heraklion were not doing anywhere near as well. At Rethymnon, the two parachute battalions of FJR2 found themselves up against the aggressive reaction of nearly 7,000 Australian troops, who, despite lacking in supporting weapons, had pushed one battalion off the high ground that commanded the aerodrome and forced them back to a new position further east, near a large olive oil factory. Further west of the airfield, the other battalion was in similar circumstances, now forced to give ground and to dig in afresh near Perivolia. They would continue to be confined to these small pockets for the foreseeable future. Communication was an added problem for them, as neither group had a wireless set and attempts to drop them one failed. The British and Commonwealth forces had also captured a number of copies of the Fallschirmjäger ground to air codes, together with the necessary flags and signal panels, which they used to their advantage. This also led to air attacks on German troops, despite the laying out of German flags and the firing of white flares, which had a very detrimental effect on the ground troops' morale.

At Heraklion the situation was much the same, despite the temporary capture of part of the town, from which the Fallschirmjäger were later evicted. They were even offered the chance to surrender,[5] but declined with the words, 'The

German Army has been ordered to take the island. It will carry out this order!' Sebastian Krug was one of the Fallschirmjäger who entered Heraklion. He writes:

'On the 21st we tried to make an advance through the west "town door" which was very well barricaded, but we managed to get through and advanced to about the centre of the town, also to the harbour. We tried to push on further, but the Englander tried to push us out of town. We made many small attacks and I saw some really gruesome sights. ... On the evening of 25 May, Oberst Bräuer gave the order that we were to evacuate the town via the "West Door" in the dark, as quietly as possible and make for Hill 182, close to the airfield. We reached it early the next morning and then attacked. The Englander put up very hard resistance but we managed to take it.

'Now we were at the top of the hill, without sleep, without shade – and it was very hot. We were also short of water and suffering from continuous enemy shelling. After six days we were so apathetic that we did not care whether we lived or died.

'The only well where we could get water was being shot at all the time, so the only possible time to get water was at night, with a long rope and our steel helmets. The British guns fired as soon as they spotted any movement there. On the 26th, a Ju52 managed to land on the rearward side of the hill. He brought ammunition, food and first aid supplies. The place he had landed was covered with bushes and very uneven, he also took some of the badly wounded back with him. When he started up he had to go down the hill, so our hearts were in our mouths waiting to see if he could pull up safely – but he did so. We could also see that he was under anti-aircraft fire all the time so it was a great achievement.

'We now had ammunition for our mortar, but whilst unloading some of the cases, one exploded and killed some of my comrades. Later we shot into the town with our mortar, until we discovered that there was an English field hospital *down there which we could not see and several mortar bombs had hit it. Oberst Bräuer gave us the order to send someone down with a white flag to apologise. I went down with several comrades to see the Englander and apologise. They did not make any distinction between friend and foe. After we had had a look round we were invited to have something to eat and drink, then we marched back to our positions and started firing again. After that Oberst Bräuer made an agreement with the Englander that our wounded would be taken to the hospital at an agreed time every morning.'*

'There was no front line,' recalled Syd Croft of D Troop, 234 Medium Battery, RA, whose troop was still manning the ex-Italian 75mm guns in support of the Heraklion garrison,

'. . .they could be all around us. If they had managed to escape death and landed safely, then we had to be really alert in case one of them crept up on our positions. All around was vegetation, olive trees, young olive trees rather like bushes about two or three feet high and right in front of the guns there was a field of crops of some kind. They were about three or four feet high and an ideal place to hide. It was a case of watching every inch of space surrounding us, and as late afternoon passed on, two of our men were shot and wounded. We, for our part, watched closely and fired at the slightest movement. Whether we were successful or not in getting a hit, one just couldn't tell. At that time, it was too risky to investigate. As early evening approached, a couple of light tanks came up to our position and swept the cornfield for us. Three or four paratroopers hastily stood up and rushed in all directions chased by the tanks. Two put their hands up and ran to our positions only yards away ... I don't remember much activity during the darkness of the night, but next morning everybody was again on alert for any movement ... Fortunately, because the German High Command imagined

that their forces would have an easy landing and would by now be in control, there was no more bombing. Every two hours or so, a lone reconnaissance plane would circle around the whole area and take pictures, then disappear. However, it did seem that the Germans realised that something had gone seriously wrong in their initial drops. They didn't repeat their catastrophic mistake of dropping more parachutists over our positions. Meanwhile, by now on this second day of the invasion, Wednesday, 21 May, the whole area around our gun positions and far beyond had been cleared. Our telephone lines to our OPs (Observation Posts), which had been cut during the heavy bombing were now repaired and we were getting requests for artillery support. Our targets were groups of German parachutists who were taking up positions ready to attack the aerodrome. There were many targets on the beaches where the Germans were making substantial drops of more paratroops and supplies, They were now also using gliders to bring in more troops and stores and these made good targets as they landed on the beaches.

'The next day, Thursday, 22 May, I was presented with an unpleasant task. In those days, I was a much slimmer and lighter man and not particularly muscular nor strong. I suppose I could have been described as rather wiry and fit! … And so I was not particularly happy when I was ordered with another gunner to escort our three POWs to the POW cage some three miles down the road towards Heraklion. We were given a loaded rifle each and standing behind these three big, powerful looking Germans, we indicated down the lane and said something like, "Marschieren! Schnell!" and pointed our rifles in as threatening way as we could. Fortunately, these German soldiers had had all the fight knocked out of them. If they had taken drugs, as we were led to believe, and if they had been told there would be no resistance in or around Heraklion and then to find such heavy opposition as they tried to land and

then to discover that none of their comrades around them were alive – well that must have been very depressing. And so fortunately for us they went quietly ... We delivered our charges to the guards at the POW cage where there were some 150 prisoners, all looking equally dejected and fed up with war. Perhaps they were secretly happy that they were at least alive. We returned to the troop rather surprised I think, that we could walk so freely through the villages when less that 48 hours ago, the whole area had been swamped with hundreds of German parachutists. ... However, not every German had been rounded up and during the day, a sniper fatally shot one of our men, Sgt Jones. Fortunately for us, we were able to find and dispose of the sniper.

'The air was now beginning to fill with the sickening smell of death, as bodies began to rot and we began the horrible business of collecting the dead from our area and burying them. Meanwhile around the perimeter our infantry were mopping up pockets of the enemy and defending the aerodrome. We gave artillery support when and wherever needed. On Friday, 23 May, several Hurricanes arrived at the aerodrome, but evidently because of the lack of fuel and ammunition almost immediately returned to Egypt. We also heard on this day that things were not going too well at Suda Bay, Canea and Maleme aerodrome areas. One of our officers had to take two gun detachments with their guns back to Suda Bay to give artillery support on the New Zealanders. They went back via a tank landing craft which also took three of the light tanks with them. But as we discovered later when we eventually met up with our party again in Egypt, things had been getting much worse at Maleme, the Allied forces there were being overwhelmed and falling back southwards towards the mountains. They were eventually ordered to Sphakia on the south coast, where after many dangerous adventures, they were evacuated and taken to Alexandria.'

Situation on 21–23 May

By last light on Wednesday, 21 May, after two days of bitter fighting, the airfield at Maleme was in German hands and, as we have seen, the counter-attack which was to have been on its way by 0100hrs 22 May had been doomed to failure from the outset. This was due to a series of unfortunate delays on the Allied side, together with the increased German resistance which had been stubbornly built up by ignoring horrific casualties incurred by continuing to fly in reinforcements whilst the battle raged about them. The fighting went on throughout the day and night, but just before first light on the 23rd, the New Zealanders were ordered to fall back towards Suda Bay. Maleme airfield was lost and, although probably no one on either side would at that very moment have realised it, the future of who would hold onto Crete had been decided, despite the failure of the Gruppe Mitte and Ost Task Forces and, as we will see from the next chapter, the destruction of the seaborne element of the assault. There would still be much more heavy fighting, with many additional casualties on both sides, but the eventual outcome of the battle was already clear and the fate of Crete sealed.

Notes

1. Oberst Bernhard Hermann Ramcke, who had earned his para-rifleman badge aged 51 in 1940, was awarded the Knight's Cross on 21 August 1941 for his actions during the campaign in Crete. In the Western Desert he commanded the crack Ramcke Parachute Brigade and earned his Oakleaves. The Swords and Diamonds both followed during his remarkable defence of Brest in September 1944. He was the 20th out of only 27 members of the German armed forces to be awarded the coveted Diamonds.

2. Quoted in *Crete – Official History of New Zealand in the Second World War 1939-45*.

3. Part of the escort went back to recover the missing items, but found the Germans already at the villa and had to leave again empty-handed.

4. General der Gebirgstruppen Julius Ringel: 'The Conquest of Crete'; Vol 13 of *WWII German Military Studies*.

5. According to Ringel's report the request to surrender was worded as follows: 'In as much as you are the only, small unit still fighting on Crete, we are asking you – recognising the brave conduct of your soldiers – to stop this bloodshed and surrender. A respectful treatment is being assured you.'

8

Naval Battles

The Argonaut expedition

At Piraeus on mainland Greece and at Chalkis on the island of Euboea, the flotillas of Greek caiques were loaded and made ready to leave harbour at around dawn on 20 May. They were accompanied by two Italian destroyers which had been assigned to protect them, one for each of the two flotillas, which comprised some 30 caiques in each party. Command of the two flotillas was vested in two of the battalion commanders of Gebirgsjägerregiment 100 – Oberstleutnant Echal of III Bataillon was in command of Flotilla I and Maj Dr Draeg of II Bataillon in command of Flotilla II. It is said that the only available 'nautical' instruments were a pocket compass, an improvised megaphone and a map of Central Europe at 1:200,000 scale! Of course they could also rely upon the nautical proficiency of the Greek crews of the caiques, who must have known the waters intimately, but it is doubtful if they would have been willing helpers. The whole undertaking was given the name the 'Argonaut Expedition' afterwards, because of its fate. 'Circled by the Italian destroyers like shepherd's dogs, the flotillas moved southward over the blue, hardly rippling Aegaeis [Aegean Sea], just as Ulysses sailed on his cruise of adventures which remained without equal.' [1]

The intention was for the leading flotilla to reach Maleme before last light on 21 May, land in the open surf and move inland as quickly as possible. In order for this operation to go smoothly it had been decided that a small naval staff would be landed ahead of the main flotilla, to mark the landing beaches with flags. However, as the official German report puts it,

'Unfortunately, expectations did not materialise as planned.' The Germans' planning does not seem to have reckoned on the Royal Navy taking an interest in the proceedings! Accordingly, a Kapitän zur See Bartels of the Kriegsmarine was landed with a small staff to mark the beaches and arrange for the reception of the seaborne mountain troops. During the evening of the 21st, many anxious eyes looked seaward from the tenuous German foothold on Crete, but nothing materialised for some time. Then, as the German account dramatically explains:

'*Suddenly, at about 2300 hours, searchlights from the north were trained on the bright sails and immediately rolling salvoes of medium naval guns, a burning ship, then quiet and calm; then again salvoes, hits upon the airfield and beach, as well as to the west, then again calm; hardly noticeable machine gunfire, no signal, no light, not a trace of the light flotilla remained. What had happened? Strong enemy surface forces had encountered the advance command vessels of the small Flotilla I, which was en route for Cape Spatha. Flotilla I had become stretched out considerably due to the varying speeds of the vessels. The flotilla itself was shot up, rammed and dispersed without the possibility of defending itself. An elephant fighting a mouse. While a small remnant escaped the British fighting force, changed its course and proceeded in a northerly direction, a still larger part of this flotilla, without accurate knowledge of the events of the night, continued further towards the south, following its original order to reach Crete. Thus, the second catastrophe was in the making. The smaller Flotilla II, which had left the embarkation harbour at Chalkis with II/Gebirgsjägerregiment 85 aboard, lagged some six hours behind Flotilla I. It headed in a south-westerly direction and reached the isle of Milos during the night. The heavy flotilla which was loading at Piraeus had not as yet received its sailing orders due to lack of an opportune moment.*

'By the evening on 21 May it became clear, and was also verified by the reconnaissance aircraft of XI Fliegerkorps, that the bulk of the British Mediterranean fleet had assembled in the waters around Crete, particularly to the north. The result of this was the inevitable duel between the Luftwaffe and the enemy naval forces. While the transport and landing of the Gebirgsjägers on the airfield at Maleme continued and thus the fighting for the fortification and extension of the small beachhead proceeded, the rest of Flotilla I followed orders and sailed further southward. So, early on 22 May, two dramatic and fateful events took place in the waters north of Crete. At dawn, strong British naval forces attacked the remnants of the small flotilla still sailing southward. Again, an unequal battle took place between nutshells and armoured giants; motor sailboat after motor sailboat was rammed, shot up, broken up and sank with its load in the blue Aegaeis. Even rubber rafts and soldiers drifting in the water were shot at with MGs and artillery. Valiantly, the Italian destroyers entered the uneven battle and one of them succeeded in laying a smokescreen, under cover of which a few ships sailing at the rear of the flotilla managed to turn about and return to the harbour at Milos. Many of the survivors, drifting about on their rafts and in life vests could still have been saved through the Luftwaffe's sea-rescue service. The British report, that the bulk of 5 Gebirgs Division had been annihilated during these dramatic events and about 9,000 soldiers had drowned, is absolutely untrue. According to my own estimate, 350-400 men had drowned. In any case one battalion of Gebirgsjäger had been lost and only the remnants could be employed. The rescue of the shipwrecked which we expected of the British did not take place in a single case. The revenge for this unfair mode of battle by the British was already in the making.' [2]

It is interesting to note from Gen Seibt's dissertation that, just in the same way as some of the Fallschirmjäger considered it unsporting of the British to shoot at them while they were descending on the ends of their parachutes (although it was perfectly acceptable for them to shoot at those on the ground with their personal weapons as they descended), clearly he felt that it was wrong for the Royal Navy to attack and sink the flotillas of caiques and then to go after their luckless human cargoes of mountain troops. There was undoubtedly an unwritten law between the opposing navies that, having sunk a vessel, neither side then pursued its helpless crew (indeed if circumstances permitted, they would be rescued) but of course the Gebirgsjäger were not a 'helpless' crew, but rather a highly lethal cargo, which had to be disposed of before it was able to assist in the struggle for Crete. In any case, the 'fair play rules' do not appear to have covered the Luftwaffe, for whom anything in the water appears to have been fair game. I don't intend to adjudicate on this issue, but it clearly depends upon which side of the court you were on as to what was fair and what was a definite 'foul'.

It was, in fact, Rear-Adm Glennie's Force 'D' which encountered the first enemy troop convoy (Flotilla I) at 2330hrs on Wednesday, 21 May, when it was about 18 miles north of Canea, radar proving invaluable in leading our ships on to fresh targets. The Germans were making for Suda Bay and were headed by the Italian destroyer *Lupo* under the command of Cdr Francesco Mimbelli. The gallant Mimbelli desperately tried to protect his charges by laying a smokescreen but was unsuccessful despite making a brave attempt, as this postwar Italian report explains:

> '*Under a hail of shells falling on his ship, Commander Mimbelli directed the* Lupo *through the British formation, between the* Ajax *and* Orion, *came close aboard a cruiser (*Dido*) and passed a few metres from its stern, all the while exchanging heavy gun and machine gunfire … While these shells killed and wounded many men, they caused no mortal damage to the ship, which made good her escape, despite the* Ajax's *claim that it had "pulverised" the Italian vessel.*' [3]

The mêlée lasted for a good two and a half hours before Glennie called off his now scattered force, having, according to British records, sunk over half the convoy, with a thousand enemy troops killed or 'flung into the sea'. This total was later accepted to be an over-estimate, the revised figure being about 800, of which some were rescued. The number of ships sunk was at least a dozen caiques, two or three steamers and a steam yacht, all of which were either sunk or left burning. Glennie's main reason for breaking off the battle was a shortage of all nature of ammunition, in particular AA ammunition, his flagship *Dido*, for example, having less than a third remaining. As he rightly expected a similar scale of air attacks on the 22nd and every day thereafter, he considered that he was not justified in remaining in the Aegean. Instead of continuing his sweep, therefore, he turned westwards and ordered his ships to rendezvous some 30 miles west of Crete, where he intended to meet Rear-Adm Rawlings' Force 'A1'. However, by that time the ammunition situation had deteriorated even further and so Rawlings ordered Glennie's force to return to Alexandria to replenish, despite the fact that, with hindsight, the presence of some of the ships – such as *Ajax* and *Orion* – would have been invaluable in the Aegean.

The following day was to prove to be one of the most difficult of the war for the Mediterranean Fleet, with many vessels under unremitting air attack. In summary, the British lost two cruisers and a destroyer, leading directly on to the situation which occasioned the loss of a further two destroyers early the following morning. In addition, two battleships were hit by bombs and two other cruisers damaged. However, on the positive side, the enemy had been prevented from making any seaborne landings on Crete and deterred from making any further attempts to do so.

It was Rear-Adm King's Force 'C' which engaged Flotilla II of enemy troop-carrying caiques, the first contact being made with a single caique some 30 miles north of Rethymnon and about 60 south of Milos. HMAS *Perth* sunk this first caique while being under heavy air attack at the time, as were other ships in King's force. Then a small merchant vessel was reported and at about 1010hrs an Italian destroyer (the *Sagittario*) was sighted accompanying five small sailing ships. The action was very similar to the battle with the other flotilla, the Italian destroyer laying smoke (after firing its torpedoes) and the British ships engaging the caiques as they tried to hide behind the smokescreen. This time the reported size of the flotilla was some 38 caiques, carrying 4,000 troops, which were aiming to land at Heraklion and were accompanied with some steamers carrying heavy equipment, including guns and tanks. The Italian postwar account of this action says:

> '*At 0830hrs on 22 May destroyer escort* Sagittario *(Lt Fulgosi) ... received orders to return to Milos because of the precarious ground situation ... As soon as a British group of cruisers and destroyers under Adm King sighted the* Sagittario *(and the 30 small vessels) they came on to meet it, opening fire from 13,000yds. The enemy shells were landing all around ... but by zigzagging rapidly the* Sagittario *succeeded in avoiding the concentrated fire of the seven opposing ships. When less than 8,750yds away from the second cruiser, Fulgosi headed straight at it and launched his torpedoes ... However, the British ships ceased firing and pulled away to the south-west.*' [4]

As Capt Pack comments, 'Probably no one was more surprised than Fulgosi who was now "attacked by several Stukas five times", but his gallant little ship was unharmed and under cover of his smokescreen much of the large convoy escaped.'

Rex Hey, the Ordnance Corps vehicle fitter we met earlier, remembered what happened to the seaborne element of Operation 'Merkur':

> '*During the night we started to hear very heavy gunfire out at sea and could see the flashes from the guns. This seemed to be it, the rumoured landing. The heavy gunfire continued but*

there was no attempted landing on the beach ... we were not called upon to repel the enemy. We found out the day after that an attempt at landing supplies and men had been made, but the Royal Navy did the job. From what we were told there had been a large convoy of all manner of ships attempting to bring in men and supplies for the Germans, but the Navy caught them and demolished the lot. We had this physically confirmed the following day by numbers of dead bodies floating up on to the beach. The attempted sea invasion had been wiped out. This gave us quite a boost despite the fact that the Germans continued to reinforce their beleaguered troops by air.'

The air-sea battle

Although the destruction of the two flotillas of caiques was vitally important to the struggle on Crete, it was but a small part of the conflict that took place on the seas around Crete. The German study of this element of the battle contains this extract from the official German communiqué as issued by the OKW on 11/12 June 1941:

'The second basis for success on 22 May was brought about by VIII Fliegerkorps. Shortly after the beginning of the operation against Crete, almost the entire British naval forces from Alexandria had appeared in the area. This should have prevented the shipping of supplies and created the possibility of reinforcing British troops on Crete or, in an emergency, embarking same and bringing them back to Alexandria. This was the reason that the first attempt on 21 May to ferry over German reinforcements to Crete by means of motor sailboats only succeeded in part, due to the arrival of British naval forces.

'On the next day, the gigantic battle between VIII Fliegerkorps and the British fleet ended with the glorious victory of the German flyers. The British fleet, after

sustaining very heavy losses was forced to vacate the area around Crete and leave the island to its fate.'

The report from VIII Fliegerkorps' sea battle also says that not less than eight enemy cruisers, several destroyers and motor torpedo boats were destroyed or scuttled. Without doubt the losses suffered were grievous, but the Royal Navy accepted them unhesitatingly as all ranks knew how much depended upon them. Typical was the action which led to the loss of HMS *Greyhound*, *Gloucester* and *Fiji* on the 22nd, as this extract from the Naval History tells:

'The Greyhound, *meanwhile, after sinking the caique, was returning to her place in Force "A1"s screen, when at 1351hrs she was struck by two bombs and sank stern first 15 minutes later. The* Kandahar *and* Kingston *were at once detached from Force "C" to pick up survivors and shortly after 1400hrs, Rear-Adm King (who was the senior officer of the forces present) ordered* Fiji *and* Gloucester *to give them AA support and to stand by the wreck of the* Greyhound. *These rescuing ships, and the men swimming in the water, were subjected to almost continuous bombing and machine gun attacks (two Bf109s machine gunned the* Kingston's *whaler, killing three officers and several ratings and wounding every one in the boat) and the* Kingston *was damaged by three near misses.*

'At 1413hrs, Rear-Adm King asked Rear-Adm Rawlings for close support as Force "C" by that time had practically no AA ammunition left. Force "A1" closed at the Warspite's *best speed (18 knots) and Rear-Adm Rawlings, who was feeling uneasy about the orders given to the* Gloucester *and* Fiji, *informed Rear-Adm King of the depleted state of their AA ammunition of which the latter was not aware. At 1457hrs Rear-Adm King ordered the rescuing ships to withdraw at discretion, leaving boats and rafts if air attack prevented the rescue of survivors.*

'At 1530hrs, the Gloucester *and the* Fiji *were coming up astern of the* Warspite *at high speed, engaging enemy aircraft; 20 minutes later the* Gloucester *was hit by several bombs and brought to a full stop. She was badly on fire and her upper deck was a shambles. In view of the intensity of the air attacks the captain of the* Fiji *(William-Powlett) reluctantly decided that he must leave her – it was hoped that some of the* Gloucester's *ship's company might have reached the coast of Crete. Captain Rowley lost his life. All available boats and floats were dropped and the* Fiji *proceeded to the southward with the* Kandahar *and* Kingston, *still being hotly attacked by enemy aircraft. (After surviving some 20 bombing attacks by formations of enemy aircraft,* Fiji *would fall victim to a lone Bf109.)'*

On board HMS *Gloucester* at that time was airframe fitter Arthur John Stevens. He would be right at the heart of the 'upper deck shambles' which the official report mentions. Although he was only, as he put it, 'a lower deck member', he still knew the importance of their task to prevent the Germans making a seaborne landing on Crete. He had heard Winston Churchill saying how vital it was to hold Crete, so appreciated the need to stop the convoys of Greek caiques, loaded with German troops, from reaching the island. He recalled:

'I think on the Tuesday morning we were under early attack from dive-bombers – predominantly the Stukas – "Screamers" as we called them. And that went on all day, with many near misses.

I was at action stations continually ... Wednesday was just the same ... and on the 22nd May, we had a signal round about noon via the tannoys that the Naiad, *which was the flagship, was in trouble and badly damaged ... and that we would take over her station. Also that the* Greyhound *had been sunk and that we would attempt to pick up survivors. Well, we went steaming into the Kithera Narrows and ... I can remember ... standing by the guard rail of the gun deck and watching the* Naiad *steam by us at about eighteen knots. I remember saying, "I can't see no structural damage." We were with the* Warspite *at the time and suddenly we were attacked by 20, 30, 40 I don't know how many, Stukas. And they hit the* Warspite *on the after turret.*

I actually stood and watched the bomb hit the turret and blow it to pieces, and all the rage and temper and tears welled up in me ... And then it became the holocaust of the Gloucester. *We were attacked from all sides by what seemed to be hundreds of planes ... there was no question now of picking up the survivors of the* Greyhound. *She disappeared and it was just too dangerous to try to pick up survivors, as we were immediately attacked by the Stukas.'*

Just then one of the petty officers in the ammunition room came on the tannoy and said they needed help below decks, so Arthur and his companions hurried to help:

'I can remember running down the ladder on the after galley flat, along the flats to the sick bay flat and down, with my shipmates, into the torpedo men's mess deck and reality came to fruition. This was the mess deck on which all those marines had been killed, where all those marines had been decapitated. And fear took hold of us. I think we all understood, but at that stage there was a continual "bummp, bummp". And we felt the ship shudder and we knew that we'd been hit again. Our leading hand said, "Get up, get off the mess deck, get up top!" And I can remember I was probably the last one going up the ladder, pushing the lad in front through the aperture, literally pushing him up. And as I turned the side of the ship, all I could see was lumps of hot metal coming through.

'If I'd been on deck level I would probably have lost both my legs, but that's one of those things, that's the luck of the draw. We got up to the sick bay flat and all the lights went out. And there was quite a congregation there, not only our party but

other members of the ship's company that had been forced by circumstances to congregate in that particular flat. I was, like everybody else, worried stiff waiting for the ancillary lighting to come on. Eventually it did and they shouted for a gangway on the starboard side to get the wounded through ... then I think that somebody, it must have been a leading hand, said, "Let's move aft." And so we moved aft along the flat. I was probably a dozen back from the front of the queue – if you can call it a queue, when suddenly the hangar deck was hit by a bomb which blew in the canteen. All I could see was cigarettes, chocolate, everything flying around and I think eight lads in front of me dropped dead. Just fell down. I shouted out, "Mind the lads, don't walk over the lads!" and there wasn't a stampede, but there was an exodus to try to get to an open part of the ship.'

Arthur eventually got to the waist deck, and up a ladder to the hangar deck where he saw someone lying beside the torpedo tubes. He turned the body over and realised that it was a friend of his, a stoker named Bunny, who had been killed by a lump of shrapnel. At the time he says that he felt different to everyone else, 'I was immortal,' he explained, but he then also realised that he wasn't wearing his life-jacket, which he had left at his action station (Port 2 gun), so he was determined to go and get it:

'I ran up the port side past the captain's barge to port 2 and port 1 and found that P2 had been blown away. The gun was hanging over the side and all the chaps were lying around dead.
I could see that the after conning direction finder had been hit and had completely disappeared ... a bomb had hit the bottom part of the pedestal of the after direction finder, chopped it off and the whole 20-40 tons, whatever it weighed, had toppled over into the sea with all the lads inside. So they didn't know what hit them. But the after galley flat was just a mass of debris, twisted metal. The gun as I say – P2 – was hanging over the side, all the lads were dead. And as I looked over to the

starboard side and I was on my jack then, because I'd gone back specifically for my life-jacket. My life-jacket was just gone. And I saw this chap, he might have been a marine, standing on the starboard two gun trying to load and fire the gun on his own. He must have been berserk the way I viewed it.

'So I ran across and saw that he was attempting to do it and I picked up with a couple of lads who were matelots … and they realised I think that things were hopeless, so the three of us started to run along the starboard side. As we did so we noticed that the captain's barge was fully alight. As I got to the open part of the hangar deck where the catapult was, a bomb hit the port "Chicago pianos" [multiple pom-poms] and the gun swung round. I can remember it now. It was still firing on automatic and the two lads on either side of me got killed – the bullets went right through them. So somebody was watching over me. The one lad went down, held his chest, and the other went down on his knees just as if he was praying. But it becomes the survival of the fittest. I've got to be frank about it. You stop and look, but you become shocked.'

Arthur knew that the Fleet Air Arm office was close by and that there had been stacks of Mae Wests in there, so he went to look as quickly as he could, only to find the place in a shambles. At that time the lieutenant commander in charge was there, although he was killed later, and he asked him to help throw some baulks of timber, benches, etc which they had used as seating for cinema shows, over the side. This done, he told him that he had received the order to abandon ship, wished Arthur the best of luck and told him to go:

'I did then what I call now a silly thing. I was alongside a bakery at this stage and I took off my body belt, counted out the money I had in it, put it back, took off my boots, we all wore boots, put my body belt and boots alongside the bakery – I was going to pick them up at a later stage. That was I think how my mind was reacting.'

Clearly in a state of shock, as he stood there, however, the need for self preservation came to his rescue, urged on by the sight of a dive-bomber coming straight at him. Arthur recalled:

'While I was standing there I can remember looking up and seeing one of the Ju87s coming down and I actually saw the pilot looking out as he pulled his stick to drop his bombs. I actually saw a 500lb bomb, with two incendiary bombs attached to it, whirling down into the ship. I believe it hit somewhere forward, at the forecastle. I can't be sure but I actually saw the pilot looking out … he was probably looking down at the ship and not at me, but my eyes were focused on him. I remember looking over the side and seeing that she was lying over at a fairly sharp angle and that the cutter on the port side was being lowered into the water by a motley crew. As it hit the water I jumped and grabbed hold of a clew which I thought was attached to the davits. Instead of that somebody in the excitement had cut it, so all I was holding was fresh air. I dropped between the ship's side and the cutter, went under the water and came struggling up to the top, then all I could feel were hands dragging me inboard.'

There were eight of them in the cutter, with a petty officer sitting at the bow end who told them to pull away, while the bombs still rained down. HMS *Gloucester* was now completely on fire from stem to stern. They got clear of the stricken vessel, but then discovered that their cutter was riddled with holes where shrapnel had hit it and it just sank beneath them. The petty officer (his name was John Mayer) shouted to them to grab any beams of timber they could and he would try to make a raft. Fortunately Arthur found some of the baulks of timber which he had helped throw over the side and the petty officer managed to lash three of them together (with their belts, lanyards, socks, etc), then all of them hung onto this makeshift raft. And all the time they were being machine gunned by the Luftwaffe.

'When the Gloucester *eventually disappeared she exploded. I don't know whether her boilers blew up or whether it was our ammunition … but we didn't have a lot of ammo left so I think it was the boilers … And I watched the planes come diving down with machine guns firing and every time they did I just pushed myself under the beam … and was protected.'*

Arthur spent several horrific hours in the water, with drowning men and dead bodies floating past:

'A chap came swimming towards me and he had on his life-jacket, name of Shaddock. And he was in the throes of death. He had what we called "The Glare" or "The Stare". The water seeps into the lungs and it comes out of the nostrils, And your eyes become glazed. He immediately grabbed hold of me because he knew me as he was a mess deck mate of mine. And he took me down with him. And we was always taught that anybody that's drowning you must get away from him. So you use physical strength to get away, which I did, sad to say. Struggled to the top and held on to the beam while he floated away.'

The next to go was the petty officer, who had made the raft, part of it broke away and he drifted off, leaving just seven of them. However, during the night one by one they dropped off. The last to go was a friend named 'Ginger' Conolly, who had managed to hang on during the night but eventually gave up, although Arthur did try to hold onto him. Then he was on his own, struggling to survive:

'It was as if somebody'd split my brain right up the middle and there were two little men with hammers, one saying, "You're going to die, you're going to die, you're going to die" the other saying "You mustn't die, your mother said you mustn't die," because I wasn't married and my mam idolised me.'

Arthur nearly gave up during that terrible period in the water, but when he was almost at his last gasp he looked up and saw a biplane flying around. He managed to wave and the aeroplane dived towards him, making Arthur think it was going to machine gun him at any moment! Instead, it circled around him, and he thought it was going to land, but he soon realised that it wasn't a seaplane. It then fired a green Very light and left him thinking in his confused state that it would not come back and was merely leaving him to die. But that proved not to be the case and about half an hour later a caique came along 'with a massive German swastika flying in the breeze and on the bow end was a paratrooper sitting with a machine gun trained on me.'

Two German sailors dragged him on board, stripped off all his clothing, then one of them said, 'Englander for you the war is over.' Then they dragged him on his bottom along the upper deck (he said that he still has a sore backside to this day), then shoved him down a hatchway where he discovered other British sailors from the Gloucester (also without any clothes) who had been picked up earlier. They were all landed at Kithera and initially lined up, still naked, against a wall to be shot by the Fallschirmjäger. But fortunately one of the prisoners – a Lt Heap – who both spoke and understood German very well, jumped forward and explained to an officer that they were cruiser men not destroyer men. 'I'm afraid if we had been destroyer men we'd have all been shot there and then.' He later discovered that this was because the destroyers had smashed up the caiques and shot the soldiers in the water. Arthur managed to obtain some clothing (a pair of calico shorts with no buttons!) and he and the other prisoners were kept on Kithera for about 10 days until Crete had been captured. Then they were put onto two caiques and taken to the mainland. So began his incarceration as a prisoner of war.

Naked under Heaven
This evocative paragraph forms an appropriate lead-in to the

actions of the 5th Destroyer Flotilla, comprising HMS *Kelly*, *Kashmir*, *Kipling*, *Kelvin* and *Jackal*, under the command of Captain Lord Louis Mountbatten.

> *'There is no spot more naked under heaven than the deck of a destroyer as a stick of bombs falls slanting towards it. The assailant may be the size of a gnat on the rim of a far-off cloud; it may be a raid approaching from four quarters, roaring down with machine guns spraying the deck with explosive shells; the bombs may fall unheralded out of the blinding Mediterranean sun or low-lying cloud; they may burst on the surface of the sea, flinging a myriad of splinters of steel abroad, killing or wounding everybody in their path, piercing anything but armour; they may burst under the surface, throwing up the water in the semblance of gigantic monoliths that, as they collapse, deluge the pom-poms and machine guns and their crews and flood the ventilation trunks. These explosions lift the ship as if a giant had kicked her, wrenching the steering gear, straining frames and plates. They are called near-misses and men, watching the bombs screaming down at the ship, thank God for them as the alternative to a direct hit.'* [5]

The 5th Destroyer Flotilla had joined Adm King's force from Malta on the afternoon of 22 May. As soon as it was dark, they were sent to search for survivors from the *Fiji* and the *Gloucester*, which had been sunk that day. They then proceeded towards Crete, bombarded Maleme and sank a couple of caiques that were bound for the island with 5 Gebirgs Division reinforcements on board.

At about 0400hrs on the morning of the 23rd, the C-in-C ordered all naval forces to return to Alexandria to collect more fuel and ammunition. 5th Destroyer Flotilla was acting on these orders, when it was attacked by enemy aircraft. HMS *Kelvin* and *Jackal* had been detached from the flotilla so were not involved, but the others had to dodge numerous bombing runs, initially, from four Dorniers. Then, at about 0755hrs, when they were some 13 miles south of Gavdos (an island off the south-west of Crete), they were attacked by some two dozen Stuka dive-bombers. The *Kashmir* was the first to be hit. Cdr King's vessel sank in just two minutes. The official record of this engagement also tells of how Ordinary Seaman Ian D. Rhodes, of the Royal Australian Naval Volunteer Reserve, was manning an Oerlikon gun on one side of the ship and when it became submerged as the ship began sinking, he climbed over the wreckage to reach the other gun on the opposite side and opened fire again on the attacking aircraft and shot it down!

Next it was Mountbatten's *Kelly* that was the target for a 1,000lb bomb which hit the vessel while it was travelling at high speed. Before coming to the Mediterranean, while serving in home waters, HMS *Kelly* had had two lucky escapes, once after being mined and once after being torpedoed, but on each occasion she had managed to limp back to port safely – but not this time. With every gun still firing, she capsized, floated bottom up for a while and then sank. The dive-bombers then, as usual, began to machine gun the men in the water, killing and wounding several of them. However, the sinking of the *Kelly* had been witnessed by the *Kipling* which was some miles to the south. Cdr A. St Clair-Ford immediately closed and succeeded in picking up a total of 281 officers and men from the water – 128 from the *Kelly* (including Lord Louis) and 153 from the *Kashmir* (including Cdr King). The *Kipling* then managed to reach Alexandria unscathed, despite the fact that during her rescue work she had been attacked by six high-level bombing attacks, and between 0820hrs and 1300hrs she was attacked by over 40 bombers, who dropped 83 bombs at her, but remarkably she survived. [6]

Reinforcing the Garrison

The Germans were not the only ones to endeavour to reinforce their ground troops on Crete after the battle had commenced.

Because of German air supremacy, such reinforcement by the British also had normally to be timed at night. The initial intention was to use the special service ship HMS *Glenroy* (commander Capt Sir James Paget) and merchant ships, but it was soon found that only HM ships were fast and agile enough to able to get through. The first run actually took place on the afternoon of the 22 May, when the *Glenroy* was loaded up with 900 men of the Queen's Royal Regiment, the staff of HQ 16th Infantry Brigade, plus 18 vehicles and sailed from Alexandria bound for Tymbaki on the south of Crete, escorted by HMS *Coventry*, *Auckland* and *Flamingo*. However, after high level discussions with Gen Wavell, Adm Cunningham recalled her at 1127hrs on the 23rd, and a further plan was worked out for reinforcing the island using the fast minelayer, HMS *Abdiel*, plus destroyers. The following day, the destroyers *Isis*, *Hero* and *Nizam* sailed from Alexandria with the headquarters and two battalions of Special Service troops (known as 'Layforce') who were to be landed at Selinos Kastelli in south-west Crete. However, the weather proved too bad for the landing and it had to be aborted.

The first successful run was made on the night of 23/24 May, when the destroyers *Jaguar* and *Defender* landed stores and ammunition at Suda Bay between midnight and 0200hrs. They returned to Alexandria, bringing out wounded, together with some officers and men who were not required on the island. The following night, 24/25 May, the *Abdiel* successfully landed some 200 men of 'Layforce' together with 80 tons of stores at Suda. She then returned to Alexandria with about 50 wounded and four Greek cabinet ministers. *En route* she was attacked by four Ju88s, but successfully evaded them. On its arrival in Egypt, the *Abdiel* took on board Brig Laycock, the commander of 'Layforce', a further 400 of his men and some 100 tons of stores. They then left early the next morning, accompanied by *Hero* and *Nizam*. In total these ships landed some 750 troops, plus a quantity of stores at Suda during the night of 26/27 May. They would be the last reinforcements to be landed on Crete and the story of their gallant rearguard action is told in a later chapter. Meanwhile the intrepid minelayer and her accompanying destroyers had collected a further 930 men not needed on Crete, and then run the gauntlet of the inevitable air attacks on the way back to Alexandria, the only damage being sustained by *Hero*, which had to reduce its speed to 28 knots.

The *Glenroy*, with its battalion of the Queen's on board, had sailed once again for Tymbaki during the evening of the 25th, accompanied by HMS *Stuart*, *Coventry* and *Jaguar*. During the afternoon and evening they were subjected to continual bombing attacks, first by recce aircraft, then by dive-bombers. They shot down one aircraft and damaged another, but *Glenroy* received some slight damage and casualties from near misses and machine gun attacks. Three of her landing craft were holed, and a large dump of cased petrol on the upper deck was set on fire, which meant they had to steam downwind until the fire was put out. With some 800 troops on board, together with the large quantity of petrol, it was a tricky situation, but they managed to control the fire by 1950hrs and resume their course northwards. Next they were attacked by torpedo-bombers at about 2050hrs but successfully avoided the torpedoes. By now the operational schedule was some three hours adrift, their landing craft capacity had been reduced by a third, while the weather on the intended landing beaches had deteriorated badly. So, regretfully, the operation had to be cancelled and the force returned to Alexandria.

Despite all the problems and dangers, it was fully appreciated that the troops on Crete desperately needed resupplying, so another attempt was made, Convoy AN31 leaving Alexandria at 0500hrs on 26 May. It comprised two slow merchant ships, plus the *Auckland*, later joined by the *Calcutta* and *Defender*. Unfortunately weather and sea conditions deteriorated severely, and the convoy had to turn back. Shortly after turning back, they were bombed by nine

Ju88s, but fortunately sustained no damage, although they did hit one of the attacking aircraft.

> *'The Army is just holding its own against constant reinforcement of airborne enemy troops. We must NOT let them down. At whatever cost to ourselves, we must land reinforcements for them and keep the enemy from using the sea. There are indications that the enemy resources are stretched to the limit. We can and must outlast them. STICK IT OUT.'* [7]

Striking at Scarpanto

Not all the air activity was German. On 25 May, the C-in-C decided to attack the enemy airfield at Scarpanto, in the Dodecanese, to destroy bombers operating from there. The strike force would be the Fleet Air Arm's Fulmars and Albacores belonging to the aircraft carrier HMS *Formidable*, accompanied by the battleships *Queen Elizabeth* and *Barham*, plus eight destroyers, under the overall command of Vice-Adm Pridham-Wippell. They left Alexandria on the 25th, and by 0330hrs on the 26th were some 100 miles SSW of Scarpanto. Four Albacores then made a surprise bombing raid on the airfield, followed by five Fulmars, machine gunning the rows of parked aircraft. The result was two aircraft destroyed and numerous others damaged, including both Italian CR42s and German Ju87s. Having all returned to the aircraft carrier safely, they spent the forenoon in contact with any enemy aircraft that approached the fleet, shooting down all they could reach (two certain, two probable, for the loss of one Fulmar). They then landed on the carrier to refuel, and while this was taking place, they were attacked by Stukas, which hit *Formidable* twice – as was the destroyer *Nubian*. Nevertheless, both damaged vessels reached port safely.

> *'Throughout the battle, the Royal Air Force, working from Egypt, did all that was possible to afford relief to our troops in*

> *Crete; but the distance was too great to maintain a scale of*
> *attack on the Germans which could affect the issue.'* [8]

Enemy positions and aircraft were attacked on the Maleme airfield by Bristol Blenheims and Martin Marylands (of the South African Air Force) at intervals during 23-27 May. These raids destroyed at least 40 enemy aircraft of various types and many others were damaged, so it was a not inconsiderable achievement. Nine fully loaded troop-carrying Ju52s were destroyed by Hurricanes on the 23rd and 26th, while RAF Wellingtons bombed Maleme on 23, 25, 26, 27 and 29 May. They also attacked Heraklion on 30 and 31 May and 1 June, and before that Scarpanto airfield on 25, 27, 28 and 29 May. All these attacks did significant damage with fires and explosions, but the extent of the damage was not known accurately. During these battles, the RAF lost 38 aircraft, all of them except for five in the air.

Notes

1. Generalmajor aD (Retired) Conrad Seibt in an account of the battle which he gave postwar, on behalf of the Historical Division HQ USAREUR.
2. Ibid.
3. As quoted from *The Italian Navy in WWII* (USNI, Annapolis, 1957) in S. W. C. Pack's *The Battle for Crete*.
4. Ibid.
5. Taken from an Admiralty account of naval operations in the Mediterranean between April 1941 and January 1943, which was sold to the general public in 1944 for 1s 6d (7.5p).
6. The *Kelly* and her captain Lord Louis Mountbatten, were of course immortalised by Noel Coward's wartime film *In Which We Serve*.
7. Signal sent to the Fleet by C-in-C of the Mediterranean Fleet, Adm Sir Andrew Cunningham, on 24 May 1941.
8. Quoted from *Naval Operations in the Battle of Crete*.

9

The Battle is Decided

It was not until 24 May that the OKW, the German armed forces senior headquarters, announced that Operation 'Merkur' had been launched four days previously, and that their paratroopers and airborne troops had been battling on Crete against the British, Commonwealth and Greek forces there since the early morning of the 20th. It was to be during the period 22-25 May that the German invaders were able to build up their strength and thus maintain their assault with ever-increasing vigour, while the beleaguered island garrison grew steadily weaker, their supplies of ammunition and other matériel being reduced by continuous action and not being replaced.

Undoubtedly, also, the lack of communications between the various garrisons and between levels of command did much to weaken the overall defence and there was little co-ordination of effort between sectors. In addition, the island of Crete became more and more isolated as the Luftwaffe tightened its grip on the skies above and around the island and began to achieve the upper hand in controlling the seas during daylight hours, despite the continued heroic efforts of the Royal Navy. Sadly, the small amount of influence which the few RAF aircraft could achieve, grew weaker and weaker.

Philip Guedalla comments after explaining how the Royal Navy had dealt most effectively with the seaborne element of the German invasion:

'Sea power, it seemed, could still bar the sea route to Crete, although it was beyond its power to open it to an effective

stream of British reinforcements; and with the enemy mastery of the air route this service might delay, but could never hope to alter the result. Indeed, the price of naval operations conducted within range of shore-based German aircraft and beyond the reach of air cover from Egyptian aerodromes might almost seem excessive ... and efforts by the RAF to intervene from Egypt were largely unsuccessful.' [1]

Galatas

Michael Forrester at Galatas recalled:

'The 23rd May passed relatively quietly on the ground, some reorganisation of positions being achieved despite periodic strafing and bombing attacks. Next day was tense and uneasy, as attacks from the air were accompanied by probing attacks on our forward positions. From first light on the 25th, there was intense activity from the air as the probing attacks increased in strength and frequency along the length of the front, culminating in a strong attack, well supported by air and ground fire, against the Galatas position. As forward positions were fiercely contested, Pink Hill was captured and a counter-attack ordered. This time the Germans were in strength and with a combination of machine gun and mortar fire halted the counter-attack, inflicting heavy casualties and scattering men of the 6th Greek Regiment.

'Despite magnificent resistance from Russell Force, the Galatas position was becoming untenable and 10 Brigade was ordered to retire behind the village. Here Col Kippenberger capless and utterly calm, paced slowly up and down, smoking his pipe, as he rallied his men with the call, "Stand for New Zealand!" Roy Farran of the 3rd Hussars drove up with his troop, now reduced to two light tanks, having just returned from a reconnaissance of Galatas which he reported as being "stiff with Jerries".

'During consultation with Brig Puttick, who felt a respite was much needed and that this could only be achieved by *hitting the Germans hard and unexpectedly, Col Kippenberger undertook to carry out an immediate counter-attack for which he was allocated additional troops, including two companies of the 23rd New Zealand Battalion. And, as the minutes went by, although I had not succeeded in rallying many from the 6th Greek Regiment, a considerable number of New Zealanders, who had become detached, rejoined their units on the track that was to be the start-line.*

'Farran led off towards the village with the machine guns of his tanks blazing. This was the signal for the whole line to advance, whereupon there broke out the most startling clamour, audible, I was told later, many miles away – blood-curdling yells and shouts rising above the sound of small-arms fire and exploding grenades – as all taking part gave vent to their feelings. Many had lost old friends, brothers had lost brothers, and all had shared the frustration of aerial attacks and of being on the defensive since the invasion began. Some believed the hubbub was started by the presence of some Maoris shouting their traditional war cry – the Haka. All this contributed to the dismay of the Germans who, in addition, were completely taken by surprise.

'The counter-attack swept through Galatas, clearing the village and the surrounding area of all Germans. Thus the aim was achieved though not without inevitable casualties to add to the many already incurred in what seemed to have been a very long day. And having completed their task, all units moved back to positions on the new line.'

In one engagement near the centre of the village, where the Kiwis were held up by machine gunfire and grenades, Sgt A. C. Hulme went forward alone and engaged the enemy with a series of grenades. This and his subsequent heroic actions during the withdrawal resulted in him being awarded the Victoria Cross, the second to be won by the New Zealanders during the battle on Crete.

One of those wounded in the Galatas battle was Roy Farran. His tanks had been shot at when they entered the village on their initial recce, but it was only when they got back to safety that he realised his second tank had been penetrated by an anti-tank rifle and the gunner wounded. The tank was still serviceable so he asked the New Zealanders if anyone could fire a Vickers machine gun and soon had a volunteer in the turret. He recalled that the second entry he made into Galatas was slower, but that he got ahead of the infantry who advanced with fixed bayonets. In the village square his tank was hit several times and all the crew wounded, the driver as a consequence, skidding into a stone wall. 'I pushed the other two out of the driver's hatch and crawled out myself. My gunner was badly wounded in the stomach and I realised that I was not in much better shape myself. I had been hit badly in the left thigh and less seriously, probably with pieces of metal from the tank, in my right shoulder and left heel. I dragged myself into the shelter of a low stone wall, while the Germans from the other side of the square continued to shoot holes in my tank.' [2] Farran would continue to cheer on the New Zealanders – even when one of them stood on him to fire over the wall, then hastily apologised when he realised that the 'corpse' was still alive!

The Kiwis had now cleared the Germans out of Galatas and all was quiet. Roy Farran was, therefore, both surprised and disturbed to hear that after all the effort which had been expended capturing the village, they had now been ordered to withdraw. Two Cretan women were going round giving succour to the wounded, one of them put a blanket over him, the other gave him some water. Then, after a couple of hours of complete silence, he was surprised to hear the noise of tank tracks coming apparently from the direction in which the Germans had retreated! To his astonishment the tanks were from his squadron, and had been sent out to look for him. They picked him up, put him on the front and drove him to the nearest first aid post. The post happened to be in no man's land between the opposing forces and was regularly shelled and mortared, but all the while gave first aid impartially to both sides. Due to the serious nature of his wounds, which soon turned gangrenous, Roy Farran was unable to join the walking wounded when they withdrew, so was captured by the enemy. He would be taken over the hill to the Maleme airfield and from thence to Athens. For the next three months he would be a patient in a POW hospital, until he escaped, made contact with the resistance and eventually managed to get back to Egypt. After such an adventurous beginning is there any wonder that the rest of his wartime service – as told in his autobiography *Winged Dagger* – reads more like fiction than fact!

Gen Julius Ringel's account of the counter-attack at Galatas is perhaps even more descriptive:

'The British, realising what was at stake, defended themselves like bulldogs. Suddenly and entirely unexpectedly they penetrated in a powerful counter-attack supported by tanks into the village of Galatas, whose defences were not ready, and almost succeeded, following behind the tanks and reaching the edge of the village.

A dreadful night-time street battle ensued, which continued undiminished until dawn. At the crack of dawn, Galatas was in the hands of the Gebirgsjägers, the British, aware of the threatening envelopment by the Gruppe Kraku had given up the key position and retreated. The rising sun shone on a gruesome picture of the nocturnal battle. Many brave, death-defying soldiers, friend and foe were lying in the streets, on the heights, and in the gardens, countless weapons and equipment covered the streets and demolished tanks were standing around alongside the roads. The price of victory was high but not too high. The last reinforced switch position before Canea and the Suda Bay was smashed and the decisive battle practically won.'

At Maleme and Canea

Eastwards, during the night of 22/23 May, the defenders had begun to withdraw from Maleme, and to form a line of positions to defend Canea, with 5th NZ Brigade at the western, coastal end, then 4th NZ Brigade to its east, followed by the ad hoc 10th Greek/NZ Brigade up to the Canea-Alikianou road, then the 19th Australian Brigade south of the road. The immediate defence of the town was made up of Australian gunners fighting as infantry, a company of Rangers (KRRC) and some Royal Marines. It had been decided to evacuate all those civilians who wished to leave Canea as it was continually being bombed and was thus increasingly difficult to live in, and this was achieved. As the German strength built up and the situation grew more fluid, rumours were everywhere, as Rex Hey the Ordnance Corps fitter recalls:

> 'Rumour was rife – good and bad – "The Germans have taken Maleme" and then, "We have beaten them back" – "They are surrendering" – "We are retreating … the Germans are bringing in supplies by sea." The latter seemed to have some truth in it as we were reorganised and deployed outside the workshop grounds (complete with rifles). Defences were erected, would you believe, made of empty olive oil containers. That night we were posted behind this formidable defence line with rifles at the ready … We were told that the situation was in hand, and although we had become rather cynical, however, we believed this after the obvious destruction of the attempted sea landing, plus the fact that we were still holding Maleme. However, in the same day we were told we could be moving out. These conflicting stories (and others) continued for days. Then unexpectedly, a supply ship arrived at Suda – the Luftwaffe would soon be on to that – I was sent down to the docks with others, to collect whatever may be there for us. The best place in Crete to keep away from was the docks, apart from Maleme, it was one of the sure targets for the bombers, so there

was no enthusiasm for the trip, but orders were orders and off we went. The sight of the once beautiful Suda Bay was more than depressing. It was a mass of ships either sunk or crippled, masts and funnels sticking up out of the water. The carnage was unbelievable. The unopposed bombers had had a field day. Anti-aircraft fire didn't seem to unduly upset them and that was the only defence.

'To my complete astonishment we collected a battered Crossley recovery vehicle – if there was one thing we really didn't need at that time was a second recovery vehicle! Coupled with that, it was long past its prime and one thing was for sure, Lt Newman had never requisitioned it. All my first impressions were justified when I started it up. The engine was really rough, it clearly had bearing trouble and when we finally got it back to the workshop it became obvious that the big end had gone. To our surprise we actually had a spare bearing in the stores, so we got to work on it immediately.

I had taken the sump off and started to remove the damaged bearing when Lt Newman appeared and announced, to my surprise, that we were leaving. I said, "Where to?" "I don't know myself yet," he said, "just leave it, we won't be needing it." And then, memories of Dunkirk – drain it of oil (which had already been done) and water and leave it running to seize. Destroy everything you can – I remember shooting at the tyres at Dunkirk, but this time we didn't do that. I asked about our serviceable vehicles and was told we should give them the same treatment. We would be walking. This was incredible, as we knew that the Welch Regiment had made advances. We knew that the Aussies and the New Zealanders were holding their own, so it didn't make sense, and then we were told that the Germans had captured the aerodrome and were now flying in supplies and heavy equipment non-stop. From historical records (and I have read many) it is said that there was a complete communications breakdown between HQ and the troops around Maleme. Instructions were given to withdraw which never should have been given and this was the beginning of the end. With heavy arms and equipment coming in, it was obvious we could not hold the island. We were told we would be taken off and taken back to Egypt. History also tells us that the Germans were on the point of withdrawing before they took Maleme. Their losses had been so appalling, but taking the aerodrome made a tremendous difference.'

What had brought about this change in fortunes had been, as Rex Hey rightly says, the capture of the aerodrome, the flying in of the additional mountain troops and Gen Ringel's positive action to outflank the British positions, which he achieved on D+5, to the east of Maleme. On the following day the Germans both entered Canea and occupied Suda Bay, after a forced march over the mountains. The defenders fought bravely throughout, and continued to defend at every opportunity, making best use of the terrain and inflicting heavy casualties on the German forces.

The German report on this period makes special comment on the fact that some positions were protected by wire and mines. It also says that armed bands of Cretan civilian irregulars fought fiercely, especially in the mountains, 'using great cunning and committing acts of cruelty such as mutilating dead and wounded German soldiers'. Although this undoubtedly occurred on occasions, it was never as widespread as post-Crete German propaganda would have the rest of the world believe. Nevertheless it gave rise to some severe retaliation against any civilian – man, woman or child – who was captured after fighting against them. It is said, for example, that if a woman was suspected of fighting against them, they would rip away her dress to discover if she had a tell-tale bruise on her shoulder (caused by the recoil of a rifle) and if so, then she would be shot along with the men. One German paratrooper recalled, 'When we were pushing forward in Crete, we were being shot at from a little house standing on its own. We surrounded the house and with a good charge of explosives blew it down. In the ruins we found two dead girls – they had been shooting at us with two old rifles and very old ammunition which gave very nasty wounds.'

By the 27th, the Allied forces in the west of the island had withdrawn to the outskirts of Suda village, with the New Zealand troops deployed along a sunken road to the west of the village – the road was known as '42nd Street' after the 42nd Field Company, RE, who had built it. The leading German troops in this sector were from Gebirgsregiment 141, their battalion-strong vanguard was pressing forward full of fight and undoubtedly not paying much attention to an enemy whom they were confidently assuming was now 'on the run'. Suddenly, as they approached '42nd Street', one Australian and five New Zealand battalions, launched a bayonet charge:

> 'They had watched the Germans coming, the efficient, almost contemptuous, drive of a victorious army ... They [the Anzacs] went forward, walking grimly at first, firing at the grey uniforms in the grass, using the bayonet ruthlessly on those who resisted ... For the enemy, the sight of troops advancing into the fire with such sharp pugnacity was too much. They fought for a moment, wavered, and then fled. And they were destroyed as they ran. In a spirit of exhilaration for which there can be no words, our men swept the Germans back from 42nd Street nearly half a mile.' [3]

The I/Gebirgsregiment 141, which bore the brunt of the attack, was virtually destroyed in this, its first ever, battle. An account by Lt-Col F. Baker DSO, ED (then a captain commanding A Company of 28th NZ Infantry Battalion) from the official history gives a vivid, first-hand impression of what took place:

> 'As soon as B Company clambered up the bank I waved my men forward and was able to keep them under control while

section commanders got their men together. B Company was subjected to deadly fire as soon as they commenced to move forward, and by the time they had moved 50-55 yards they were forced to the ground where from the cover of the trees, roots and holes in the ground they started to exchange fire with the enemy, who had likewise taken up firing positions as soon as the attack commenced. I, therefore, gave immediate orders for A Company to advance. We moved forward in extended formation through B Company and into the attack.

At first the enemy held and could only be overcome by Tommy gun, bayonet and rifle. His force was well dispersed and approximately 600 yards in depth and by the time we met them their troops were no more than 150 yards from 42nd Street. They continued to put up a fierce resistance until we had penetrated some 250-300 yards. They then commenced to panic and as the troops on either side of us had now entered the fray it was not long before considerable numbers of the enemy were beating a hasty retreat. As we penetrated further their disorder became more marked and as men ran they first threw away their arms but shortly afterwards commenced throwing away their equipment as well and disappearing very quickly from the scene of battle.' [4]

I could not find a detailed German record of this counter-attack, except to say that the fighting around this time was very fierce and that they sustained numerous casualties. One Gebirgsjäger wrote, 'When we did meet the Tommies they fought very hard to hold us and several times attacked with rifles and bayonets. I think they were desperate men knowing if we won it was a prisoner-of-war camp for them. Their attacks cost them a lot of men and I remember Crete as the place of black corpses.' [5]

The garrison reinforces Heraklion

As explained in an earlier chapter, the 1st Battalion A&SH were landed in the south of the island at Tymbaki. It was the intention that they would cross over and join 14th Infantry Brigade in the Heraklion garrison, but as there was no transport, they would have to march. Maj Richard Fleming, 2BW, who had been appointed first as Garrison Adjutant Heraklion, then as brigade major of 14th Brigade, would be the 'link-man' for the journey. He recalled:

'Chappel then ordered me to find my way across the intervening area on the road under Mount Ida, where I was to meet with them and bring them back to our defensive position, unless we could fight our way through the German lines of resistance.

We set off in the dark in a south-westerly direction. "We" consisted of only two others. One being Eddie Welch my superb batman who had been with me for the past two years. The other was Spiro Davis, a corporal from the Rhodesian platoon, but he, being of Greek extraction, was to act as my interpreter. I was fortunate to have such excellent companions. Luck was on my side, for fairly early on we met three Cretan shepherds, dressed in their wonderful outfits. Baggy trousers, bandoleers strung all around their bodies, shotguns, knee-high boots, enormous moustaches and a sort of black tam o'shanter head-dress. Unless they were for you they could have been a very terrifying group. They so easily might have despatched us, as they delighted in telling us that they had already done to many of the parachutists. Thanks to Spiro's Greek, they took us under their wing. They said they had heard of the arrival of some British troops on the road up from the south and that they could lead us up to them. They took us to a nearby cave, where they played host, giving us lavish cups of krassi, the local wine. I can still visualise that cave, with its candles stuck in wine bottles, the bombastic chat of how they had dealt with so many (they claimed) parachutists.

'When we set forth again, the going was pretty bad, the ground very rough up and down the valleys endless and exhausting. However, they did their task wonderfully and

delivered us safely to the centre of those of the Argylls who had arrived. The battalion had little, if any, transport and had left their HQs behind. However, they did start to proceed down the road towards Heraklion, when they encountered a certain amount of German opposition. There was nothing I could do as I had only been sent up in a welcoming role. As they were unable to break through the opposition, I told them that I had come across country with three excellent Cretan guides and so supposed we could take them on that route to the Brigade. This was considered a good plan, so I started to look for my friendly Cretan guides. They had promised to wait for me should I need their services again. But I can only suppose that they had got bored with the apparent inaction and so pushed off to more exciting and profitable pursuits.

'*By this time darkness was not far off, so Spiro, Eddie and myself told them to get into single file and follow us. What followed was a nightmare. For one thing it is well known that in any convoy it is extremely difficult to keep any semblance of control however steady a pace the leading file may endeavour to maintain. Messages kept coming up to us to go slower. The darkness was soon upon us and we had no knowledge of the very rough terrain. However, there was one saving grace and a very important one it was. The town of Heraklion had been bombed unmercifully and so was a heaven-sent landmark to give us somewhere to aim, being a blaze of light.*

'*We must have stumbled our way across that very rough going for eight hours, up hills, down gorges and cliffs, before I was beseeched from the rear to call a halt. This I was only too prepared to agree to. The three of us – Spiro, Eddie and myself – had been on the go without sleep for quite 44 hours. We all just flopped down and passed out, until about four hours later my alarm bells must have got through to me. I awoke with a start, realising that no sentries or look-outs had been posted. Not really my concern, except that it was my responsibility to get that unit into our base, intact and safely. Somewhat refreshed and after only another three hours' marching, what joy to find ourselves being welcomed into the Yorks and Lancs lines. Not all that much joy, for I discovered that we were one company short. Horrors, but before I set off to discover what had happened to them, dear Gilly – Lt-Col Alistair Gilroy, the CO of the Yorks and Lancs – made me sit down and eat a very welcome breakfast with my tea well whisky-laced. He then detailed two of his young officers to accompany me back along our trail. I cannot now remember how far we had to travel, but that is of no import as find them we did and brought them in. They had somehow been left behind along our trail so had then waited until daylight before moving forward. How lucky we were that we did not meet up with any Fallschirmjäger who by then had had time to get their act together.'* [6]

A member of the Argylls who was to make the difficult journey northwards, was Lt-Col Andrew Brown, then the battalion intelligence sergeant, who had been helping to guard the Messara Plain and whom we met in an earlier chapter. He was then at the Bn HQ at Ay Deka and recalled how, although the Germans had been cleared out of the Heraklion area, they did establish themselves astride the main Ay Deka–Heraklion road which cut the Argylls off from the main garrison, physically and on the radio because the battalion wireless sets refused to work over the intervening hills.

'During 21 May, I with my section climbed the hill and scoured the plain but saw nothing. Little news was coming to the battalion and as the wireless sets refused to work, we had to rely on the local telephone service. During the night two British tanks had landed on the morning of 22 May, they, along with our Carrier Platoon, set off to clear the road to Heraklion. The tanks got through but the Carrier Platoon was forced back. I spent the day once again up the hill with nothing to report.

'On 23 May, the Carrier Platoon along with A Company were given the task again of clearing the road to Heraklion. Progress was being made until an unexpected landing of 150 German paratroopers in their midst caused them to withdraw to a defensive position. Our casualties numbered two officers and 20 Other Ranks, but the Germans had very heavy casualties. Many of the parachutists got caught in the trees and were easily picked off. One of our sergeants, Sgt Bloomfield, was awarded a DCM for his efforts. I had again spent the day up the hill with my section – nothing to report.

'On the night 23/24 May, a message arrived via numerous police stations from Brigade HQ in Heraklion, ordering the CO to attack and clear the road south of Heraklion. Battalion HQ included the Intelligence Officer, Lt John Phillips, and three companies set off immediately and were in position by 0445hrs.

I was left in Ay Deka with my section. I learned later that the attack was not successful and heavy casualties were sustained. More Germans had arrived by parachute. Orders were received from Heraklion – sit tight and after dark, with the help of guides (as we know, these were the 14 Brigade BM, Maj Richard Fleming and his two companions), this part of the Battalion should march across the mountains to Heraklion.'

Because of the problems which have already been explained by Maj Fleming, they did not reach Heraklion until the afternoon of 25 May. Andrew Brown was meanwhile still in the south of the island, still climbing his hill and still looking over the countryside, with little information coming back to Ay Deka. Most worrying was the fact that they now had half the Battalion in the north of the island and half in the south.

'Shortly after this a convoy of six vehicles arrived from Heraklion with some wounded. Among them was Lt Phillips, the IO. The Mortar Platoon was ordered to embus, along with

*blankets and greatcoats, and travel back to Heraklion. The road
to be used was a mountain track and I talked my way on to the
convoy. I implied that as the IO was wounded, I as his second in
command should take his place with the Commanding Officer.
No one objected and I set off as NCO in charge of the convoy in
late afternoon by the same mountain track. Shortly after we left
we were buzzed by a German plane, dropping a few bombs
harmlessly before taking off. I was travelling in the Gun
Carrier at the front of the convoy. This restricted the speed to
about 20mph. As darkness fell, we crawled slowly along,
climbing all the time. After two or three hours of slow
travelling, suddenly out of the darkness appeared two figures
waving their arms telling us to stop. Much to my relief they
were two members of a Black Watch platoon stationed in this
village. They took me to their officer who told me that the
platoon was cut off from Heraklion as there had been another
landing of German paratroopers. He suggested we stay with
him for the night and make a break at first light. With him
was a Royal Engineer officer who had been surveying the
Messara Plain as a possible landing ground for RAF planes.*

*I should mention here that we had no RAF presence on the
island. I told the Black Watch officer that I had been instructed
to get this convoy and this I must try to do. On reflection it was
not bravery on my part, but more fear on my part as to what
the CO would think if I did not make the effort. When it was
realised that we were definitely going on, the RE officer said he
would come also as he had a very important message to get back
to HQ Middle East. He travelled in the carrier and I travelled
in the rear truck. Before I left the Black Watch officer said that
if we could not get through we should return and join his
platoon and attempt to clear the road in the morning.*

*'Before we could get going we had a helluva job getting all
the men together. They had found a baker's shop and were
tucking in to buns and milk! Eventually we were all aboard
and we set off. We travelled for two miles when we were again*

stopped, by local Cretans this time. One of them could speak English and he told us not to go on as a large paradrop of Germans had taken place that afternoon. They were very upset when we decided to go on. Very slowly we made our way along the mountainous road. The carrier heralding our approach, the noise of the tracks echoing and re-echoing though the valleys. Suddenly the carrier noise was drowned by a hail of machine gun bullets with tracers coming from our left but fortunately flying harmlessly above our heads. As I was in the last truck I kept hoping their aim did not improve before we got past. We weathered the storm, and passed through another village that was completely deserted. Shortly after this we descended a very steep hill and the convoy came to a halt. I got out of the truck and went to the head of the convoy. The carrier had come to a halt on a bridge where an old car loaded with bricks was blocking the way. The carrier had attempted to push the car out of the way but the car was so weighted that the carrier, in backing for a second attempt in the dark, had reversed down a steep bank leading to the river. I got everyone out of the trucks, detailed some for look-out and we all got down to pushing the obstruction out of the way. The carrier, after many attempts, managed to get back on the road. We quickly got back in the trucks, crossed the bridge and climbed the steep hill on the other side.

'To this day I do not know if the road block was German or the local militia. A few miles after we passed through a village smelling of death. I learned later it was the village called Knossos. A few hundred yards later we came to a British checkpoint, much to our relief, and were directed to Brigade HQ. It was 0300hrs and I reported to the Orderly Officer who was very surprised when I told him where we had come from. He told me to bed the men down and he would arrange for a guide to take us to our Battalion HQ at first light. A few hours' shut-eye were very welcome and we duly arrived at Battalion HQ at 0630hrs.

I reported to the Adjutant, Capt Pearson, who also expressed surprise that we had made it. Shortly after I saw the CO and made my report. I showed him on the map the location of the road block and also the approximate area where we had been shot at. Later that morning a convoy of six lorries and the carrier were sent back on the same route I had taken. It came under heavy fire – I think we had been lucky. Two lorries were destroyed, also the carrier, but Lt Valentine made good his escape and returned to Bn HQ to make his report.

'The Mortar Platoon was soon placed in its combat position and I was allocated a fine deep slit-trench at Bn HQ. I remember I sat down and mused over what had been quite a night. I was really full of admiration for our drivers. We had examined all the vehicles at first light and found evidence of only one hit – on the towing arm of one of the trucks. My musing was interrupted when suddenly the sky was full of German dive-bombers – Stukas. As we had no anti-aircraft guns they came very low and the pilots were clearly visible. The bombing raid lasted for about half an hour and was followed by troop-carrying aircraft and suddenly the sky behind Apex Hill was black with parachutes descending. They were out of range of our small-arms fire and all we could do was sit and marvel at it. They dropped behind Apex Hill, then shortly through my binoculars, I saw them coming up and sitting on top of the hill looking in our direction and sunning themselves. During the bombing raid I had a little satisfaction as I sat at the bottom of my deep slit-trench firing a .303 rifle. I don't know if I hit anything but one felt a little better. 27 May had been an eventful day.'

Patience and courage of the wounded

2nd Leicesters, nicknamed the 'Tigers', were another of the British battalions defending Heraklion. Maj A. W. D. Nicholls MC, who was at the time commanding A Company, later wrote a personal account of the battles, which included some words about the medical staff. He had had what he described as a 'slight misunderstanding' during the rounding up of the enemy Fallschirmjäger when they had first dropped:

'I told a soldier to shoot when I should have told him to use his bayonet, and the bullet went through the German and then into me. I'd been told before that ricochets were dangerous! Now I knew. Doc McLeod did a little carving and a few hours later I was taken to the casualty reception station on the outskirts of the town. This was a cave; it had few, if any, lights and it was fast filling up with casualties in varying forms of distress. I was the only officer in the place and could not have been called combatant as the morphine was now doing its work. The cave contained about six or eight RAMC orderlies, but no doctors. There had been two doctors but at the time of the attack they were both away in hospital. The RAMC orderlies had never been under fire before, and were only too relieved to find that their first visitors were wounded British and not combatant Boche. Still they coped and the night passed. Early next morning a medical officer and a padre arrived, and we all felt better as a result. The next few days were distressing. We very soon overflowed the cave and occupied a house. More and more of our chaps were brought in. I was glad to welcome a Royal Marine officer who also had a hand injury, and between the two of us we almost made one combatant body. After a further 24 hours, when the MO had been operating by the light of a gas-jet without sleep and without stopping, some order had been obtained and the flow of casualties had eased. Many stories have been told of the patience and courage of wounded men. In the cave in Heraklion were many examples.

'After moving from the cave to the house, we were visited by the owner and his wife, who couldn't have been more delighted that their bedroom and sitting room contained bodies in different forms of life and semi-death. Nor did they mind

when they saw that a box of books which they had no doubt carefully packed before leaving, had been broken open. The sight of a picture of a bottle of Haig on the box had been too much for a Tiger and a Royal Marine! A few days later I visited the battalion area again to collect some kit before being moved to the hospital at Knossos. This was about five miles outside Heraklion to the south. I collected my kit and next day moved off. The hospital was in a large mansion and there was a small lodge in which the officers were housed. It was fortunate that I had collected my camp kit because if I had not I should have lain on the floor.

'The day after the Boche visited us and wished to occupy the hospital. It was only with great tact and force of personality that the MO persuaded them to respect the Red Cross and not to place a platoon of infantry in the grounds. During this argument we heard the ominous click of an automatic being cocked just outside the room in which six of us were lying. Thereafter, both the Germans and ourselves evacuated their wounded to the same hospital. During my stay in Knossos I saw a number of our people and all were high in their praise of the two MOs, who were equally impressed by the behaviour of the soldiers under duress. Knossos was a queer experience; we all knew we were safe from the war for the time being, but it was obvious that the situation could not remain static for much longer. Food was running out for one thing, and medical supplies were being used only for the most serious cases. Every now and again an odd straggler, German or British, would turn up and be given shelter.'

One of those on the hospital staff was Basil Keeble, RAMC, who recalled of that period:

'We made ready for casualties as we were fully committed during the action to administer medical and surgical help not only for our own forces but for the Germans and Greeks of

which there were many. This continued for a further 11 days; at times we were completely cut off by the enemy forces, unable to evacuate the more serious casualties for further treatment or to restock medical and surgical preparations, nor able to collect food, etc. However, as the forward position fluctuated with constant changes, our forces were able to reunite the front, but what was most agonising for us, we were subjected to mortar and machine gun fire. These attacks caused some casualties to our very small, overworked unit. This was due to us not displaying the Red Cross flag and marking the area. We had been instructed not to display, as the 7th Tented General Field Hospital, west of Canea, was bombed by the Germans who dropped a stick of bombs across the tented area causing many casualties and the death of the senior surgical specialist, Maj Wardrop; also the hospital ship was attacked in Suda Bay. This did happen on a few occasions, but our problem was subsequently settled by meeting a high-ranking German officer who stated, "Fly the flag," and we had no further problems. We also gained medical supplies to assist in treating the German casualties.'

Germans reinforce Heraklion, 28 May

The news, mentioned by Syd Croft in an earlier chapter, that British aircraft had visited Heraklion on 23 May, coupled with the arrival of reinforcements by sea decided the German High Command that it was necessary to reinforce their troops in the Heraklion area. Accordingly, four companies of paratroops were taken from Maleme and dropped in the vicinity of the Heraklion pocket on 28 May. The fighting there was every bit as fierce as in other areas, as graphically recounted in the memoirs of the late Maj J. W. Stewart-Peter, then a platoon commander in 2BW:

'At dawn a runner came up bearing a note from the post at the western extremity of the aerodrome. "During the night," it said,

"the Germans occupied Sangar Post. It has now been cleared. Sgt Sutcliffe is dead." I failed to elicit any further information out of the runner about how this disaster had occurred and then made the odd quarter of a mile to Coy HQ to report in safety. The return journey, however, had me considerably tied to the ground by fire from stray machine guns, planes doing their morning terror blitz and odd sniping; the latter mostly at long range from the barracks. It was not until after 11 o'clock that I got down to the position near Sangar Post. It was about 100 yards between the two posts and in the middle lay Sgt Sutcliffe: he must have been killed instantly. Cpl Brown told me that he had taken himself and the two men out of Sangar Post and put them on as "prowlers" during the night. While they were out of the post the Huns occupied it; it seemed a very peculiar performance to me and I shall never know how Sutcliffe died. The post was now clear of Germans, I was assured. "Have you been to see?" was my first question, the answer being, "No." I got my corporal to cover me, while with a rifle and bayonet slung, and my untried but no doubt trusty Smith and Wesson (revolver) in my left hand, I advanced fairly cautiously to the Sangar Post. Within 10 yards of it, a crouching figure with a crash helmet on and two men squatting behind it, looked up from a depression in the ground surrounded by a low wall – and pointing a Luger at me said: "Hands-up!"

'Somewhat uncourageously I shot in his face without aiming my pistol, which shocked him so profoundly that he missed me. As I fell "dead" – screwing myself round with my head for home, Cpl Brown bless him, had loosed off a burst which kept their heads down. The rifle and bayonet slipped from my "dead" hand as I fell, but the other limply covered my pistol. I had no grenades. "Here's a to-do," I thought sweating profusely. No heroic thoughts went through my mind, but only to extract my body alive and not to be killed ignominiously on my first full day in action. There were obviously more Germans in the Sangar Post proper, probably eight all told. How many could see me? About a quarter of an hour passed

during which life seemed ever more sweet, even with a war on. Then deciding to move, I started to crawl, absolutely flat, an inch at a time, my pistol still with me. I got about 15 yards and thought I was going to get away with it, when "rrripp!" burst went just over my head. It was answered by a burst from my own gunner. I died a second death – more perfect and practised than before: I hope a death not altogether unseen: I should hate to think it had been wasted. I drummed my feet on the ground, ever more faintly, until with a few horrible gurgles they ceased, and with one final convulsion I ended up with an eye under my arm, viewing the scene from my new position. I was still not under observation from the main post, and I hoped the three known Nazis could not see me without standing up. More sweat and thinking and then, trusting that as soon as he saw me, Cpl Brown would blatter off and keep their heads down, I jumped to my feet, and, lurching from side to side, more I'm sure like a drunken elephant than a perfectly sober sniper, ran for the old Turkish trench.

'A few shots came after me, but missed, and I leapt into the 12ft deep trench as if the drop was nothing. Having only three men and being afraid the Germans would escape into the rocks and take a lot of rounding up, I went round the flank and realising that Sangar Post was a menace without the support of the two positions I had not had time to complete, got the Bofors to depress their gun and demolish the Germans. Not a brave action but a practical one. When I examined the remains of the post I found a boot with four of our grenades in it and a German one tied down on top – all ready to sling into our position that night. So the little dears had found something to occupy themselves during the long hours of waiting.

'It is a sobering thought to think that out of the foregoing situation could be built a story, my story and with its aid – if God spares me – I can, and presumably will – become an IB (an interminable bore). As I go on, and reach my eightieth year it will ever gain in length if not in interest – and it will

become – "for God's sake leave him, before he reaches HIS STORY!" The really sobering part of this thought is that there will be approximately five million storytellers, each with "His Story" – the aftermath, the awful aftermath of war.' [7]

Evacuation

In spite of the fact that the eastern-based garrisons were doing quite well and holding their own, as we have seen, the western enclaves in the area Maleme-Canea-Suda Bay were in a much more perilous position. This continued to deteriorate over the 25th and 26th. At 0824hrs on Tuesday, 27 May, Gen Wavell informed the Prime Minister that Crete was no longer tenable and the Chiefs of Staff ordered evacuation. A provisional plan had been worked out already, involving the use of Sphakia, a small fishing village on the south coast, accessible only by a rough mountain road across extremely difficult terrain. Those in the east would have to look elsewhere. Just seven days after the first paratrooper had landed, the final act of the drama was about to commence.

Notes

1. From *Middle East 1940-1942, A Study in Air Power*.
2. 'Crete and Greece 1941, a Testimonial' from the *Parnassos Bulletin*, May 1991.
3. As quoted in 'Crete – A Tribute from New Zealand' from *Mark of the Lion* by Kenneth Sandford.
4. As quoted in *Crete – The official History of New Zealand in the Second World War 1939-45* by D. M. Davin.
5. As quoted in *Hitler's Mountain Troops* by James Lucas.
6. As quoted in *The Red Hackle* December 1996 edition and published here by kind permission of RHQ The Black Watch.
7. Memoirs of J. G. Stewart-Peter: *Experiences of a Platoon Commander in Crete, 2 BW*; BW Arch 0716, summer 1941.

10

Withdrawal

As has already been mentioned, on the nights of 24/25 and 26/27 May, a very important element towards the success of the coming withdrawal arrived in Crete, namely 'Layforce', which was in essence one half of a commando brigade, that is to say two battalions (A and D), plus the brigade headquarters. It was called Layforce after its commander, Brig Bob (later Maj-Gen Sir Robert) Laycock.[1] Serving in brigade headquarters was Maj (later Maj-Gen) Freddie Graham, then the brigade major, who would later command the 2nd, then 1st Battalion A&SH and go on to become colonel of the regiment for 13 years. In a reminiscence, now held by the IWM and entitled Cretan Crazy Week, he tells of those days on Crete thus:

> 'The news filtering through to Egypt regarding the progress of operations in Crete was sporadic and vaguely optimistic in tone and it was not until late May, when orders were received for two battalions and HQ of the Commando Brigade to embark on three destroyers and proceed with all possible speed to Crete, that it was realised things on the island were not going well. The orders with which we were issued were sketchy – to land at a point on the south coast, where MT and mules would be waiting for us, to march across the mountains to join and assist the forces battling to hold Maleme airfield, which we gathered was very seriously threatened. Half of A Battalion was to go ahead of the main body as an advance party.

'We duly embarked in the destroyers: the only delay caused by a naval rating who fell overboard just as one of the ships was casting off. When this unfortunate lad had been fished out of the harbour, the little convoy sailed for Crete under full steam. The Mediterranean was in one of its worst moods and the passage was extremely uncomfortable. Everyone was very sick and the Senior Naval Officer flatly refused to try to land troops through such a sea. Back to Alex! On our arrival we found new orders waiting for us. We were to transfer at once from our destroyers into a mine-laying cruiser, which would sail as soon as possible and take us into Suda Bay the following night. That meant passing through the Stuka and submarine infested straits at the eastern end of Crete in daylight – not a happy thought! The transfer from destroyers to minelayer, although carried out in darkness, was safely and speedily accomplished, thanks to the guidance and patience of the Royal Navy, and the ship sailed in the early hours of the morning. The passage to Suda was, most unexpectedly, completely uneventful and at approximately midnight on 25 May the ship crept up to the mole at the western end of the bay. All was quiet and only distant gunfire and occasional flashes of light from the direction of Canea marred the peacefulness of the night.

'Just as the Brigade Commander, myself and other officers were bidding farewell to the Captain of the minelayer, the door of the latter's cabin was flung open and a bedraggled and apparently slightly hysterical Naval officer burst in. In a voice trembling with emotion he said, "The Army's in full retreat, everything is chaos. I've just had my best friend killed beside me. Crete is being evacuated." Cheerful to say the least and something of a shock to the little party of Commando officers, armed to the teeth and loaded up like Christmas trees, who stared open-mouthed at this bringer of bad news. "But we are just going ashore," I faltered.

"My God!" he cried, "I didn't know that: perhaps I shouldn't have said anything."

"Too late now old boy," I said. "You can at least tell us what the password is."

'But he had forgotten it. We had no time to stay and check up on his story, which in any event was likely to be unreliable in view of his state of mind. Disembarkation started at once and as soon as we were ashore we were met by a young officer from A Battalion advance party, who had been sent to give us "the form". He brought grim news. Maleme had fallen, the garrison was retreating towards Sphakia on the south coast. The Commando was to cover the retreat. There was no transport, probably no food and probably no ammunition. The Brigade Commander was to report at once to Gen Freyberg. There did not seem to be one bright spot in this tale of woe! The Brigade Commander discussed with me, on a small-scale map, the position we should take up, and we agreed that the hills astride the main road from Canea to Sphakia just above Suda Bay were the most suitable delaying line we could find. This line would be held by A Battalion, while D Battalion would go further inland to form another "firm base" on the Sphakia road. After the decision was made the Brigade Commander said, "Well Freddie, you'd better get off now as it's a good long hike and it looks as if it's all uphill: use your discretion about dispositions and administration when you get there. Goodnight!" And with that he disappeared into the night!'

Tom Caselli of Huddersfield was one of the commandos in Layforce (D Battalion) who landed that night and he remembers:

'. . . in view of the situation, we loaded ourselves up with tins of corned beef, biscuits, ammunition and magazines, as much as we could comfortably carry. Regrettably the wireless sets went overboard with various other items. The ships were desperate to unload quickly, as they were under orders to embark 1,000 men and to get away from the island well before daylight, because of the overwhelming air supremacy of the Germans who, by now, were airborne at dawn and looking

for targets not only on Crete but anything up to 100-150 miles from the island. We had to transfer to a lighter to get to the quay which, to say the least, was chaotic. However, we assembled by companies on the quay, by forcing other military personnel milling about out of the way. Brig Laycock went off to find Gen Weston, RM, who had been put in charge of the forward area who confirmed that the evacuation had been ordered and that "Layforce" was to form a fighting rearguard … In the darkness we formed up in column of threes, company order, and set off out of the dockyard and Suda. When we got onto the actual road it was clogged up by disorganised soldiery – only two words to describe them – a rabble! Consequently our progress was impeded and it was not until about 0500hrs that we got to our destination. Three companies were deployed to cover the road, with the other two, one on either flank, and we had to hurriedly scratch out some positions on the ridge and wait. It was to our advantage to be able to look down the slope.

'It wasn't long before a Fieseler Storch spotter plane turned up and had a good look round. Ground troops appeared later on but we kept them at a distance. Flares went up and very shortly, the first of the Ju87 Stuka dive-bombers attacked – very noisy due to the screamers fitted to them. Our cover and positions must have been good as we had no casualties from either the air or infantry attacks which went on all day … During the afternoon, Col Young and Maj Borthwick reported to Brig Laycock for further orders and were told to reconnoitre a new position for the battalion and when such a position was found, we would pull back and occupy it.'

'The Commando force lay with the sun on their backs,' recalls Freddie Graham, 'straining their eyes to catch the first signs of enemy movement on the road to the south or the mountains to the west. Thanks to strict orders and discipline, good use was made of any available cover and with a minimum of movement enemy aircraft failed to spot the rearguard. I know, from that day, exactly how a partridge feels on September the First!'

Thanks to Layforce, for many of the garrison the
withdrawal was going to be more a test of physical endurance
than a running fight, although that did not make it any easier,
as Rex Hey recalled:

*'Although we didn't know it then, we were going to walk
somewhere between 60 and 70 miles across the island to the
south coast. It was perhaps as well we were completely ignorant
of the length of the journey and the tough, uncompromising
terrain. It was a most traumatic march through mountain
ranges, along primitive roads which consisted of dozens of sharp
hairpin bends. In the later stages we would, perhaps, wearily
traverse seven or eight of these bends and looking down would
realise the actual distance covered was minimal. The beautiful
mountains we had always admired became pure torture. We
had started off from the workshops pretty fit, but it wasn't long
before we began to flag.*

*We were constantly attacked by aircraft, strafed by day and
bombed by night (with the aid of flares). Before we actually
reached the mountains the machine gunning was almost
continuous. We would scatter frantically off the road into the
olive groves in an attempt to get some protection, but the olive
groves were strafed from every direction – north to south, east
to west and then diagonally. The planes were little higher than
the olive trees. There would be desperate efforts to find some
form of protection. Obviously now under this incessant attack
there were bodies in the ditches and amongst the olive trees. I
still remember coming across one Australian with his back
blown away, still clutching the tree which he had obviously hoped
would give him some protection. This was towards the end of
May so the weather was hot and the sickening smell of death was
everywhere mingling with the sweet smell of thyme – I can
smell it as I write. The little food and water we had started off
with had long since gone and there didn't appear to be any hope
of supplies. Our wanderings became almost timeless and without*

meaning. Days passed into days – we must have been on the march six or seven days – many were now becoming exhausted from lack of food, the most arduous trek through the mountains, and of course, lack of sleep. On odd occasions there would be a wonderful lull in the air attacks and we would come across a grassy slope where we flopped in sheer exhaustion. Kit of all kinds had been ditched – steel helmets, gasmasks, packs, rifles, anything of any weight was discarded, even cameras and treasured personal possessions were abandoned.'

Freddie Graham, brigade major of Layforce, writes:

'About midday, the Brigadier returned triumphant with a truck, complete with Royal Marine driver, which he had stolen. To such expedients, in dire emergency, are even the most upright officers reduced! He brought the news that the essential task was to evacuate the island, that our task was to cover the withdrawal as long as we could – we had only some 700 men all told – that we were being given three tanks – the only tanks left on the island – and that in the view of the Commander-in-Chief, we were safe from outflanking to the west because "the Boche had stuck to the roads to date and would probably continue to do so". We were commenting on this last remarkable piece of reasoning when we spotted, away on the tops of the mountains to the west, an enemy force complete with mules and what looked like mountain guns. It was beginning to get dark and, leaving a senior officer in charge of Bde HQ, the Brigadier and I set off to contact the tanks, issue final orders to A Battalion, see that the road in front of them was "blown" after the last stragglers had passed through and then to move Bde HQ back to join D Battalion who were on their way to make a firm base further inland. The stolen truck was invaluable; we found the tanks, gave the officer in charge a rendezvous and a small escort from A Battalion and then drove back to the rearguard to see the road

blown and say goodbye to that gallant company which, we heard later, held on until the next morning, when they were completely overrun. After that we lay down to snatch an hour's sleep, for we had had none for 36 hours. A few hours before dawn – I find it impossible to give any exact timings as events were so confused – we went to pick up Bde HQ and move back to join D Battalion. Bde HQ had completely disappeared and, cursing all and sundry, we set off alone down the road to try to find them. We arrived safely, the Brigadier, myself, Royal Marine driver and my batman, at the tank RV and were just heaving a sigh of relief that we had at last some local protection, when a storm of small-arms fire was opened up on us from a small scrub covered hill about 50 yards away. Luckily we were in a dip, which although it prevented the tanks from manoeuvring, it obscured the enemy paratroopers' fire and no one was hit, though the bullets were humming through the trees like large bumble bees. The Brigadier mounted a tank and got a lift out of the line of fire. My batman and I were not so lucky and had to run for it – our precious truck, loaded with food, was abandoned. The tanks, with their escort of A Battalion, organised a counter-attack and the Boches, temporarily, retreated, enabling us to run up the road and recover the truck. Of my batman and the Royal Marine there was no sign. The former, I later discovered, ran the wrong way, slap into the arms of the Boches. He later escaped into the hills and lived as a Cretan for nearly a year before escaping to Egypt in a caique. Just after this alarming ambush we came upon Bde HQ sitting peacefully beside the road. There was a good deal of good round swearing by the Brigadier when he discovered that the senior officer whom we had left in charge had moved because he "thought they might be outflanked". He was left in no doubt as to the Brigadier's opinion of him! Shortly after this we joined up with D Battalion who had found themselves an excellent position which had only one serious weakness – there were no supporting troops on either flank!'

Tom Caselli had marched back to D Battalion's new position which he says was located just north of Babali Khani, arriving there in the early hours of 28 May:

> 'Col Young had decided to deploy our four companies in line, two each side of the road. My company (E) was the left flank company. We all deployed roughly in our company areas and as dawn broke, occupied the positions in detail, arranging inter-company junction points, tidying up arcs of fire and getting ourselves fixed up with individual sangars – plenty of stone about and using the steel helmet rim (the back portion only) to scratch out a hollow. If we had used the front of the rim the sun could catch that part where we had scratched off the paint and give our position away, While this was going on, there was a continual procession of unattended, retreating men, straggling through our lines and along the road south, very few carrying any weapons … Our battalion had been joined by the remnants of the 2nd/7th Australian Infantry battalion, who were giving us invaluable back-up. Gen Weston had given us three of the Matilda Infantry tanks (7RTR) as a reserve. There was a ravine on the left of our company running roughly east-west, capable of giving the enemy a covered approach and during the morning we had mounted several patrols there, so as not to be surprised, but Jerry was not encountered.'

Tom then goes on to explain what had happened to A Battalion and B Company of D Battalion, who were still further up the road to the north. A Battalion had spent most of 27 May covering the withdrawal of the remnants of Creforce, which included 1st Welch, the only troops to escape from the Akrotiri peninsula. Their orders were to withdraw during the night, once everyone else had passed through. Achieving a clean break proved difficult because the Germans were hard on their heels; however, they had been strengthened by two companies of Maoris who had asked if they could stay with them and fight! Later the enemy did attack their positions and eventually the remnants of B Company, together with their Maori comrades, made their way back to the main battalion position, where they were also joined by the remnants of A Battalion. His narrative continues:

'Babali Khani stands at the head of a small reasonably flat valley extending east towards Georgeopolis and Rethymnon. About four miles south of the village the road forks and runs due south to Sphakia. It enters a pass through the White Mountains, narrowing as it goes along. The "road" being just a stony vehicle width track in the valley bottom and as it climbs up it is scooped out of one side of the pass. About half-way up and nearly 3,000 feet up is Askifou Plain – a small green oasis among the rocks. From Babali Khani to Askifou would be 10-11 miles of successive hairpin bends and precipices rising all the time, continuing all the way to the end of the pass. Coming out of the pass above Sphakia the road disappears down hairpin bends into Sphakia with its tiny beach, falling 2,000ft in two miles.

'So there we were in our little stone sangars, watching for Jerry to appear and with our forward scouts posted to spot men or vehicles making an appearance. About midday the first German patrols appeared on motorcycle combinations. They were allowed to get well within range before we opened up with concentrated machine gun and rifle fire and some grenades, which sent them hurtling off the road into a quarry. The follow-up troops got the same treatment. Sure enough, up went the blue flares and the mortars began to range in. Star-shells followed and the Stukas turned up and plastered our positions in their own noisy fashion. Curiously enough they caused few casualties and many bombs went wide of the mark. They did manage to set some of the scrub on fire, but their ground troops didn't take advantage of it, but it was hectic

whilst it lasted. Then they tried a change of tactics – turning our flanks, but were beaten off. A Fieseler Storch appeared again, disappeared and the same tactic was repeated. However, the field grey uniforms were soon spotted as they came on and they were easily picked off. They must have had heavy casualties. About 1530hrs, things quietened down, but we remained on stand-to and kept our eyes open.

'Our HQ position and right flank were bothered by a sniper who was located on the roof of the village church near the crossroads. One of the Matildas did a super job and gave him a hard time. When a patrol went up there they found him riddled and very dead. The other two tanks also did a good job bolstering our fire during frontal attacks.

'Brig Laycock must have had a guardian angel because he was here, there and everywhere, wearing his brigadier's cap with its red band and gold peak, which must have been very obvious to the snipers as we were all in steel helmets … It wasn't long before the Stukas turned up again and we got plastered, with the infantry following up, but about 1500hrs we noticed a difference in their tactics – the pressure was increased on our left flank, so much so that the 2/8th Australians were moved up to our left on the edge of the ravine. Brig Laycock, plus cap, also arrived to assess the situation.'

We can turn again to Freddie Graham for the 'bigger picture', which involved deciding when to blow the main road. He recalls:

'By this time the bulk of the retreating garrison was south of D Battalion, but there were still many wounded, all of D Battalion itself and Brigade HQ eventually to be withdrawn over the mountains to the assembly area near Sphakia, so there was, as yet, no question of "blowing" the road. Imagine my horror, when, on being sent back to report to Gen Weston, our immediate superior commander, I found a huge crater which was being admired by the sapper party who had done the

deed. In a fury I cross-examined the officer in charge, but all he could say was that a "senior officer", who said he was commander of the rearguard, had ordered him to blow. To this day no one knows who that "senior officer" was. There was no time for recrimination – desperately we organised working parties to at least partially repair the damage. No vehicle tracked or wheeled, would ever get through, but we might make it passable for marching troops. After some hours of backbreaking toil, we succeeded in getting the wounded across to the other side, where some ramshackle Cretan lorries were waiting to evacuate them.

D Battalion meanwhile had been fighting a desperate rearguard action, but they had been outflanked and had to pull out. Two tanks had run out of petrol and been destroyed and the third was slewed across the narrow road on the enemy side of the crater and, after removing oil and water, we abandoned her with her engine running. Our precious truck was driven over the mountain edge after her store of tinned food had been distributed to D Battalion as they trickled past across the partially repaired crater. Then began the weary march across the mountains to the Sphakia assembly area; by this time we had been relieved of our rearguard duties and a New Zealand brigade had taken over. The commando assembly area was a deep gully to the east of and some nine and a half miles distant from Sphakia beach. We arrived after an exhausting march, the chief features of which were heat, thirst, hunger and Stukas. As soon as we had had some rest it became urgent that we find Gen Freyberg and get some orders – there was only one way to do this – one of us had to go and find him. The brigadier set off first, with the intelligence officer, but returned some hours later, exhausted and unsuccessful. I took up the hunt. Twelve miles I walked on that warm summer's day, with only a spoonful of jam as "iron rations" to sustain me. At last a kindly cavalry officer, sitting in a derelict armoured car, admiring a wound in his leg, half *a bottle of gin in his hand, gave me the necessary clue – and a swig of gin – and I found GHQ. Although swaying on my feet with weariness I was able to gather the gist of Gen Freyberg's orders, which were that the Commandos, now only some 300-400 strong, would take up position round the beach and cover the evacuation of the other troops. As to how the Commandos eventually acted after the evacuation was complete was of little interest to the General! I saluted and was limping thoughtfully away when a friendly voice hailed me and an almost full tin of M and V was thrust into my eager hands. This manna from Heaven revived me and I was able to complete my return journey to our cave without mishap. On receiving my news the Brigadier set about implementing Gen Freyberg's orders and, after a square meal of rice, potatoes and sucking pig, which had been scrounged by Spanish troops serving with A Battalion, I was sent to Sphakia to arrange for as much ammunition and food as I could lay my hands on. I spent a fruitless day and got nothing; moreover enemy aircraft made life anywhere near the beaches very unpleasant. It was now late afternoon on 31 May and there was a rumour abroad that the evacuation was to be completed that night. Gen Freyberg had been flown out the previous night* [2] *and Gen Weston was now in command. Before I left Brigade HQ, the brigadier had told me to meet him in the evening at the GHQ cave which was in the next ravine to ours.*

'Accordingly, after my unsuccessful afternoon in Sphakia, I set off to make the three-mile walk, always uphill, to GHQ. Arriving there after dark, I could find no trace of the brigadier so sat down to smoke a cigarette and meditate on the situation.

As I sat there a voice called out of the darkness: "Is Brigadier Laycock there?" "No!" I shouted, "but his brigade major is."

"Well, please come in at once and bring a notebook," was the reply. Wearily I clambered to my feet, wondering what new horror was going to be sprung upon us and went into the cave.

There I found Gen Weston, a staff officer and another officer, who shall remain nameless. Gen Weston asked if I had paper, pencil and carbon paper – quite remarkably I was able to reply in the affirmative, thanks to that old friend the Army Book 153 in my haversack. Gen Weston said, "Sit down on that suitcase and take this letter to my dictation – make three copies."

He then proceeded to dictate the capitulation of Crete.

'The letter was in the form of a short operation instruction, addressed to the officer, whom I have already said shall remain unidentifiable, instructing him, in view of certain considerations, to go forward at first light and capitulate to the enemy. Gen Weston took two of the copies I had made, handed one to the officer concerned, put the other in his pocket and with the words: "Well gentlemen, there are one million drachmae in the suitcase, there's a bottle of gin in the corner. Goodbye and good luck!" – He walked out of the cave and down the hill into the darkness. Later he was flown out by Sunderland flying boat which had been sent to fetch him, under orders from GHQ Cairo. I was left staring at the miserable little piece of paper which, only too forcibly, confirmed my worst fears. There was to be no further evacuation after that night and already the ships were in Sphakia Bay and filling themselves to bursting with weary troops, but there were many thousands more.

'Rousing myself, I went out of the cave and shouted for the brigade sergeant-major, telling him to gather together a crew for a motor landing craft which I had seen on the beach and which I had every intention of laying my hands on with a view to sailing it down the east coast. Just after he had gone off to do this the brigadier, whom I had not seen all day, came panting up the hill. Full of news I started to pour out my story when he cut me short, "Yes, yes, I know all that old boy, but I got counter orders this evening and that's why I am so late back. As we have two battalions in Egypt we are to be evacuated tonight, taking as many troops with us as we can. It's going to be a hell of a rush for some of D Battalion, but I

think they can make it." This was the only piece of good news I had heard since landing in Crete. There was no time for questions; we collected as many Commando troops as we could and set off hot foot for Sphakia. We ran it very fine but at last succeeded in fitting into what was almost the last ship's boat to leave Crete.

'It was only after we had had some sleep and food that I learned how our deliverance came about. While I was at Sphakia beach on the afternoon of 31 May, the brigadier attended a conference at GHQ at which Gen Weston announced his intention of capitulating the following morning – and ordered my brigade commander to carry out that capitulation! The brigadier accepted the order and that was that until a few minutes later a staff officer of Weston's passed the remark to Weston that there were two battalions of the Commando Brigade still in Egypt. "Is that true?" said Gen Weston, turning to my brigadier. "Well, yes Sir," he replied. "Oh, in that case I must reconsider my order: you and your staff and as many of your troops as you can get away must go tonight – my staff will see to it."

'We never even knew who the staff officer was to whom we owed our deliverance.' [3]

Captured

Tom Caselli was not as lucky as Freddie Graham, the order that the commandos were all to withdraw on the last destroyer (HMS *Kimberley*), being clearly delayed in some places:

'I don't know when we withdrew from our positions; our two groups met up and withdrew in good order down to Sphakia. But the nearer we got to the village proper the greater was the problem with stragglers. We just could not force our way through the mass of leaderless and confused men to the beach. We didn't even reach the armed cordon round the evacuation beach. Later on we were told that Laycock and his staff tried

to delay the sailing of the last boat for us, but at 0245hrs the senior naval officer said that he could not jeopardise the safety of his ship and crew any longer and weighed anchor. By then Brig Laycock and his staff were already on board HMS Kimberley. [4]

'When we were told that the last boat had sailed without us, it took a long while for it to sink in as we stood around in the darkness. Nothing we could do about it, but suffer the huge sense of disappointment and, as nothing could be gained by remaining with the rabble, we made our way out of it and back up to the cliff top on the east side where it was a bit more peaceful. We were still a fully armed and disciplined unit, just the same as the Aussies, New Zealanders, Maoris and Marines, and we could have mounted another action if required. Our Layforce had found out the hard way that the Germans were not invincible. We had shown that they could be held and although outgunned, both by mortars and dive-bombers, they did not penetrate our lines at all, so I think we could hold our heads high in any company – very much later we heard that our fighting rearguard had enabled 15,000 men to be evacuated from the island.

'So we found a reasonable place and settled down, got a bit of sleep until dawn to await whatever came. When it was daylight RSM Howland moved among us ensuring our rifles, Tommy guns, etc, were smashed on convenient rocks and our ammunition ditched. We removed our "fannies" [5] and stuffed them between the stones in nearby dry stone walls. I inspected my possessions, apart from webbing equipment – pullover, shaving kit, mess tin with knife, fork and spoon, jack knife and lanyard, pair of socks and underpants, sidecap, one tin of bully beef and a pack of army biscuits. I looked at my mucker – Teddie Abdale (Coldstream Guards), both of us dog tired and dirty, covered in red dust, unshaven, and on looking round we were all in the same boat. We hadn't washed or shaved since leaving Alexandria, nor had we taken anything (including webbing) off whatsoever!*

'White flags were appearing here and there, so we sat down against the rocks and walls in the sunshine and enjoyed our quietest morning since arriving in Crete. By now it was sinking in that we would soon be prisoners of war and facing an uncertain future. That is how things were on the morning of Sunday, 1 June 1941.'

Another prisoner

Rex Hey was another who had made a futile attempt to reach the boats. In the darkness he had first 'smelt the sea' rather than seeing it, and now could hear the gentle lapping of the water:

'I honestly don't know how we ever found out that we had reached Sphakia from which we were supposed to be evacuated. Evidently there was a small jetty from which the evacuation was to take place. Among the milling, disordered crowd of men, if I remember rightly was a regimental sergeant-major, who was organising the selection of those who were to stay and those who were to go. First of all he said that all men with rifles must hand them in for use by the rearguard. Being a dutiful soldier I still had mine (it was a relief to get rid of it!). We handed over the rifles as instructed and were then informed that married men would be the first to go and then lots would be drawn by the others. How this was done I can't remember – if I ever knew – it was almost a lottery for one's life but I can't remember taking part in any lottery – but if I did I didn't have any luck, neither did Eric Lacey. In fact none of our unit had any, married or single ... We were told that we would be moving into a valley nearby in which there were many deep caves and here we would be safe from any air attack. I think at this point we were all so tired that we didn't even think or care what was going to happen next. There was the strange "out of this world" feeling I had experienced at Dunkirk – a feeling of complete unreality. We started to move away and had the pleasure of seeing the "rearguard" forming

up to get on the boats complete with our rifles – not that it now would make much difference. We eventually reached the valley and there certainly were many deep caves. We settled down in the caves as best we could and probably for the first time in a week fell into an exhausted sleep, without any fear of being awakened by the Luftwaffe.

'We were rudely awakened in the early morning by angry and excited shouting from the valley and immediately ran out of the cave to see what it was all about. There was an Australian captain in the valley giving some sort of instruction which at first we couldn't understand and then to our complete astonishment we found he was announcing that we had surrendered and that we should spread anything white we happened to have on the floor of the valley and if any of us still had rifles they should be stacked outside the caves. At first there was a stunned silence at these commands – utter disbelief and then the silence was broken by shouts of frustration and anger. There was no respect for rank and four-letter words of abuse were hurled at the officer. He accepted the insults and I am sure appreciated the reaction to what seemed his impossible orders. Men clamoured around him demanding some clarification of his orders and many telling him in the crudest terms what he could do. It really should have been more obvious to us that this was the only possible end to our stay on Crete. There was nothing we could have done about it, but strangely enough nobody had expected the unbelievable order to surrender. Fate has many twists and turns. We had been distraught that we had not been on the list for evacuation, but we discovered later that many ships had been sunk in the evacuation with terrible loss of life, so many of those lucky (?) enough to get away did not survive. We started to hear machine gun fire from the hills around us and eventually troops appeared. As instructed, everything white had been spread out on the floor of the valley and we waited with some apprehension for the arrival of the enemy advanced troops.

Most of the men were now wandering despairingly in the valley, unable to accept the magnitude of the disaster. Suddenly planes appeared over the mountains and started strafing the men. At the same time mortar bombs began to explode amongst us. Apparently (we were told) frantic messages were sent by the Germans to their headquarters and the attack ceased, but not before quite a number of men had been killed or wounded ... The troops we had heard in the mountains now started to appear in the valley (we never heard or saw any signs of the rearguard who had taken our rifles by the way). They turned out to be Austrian alpine troops and were not at all as we expected German troops would be. They were met immediately by considerable abuse over the air raid and mortar attacks. I never saw anybody who was intimidated by their presence – rather the reverse. Despite the obvious language barrier they certainly understood our fury at the actions of their troops. They seemed genuinely to be as angry as we were and immediately made radio contact with their headquarters to ensure there would be no further such actions. We were told for what it is worth that the Luftwaffe had not been informed of the surrender and had thought we were regrouping in the valley, but this didn't quite explain the mortar attack.

'The Alpine troops, to our complete surprise, were almost friendly. They made no effort to take control, but asked our officers to remain in command while arrangements were made for our eventual accommodation. It all sounded very civilised. Under the circumstances we were reasonably impressed by their treatment – but how wrong this assessment turned out to be when the occupational troops took over.'

A German view

'What a sight is presented by our Mountain Infantry. Sun-tanned and parched, their uniforms in rags, caps flattened and caked with sweat and mud. Our mountaineering boots are patched up with insulating tape and leather straps, soles worn through, nails torn out from jumping and falling. Arms and legs are grazed. Every group has its wounded and yet we carry on with unheard of elan. We no longer feel the heat and have overcome extreme exhaustion ... Below us is the sea and the port of Sfakia with the white cubes of its serried buildings. The rugged mountains drop steeply to the ground below. Crete's southern coast towers over the blue waters of the Mediterranean.' [6]

It is perhaps also relevant to quote from Gen Julius Ringel's account of this last day where he says:

> *'On 1 June, everything was set. After an air attack with Stukas and twin-engined fighters and the well-aimed fire of the only infantry gun, the enveloping companies forged ahead towards Sphakia, Wraskas and Komitades. On its own initiative, the first combat group entered Sphakia, while the running air attack was still in progress. Large groups of British, worn down by the air attacks, immediately waved white sheets but others were still determined to fight. Uncertainty prevailed as to the success of the small attack group. But more and more hands were raised and white sheets appeared; then news came that Komitades had been taken, and the British collapsed. The pincer movement attempted in most difficult mountain terrain had been a complete success. Difficulties with food supplies and, perhaps, the fact that the British fleet had left its fighters on Crete in the lurch, might have been a deciding factor in the capitulation of the British. Only a fraction of the British main body was embarked and escaped to Egypt. About 10,000 British soldiers moved as prisoners for two days on laborious marches to the north. Thus, 1 June 1941 brought the battle of Crete to a dramatic conclusion.' [7]*

Slightly earlier, after their successful breaking of the British line, Generalfeldmarschall List had said in a radio message, 'Bravo Ringel! Congratulations and praise to the Gebirgsjägers!', while on 1 June, Generaloberst Loehr, the commander of Luftflotte IV, with whom responsibility for Operation 'Merkur' lay, was able to signal to OKW, 'Mission completed, Crete is clear of the enemy as of today.' There were two other significant radio announcements: first, the British War Office announced on 2 June, 'After 12 days of, doubtless, the hardest fighting of the war so far, it was decided to withdraw our troops from Crete.' On the same day OKW stated, 'The battle for Crete has been concluded. The entire island is clear of the enemy. Yesterday, German troops occupied the last base of the defeated British, the harbour of Sphakia.' [8]

Notes

1. Nos 50, 51 and 52 Commandos had been raised in the Middle East in the late summer of 1940. Nos 50 and 52, which had been drawn from Regular and Yeomanry regiments in Egypt, were amalgamated to form 'Z' Force. However, instead of being called by that name or 'Commandos', they were instead called Layforce after their commander. It should be noted that the battalions comprised five companies, each of two 50-man troops, but they lacked both the infantry heavy weapons and transport of a normal infantry battalion.

2. Gen Freyberg sent the following signal to Gen Wavell before he left Crete on 30 May: 'I leave Crete tonight in accordance with your orders. I have handed over command to Gen Weston. I again urge you to do all that is possible to send ships tomorrow night to evacuate the gallant remnants of the British, Australian and New Zealand troops who have borne the brunt of the fighting in the battle for Crete.'

3. *Cretan Crazy Week*, written by Lt-Col (later Maj-Gen) F. C. C. Graham, at Latimer, 4 April 1948, and held by the Imperial War Museum, who have given their approval to my publishing these extracts, as both Gen Graham and his wife are deceased.

4. Tom Caselli comments that much later, after the war, he was astonished to find that although there were some 23 officers and 186 other ranks of Layforce evacuated, none of them were of his battalion.

5. Fannies were the combination commando dagger and knuckle-duster, which was an obvious 'give-away' of a commando.

6. As quoted in *Crete 1941 Eyewitnessed*.

7. From *The Conquest of Crete* by Gen Julius Ringel.

8. Ibid.

11

Journeys from Crete

Before telling of some of the daring individual escapes made from Crete, we must deal with the evacuations that took place, thanks primarily to the bravery and determination of the Royal Navy. Typical was the withdrawal of the garrison from Heraklion. The late Maj Richard Fleming of the Black Watch was brigade major of 14th Infantry Brigade and had recently returned to Brigade HQ after guiding part of the 1st Battalion A&SH from Ay Deka to Heraklion. He wrote later in his regimental magazine The Red Hackle:

> 'After this excursion, I don't seem to remember much until word came through that we were to organise for evacuation from the island on 28 May. We had to get down to work out a plan of withdrawal. This was very much the work of Brig Chappel, for at that time I had had no training in staff work at all. It was an excellent plan and worked extremely well. The brigadier, who had stationed himself down at the harbour, rang me and said, "The Navy have come in, but want to push forward the whole exercise by one hour. Get cracking and act on that." We were indeed fortunate that a naval force of two cruisers – Orion and Dido – and six destroyers, all under Rear-Adm Rawlings, was to evacuate us from the harbour of Heraklion. The need for the hurry was in order that the fleet could pass the Strait of Kasos and be away from the island of Scarpanto before first light.

'*Alerting the various units was not an easy task, but I did manage to contact by telephone all the many units except my own battalion. The Black Watch, who were positioned on the extreme eastern perimeter, for some reason were out of contact. We had by then started packing up Brigade HQ, burning all so that nothing was left, and sending personnel down to the docks. Eddie and I, therefore, found a 15cwt truck and motored off to pass the instructions by word of mouth. We got the message through and so back to the HQ cave for a final look around and gather our belongings. Down at the docks there was a long, long mole out into the harbour, with the destroyers alongside. Standing at the start of this, we waited until all had reported and gone through, the BW being the last. No more came, so we suddenly realised we had better get a move on ourselves or we would be left behind. Trust me, but I managed to trip on a hawser or something and spread-eagled myself, everything I was carrying going to the four winds. It seemed a very long mole indeed but we did manage to get up to the last destroyer (HMS* Imperial) *to be met by a naval officer who said, "Thank goodness you have come, as the Brigadier asked us to wait for you if possible. So now off we go." I was shown to the wardroom, where I literally passed out.*

'*This cannot have been for long, as I can still remember being shaken awake by a naval officer. He apologised most profusely, saying, "I am most awfully sorry to awaken you, but would you mind coming aloft, as I fear we are going to abandon ship." This in a most courteous, unruffled manner, in fact rather as a mess waiter would say to us, "Will you please come into the dining room as dinner is served." Up we went to find another destroyer alongside us. We scrambled across to her. This was HMS* Hotspur, *who had been ordered to await and collect all aboard the* Imperial. *How lucky we were, as this meant delaying the force to a reduced speed of 15 knots for our overloaded* Hotspur *to catch up – a very brave decision for*

Adm Rawlings to have taken. HMS Hereward *was hit later and was told to turn in and beach on Crete. I kept awake for a short period as we swept away and fired torpedoes into the poor* Imperial *and so saw her sinking rapidly. Beside me was a naval officer in tears. He was the chief engineer of his beloved vessel, which evidently had just come from a refit in Malta and was in prime condition. On her way into Heraklion, I believe she had a near miss from a torpedo. This did not affect her until an hour and a half after leaving port when her steering gear jammed ... I regret to state that once again I passed out and only awoke to realise that we were sailing into Alexandria harbour with one of the regiment's pipers playing a lament on the bridge. The squadron had had a terrible pounding, as due to our delay, it was an hour late getting past the Strait of Kasos and the island of Scarpanto with its enemy airfield. The bombing which had started with five Stukas went on in waves for five hours. The cruisers* Orion *and* Dido *were hit several times, with one bomb breaking right through to explode in a canteen packed with troops. In fact the brigade lost one fifth of its strength, the majority at sea and not in fighting the paratroopers.'*

Another member of the Heraklion garrison who managed to escape that night was Bdr Syd Croft of D Troop, 234th Medium Battery, RA. They had received the news to evacuate at about 2000hrs on the 28th. They had felt reasonably secure in their 'little patch' but were running short of ammunition fast. They weren't given much time to think about leaving and he remembers being a little surprised when they were told to put the guns out of action (as quietly as possible) and then, when everyone was ready, march silently down the rough track to the harbour:

'As we neared the German prisoners' cage we were warned to be especially quiet. We didn't want the prisoners to get an

inkling of what was happening. They could have quite easily attempted to escape or cause some kind of disturbance and that might have spoilt our plans. But all went well and we reached the harbour safely where we were directed to the mole, and before long we could just make out the dark shapes of destroyers slipping through the harbour opening. Two or three ships tied up alongside the mole and nets were immediately thrown down the sides and we were ordered to clamber up as quickly as possible. We were only allowed to keep light kit and, if you had one, your rifle.

I naturally clung to my gasmask case with its precious contents (to me) of camera and photographs. We crowded onto the decks, taking up every inch of space and we were told to stand as tightly as possible as we were being taken to another ship. When the destroyer was fully loaded, it moved out to sea just outside the harbour to where I now know two cruisers were waiting – HMS Orion and Dido. By now, I was completely cut off from my own troop comrades and huddled closely to other soldiers anxiously waiting for the next step. We soon discovered what that was to be. The destroyers eased up to one of the cruisers and more nets were thrown over the sides. We now clambered up these nets to the giddy heights of the cruiser's deck where sailors were ready to haul us unceremoniously aboard. We were quickly directed to a mess deck where that magic and lovely big hot mug of cocoa which the Navy seemed to produce at just the right moments awaited us. We then settled down on the benches and awaited events. Time appeared to go very slowly and we seemed to be very isolated from what was happening all around us. We discovered that we were on the cruiser HMS Orion and later, much later after the war had finished, we learnt that the cruisers were too big to enter the harbour and the six destroyers had to go to and fro, ferrying the troops to the larger cruisers. This was what was taking up the time, but the whole garrison was embarked by 0300hrs when the force set sail for Alexandria.

'*All did not go well that night, and the destroyer Imperial had steering troubles and had to be sunk. When dawn appeared, so did the German bombers and they continued to bomb the force until well past midday. The destroyer* Hereward *was hit quite early on, fell out of line and had to be left, sinking ... HMS* Orion *suffered several near misses or grazes and two or three direct hits. We who sat in the mess deck knew little or nothing of how things were going up above ... I can only recall going down one set of steps to one of the mess decks after we embarked ... so that placed us immediately below the main deck and I did know we were at the front of the ship. ... As dawn approached it also confirmed that we were well up above sea level as we had portholes on our mess deck. In the cold light of today, 60 years later, that appears patently obvious. But in the confused state we were in at the time, tired, partially "bomb happy", being soldiers not sailors and knowing that daylight would bring bombers, we were not a little disorientated to say the least. We did not have to wait long before the bombers attacked and we heard large explosions all around us. Above we could hear the ship's armaments and AA guns firing almost continuously. At one point the ship shuddered and we now know that this was what the Navy called a grazed hit, which had exploded very close to the side of the ship and done damage. This and the near misses were playing havoc with the ship – serious leaks, water getting into the fuel tanks, damage to the electrics, telegraph system and so on. Obviously we didn't know anything about this at the time, but we had the feeling that the ship was slowing up and that there was more than just an air of emergency in the way the crew was operating. These attacks went on almost continuously and blackouts were happening intermittently.*

'*It was during one of these air raids, around 0900hrs that there was a sudden crash above us, a huge flash and explosion and the ship appeared to jump six feet into the air. I repeat, it seemed to jump. One cannot explain what actually happened but it seemed as though we were taken up in the air and dropped again. The whole mess deck, except one end was now completely pitch black because all the lights had gone out. On that side of our deck where the bulkhead door was, a fire had started and was beginning to take hold. Although two or three of the portholes had been opened earlier allowing in a little light, as our eyes grew accustomed to the dimness, there didn't appear to be any immediate damage to the part of the ship where we were except for the fire. Most of the soldiers appeared to be alright although we were frightened out of our skins. There seemed to be complete silence. As individuals we knew we had been hit – but where? How seriously? Were we about to sink? And then suddenly piercing screams broke the silence. They came from the area where we had entered the mess deck which was now ablaze. In that part, there appeared to be a shaft of some kind, a hoist or mechanical lift where shells, charges, etc were lifted from the magazine in the bowels of the cruiser up to the gun turrets somewhere above us on the forward deck. To our horror, we found a sailor trapped in the mechanism of the hoist and he was horribly injured and being consumed by the flames. Try as we might we could find no way of releasing him. After the immediate shock of the accident the sailor was now in terrible pain from his injuries and wounds and yet still conscious. We had no first aid equipment at all to help him or ease the pain and no one on the mess deck could find any crew member or medic around to help. Little did we know at that time that many of them had also been wounded or killed during the continuous air attacks we had endured that morning. Sadly, we took it in turns to try to comfort the sailor as he slowly sank into unconsciousness and his precious life ebbed away.*

'*Meanwhile, water had begun to enter the mess deck and didn't appear to be draining away. It began to rise higher and higher until it reached the table-tops. In our innocence and shock we imagined the ship to be sinking. We seemed to be paralysed with both fear and ignorance. The exit to the deck was jammed and there was no way of escape. One poor devil, convinced that we were definitely sinking, managed to open a porthole and escape through it into the open sea. I cannot imagine he lasted long out there. I'm sure all eyes were on the skies and all hands manning the anti-aircraft guns and no one on any of the ships would have seen him. And if he had been seen, who was going to risk turning round to save him when already many thousands of lives were at risk? At that point we didn't actually seem to appreciate that, in fact, we probably weren't sinking even though we could still see through the portholes and we could still see the sea and the horizon and we still appeared to be quite high above the actual sea. But there you are, unless you have been in such conditions and circumstances, it is quite impossible for you to imagine how you would have reacted. We all like to think that we would behave coolly and calmly, assessing the situation and taking the necessary action. But you have to remember that we had already suffered defeat in Greece, taken a very big hiding from the German Luftwaffe, struggled to be evacuated where, unlike Dunkirk, there wasn't the tremendous support and back-up awaiting the survivors when they eventually reached a "safe haven". And then to find that in a few days' time, that so called "safe haven", Crete, that we had reached only a few days ago was going be an even worse living hell than before, a place where for most of the time, you didn't for one minute think you would ever survive or escape. And now that we were escaping from there, the Germans wouldn't even let us go in peace!*

'At the time, as I have already said, we imagined that the water was the result of the sea flooding in because we were sinking. I don't think any of the soldiers on that particular mess deck realised as we sloshed around holding onto the fixed tables for support, that we were standing over the forward ammunition magazine of the cruiser, and because of the fire in the shell hoist, someone had decided to flood the magazine.

*In doing so, our mess deck prison, as it was at that particular
time, was also being flooded. Naturally, the men were more
than anxious now and were banging hard on the bulkhead door
and shouting to attract attention. In the end, we were heard,
and for some reason or other, the door had locked or become
jammed and luckily could easily be opened from the outside.*

*We rushed out and up the ladders to the forward deck,
which was, of course, open to the sky. We were just not
prepared for the sight that greeted us. Where obviously there
had been two large gun turrets one above the other, immensely
strongly made and heavily armoured, lay a mass of twisted
metal, wood and asbestos, and the charred bodies of sailors and
marines who had manned the large and powerful guns, were
scattered all over the place ... A large Alsatian dog was
walking over and through the wreckage sniffing at the bodies
as he passed over them. It was a horrible sight and one that
haunts me to this day. And to think we were almost
underneath those gun turrets. If they hadn't been there, or if
the bomb had fallen just a few feet to one side, it would have
crashed through the deck onto the mess deck where we had been
sheltering. In the resultant explosion we would have been
annihilated, completely evaporated into the surrounding air
and my dear parents would have never known what had
happened to me, because no records were or could have been
taken when we embarked at Heraklion in those wonderful
rescue ships of the Royal Navy. Like so many other dear brave
sailors and soldiers in other parts of that and other ships, we
would have died and disappeared and nobody would have
known exactly how, where and when.*

*'The attacks went on throughout the morning and round
about 11 o'clock a formation of Ju87s made another
determined attack, especially against us, one of the bigger
ships. This time they were lucky and we were very unlucky.
A bomb hit* Orion *somewhere amidships and did terrible
damage through several decks. I later discovered from a*

comrade that several of our own 234 Battery were sheltering in that area and had been killed.

I read that the actual casualty figures on the Orion *on that fateful day were 304 sailors and soldiers killed and over 300 wounded, perhaps more because of the way explosions in a confined area can often make bodies disintegrate or evaporate or disappear completely.*

'After that last bombing, attacks became less frequent and by midday, had stopped altogether. We limped (or whatever ships do) back to Alexandria feeling absolutely exhausted, a little bomb happy, hungry and thirsty for we had had nothing to eat or drink for over 30 hours. We tied up and disembarked around midnight at the end of a very eventful day – a day I hoped I would never have to live through again. On the quayside, we were quickly herded as far as possible into our units. Then members and lorries from a local HAA Regiment took us to their Londonderry Camp in Alexandria and treated us to a lovely (yes, you've guessed it) M and V stew with fresh bread (a real treat) and a glorious brew of good old army tea. But on that particular night, it really was delicious! During that night there was an air raid on the harbour of Alexandria and our hosts were in action.

Us? We slept through it all!'

Andrew Brown of the Argylls was another of the rescued. He was taken on board the destroyer HMS *Kimberley* – the only vessel to escape from a direct hit in over six hours of intense bombing. He recalled that he saw little of the action because,

'I was sitting on a mess deck but at regular intervals we were suddenly shot across the floor! We learned afterwards that the captain lay on his back, spotting the aircraft and as the bombs were released he would order, "Right hand down" or "left hand down". We literally zigzagged from Crete to Alexandria.

The cruiser Orion *carrying 1,000 troops had a direct hit. Two bombs penetrated three levels of deck causing 260 killed and 280 seriously wounded. The cruiser* Dido *was also hit causing over 100 fatalities. A considerable number of Argylls were among the fatalities. The* Imperial *was damaged and personnel including Argylls were transferred in the dark to the* Hotspur *before the* Imperial *was sunk. The return from Crete was a nightmare and all my compatriots for so long have thought the same. None of us will ever forget the superb discipline and kindness of all ranks of the Royal Navy who made the whole thing possible. When we were dropped in Alexandria, all the ships literally turned round and headed back for Crete to attempt further evacuation. It was a sad battalion disembarking in Alexandria. Of the 655 all ranks who had embarked on 18 May only 312 disembarked on 29 May. Besides those killed and wounded, over 300 were taken prisoner.'*

And those who remained behind

'I myself did not leave Villa Ariadne, our Casualty Reception Station,' writes Basil Keeble, RAMC, 'having to remain behind with six others to tend the casualties who could not be moved to the waiting ships – 100 British, 50 Germans and a few Greeks ... the next morning on waking everywhere was still and so quiet – no gunfire or aircraft. We then realised the battle was over, but we had had no mention that we were to be left behind. Later in the day the Germans moved in and we became POWs – not a very pleasing experience with the hazards of the life of the unknown.'

Commando Fred Dashfield of Swanage was one of a remarkable band of 140 all ranks who included Royal Marines, Commandos, RAF, Royal Navy, Palestinians, Australians and New Zealanders, who on the beach at Sphakia, answered Royal Marine Maj 'Kipper' Garrett's call, 'Anymore for the *Skylark*?' and joined him in a desperate dash for freedom. Garrett, who was determined not to be taken prisoner, had seen an abandoned landing craft in the bay. He swam out to her and discovered that she appeared seaworthy, but that there was a wire fouling the port screw and that the engines weren't working properly. However, undaunted by these problems, he went in search of an engineer and found one. Together they managed to get the engines started and sailed the craft inshore. Then 'Kipper' asked others to join him and to help him sail to North Africa. His 'crew' assembled – they collected all the fuel, water and rations they could lay their hands on and, at 0900hrs on 1 June, cast off in a light mist. 'We made for a small island called Gavdopula and sheltered under a cliff away from the Stukas on their way to strafe the beaches,' recalled Fred Dashfield. 'We then went ashore and filled all our containers with water from a well – it would have to last a long time.' They stayed on the deserted island all day, while the 'engine room staff' (four Australian corporals and a Commando sergeant) overhauled the engine and the rest of the crew were 'exercised in seamanship'. Then at 2130hrs that evening off they went. With the aid of two maps, but without a sextant or other instruments, they set a course for Tobruk, which they knew was in Allied hands.

> *'All hands had dinner – an inch square of bully – the last solid food for nine days, plus a last drink from the well … our petrol ran out after the first day and it was decided to try to convert the engine to run on diesel, as we had a drum. An Australian called Keith Walker said it had been done in the outback and gave it a try, but he had no luck. The next thing we used was a sail made out of blankets, which helped when the wind blew, but most days were calm and it became very hot, with no shelter from the June sun. Garrett said, "Right lads all who can over the side and keep her heading for home!" I liked the idea of cool water over my body so had a go. With men each side we did manage to keep her on course. That night an RAF man died of wounds. We tied his body to an iron plate and Kipper said a few words and away he went into the sea.*

'We had a water ration each evening – the lid of a cocoa tin was the measure. It had to last and we had no idea for how much longer. Each day got hotter and hotter and we welcomed our swim. With just a little wind from the north we liked to think we were nearer land. One chap tried drinking sea water and, being in the sun, went a bit off his head, but his mates restrained him and he settled down. On the sixth or seventh day a Palestinian shot himself with a revolver, why no one knew, but he must have thought the end was nigh. If only he had waited two more days. The revolver was a lovely .38 Smith and Wesson which I took a liking to, but another Palestinian grabbed it before me. On the eighth day I was in the bow, sitting on the landing ramp with a Digger, when I thought I saw breaking surf. We had a good look and shouted together: "Land Ahoy!" It was a few miles away, but sure enough it was Africa. But where? And it's a long coastline! Garrett had a surprise for us, he had hidden a two gallon tin of petrol which we used to get over the last few miles. The next thing was to find out where we were and to find some water. The sun had set and some Maoris wandered off along the beach, to come back later and say they had found a well, so we all trooped off and sure enough they were right. Of course everyone drank their fill and that gave a lot of us a very quick bowel movement – it was funny to see perhaps a hundred men squatting in the desert relieving themselves! When daylight came, the reason became clear as in the well was the carcass of a sheep or a goat, covered with little red creatures. How long it had been there no one knew and we thirsty men had only cared that it was water!

'Two marines struck off across the desert to discover where we were and came back some hours later to say that we were about seven miles from the coast road and an RASC camp. They couldn't pick us up, but if we marched to their camp they would ferry us back to Mersa Matruh where the railway began. We were lucky, we had landed about half-way between *our lines and the enemy ... we formed a column and trudged up to the RASC camp where they put up tents for us and the cooks made us a bully stew. Unfortunately most of it was wasted as we hadn't enough saliva in our mouths to do it justice. However, the cooks had another surprise and very welcome it was – a big Jaffa orange. Never had the humble fruit been more appreciated! Many years later after the war, I did a programme about escaping from Crete on Solent TV, with the marine who dished out the water ration at sea. His name was Reg Pilgrim and his first words on meeting were, "Remember that lovely orange?" Who could forget – not me!*

'The RASC took us to Mersa Matruh for the train. During the night an Italian bomber dropped some bombs from a great height and one landed directly onto a slit-trench killing two of our marines – what rotten luck. After all they had been through they didn't deserve that. On arrival in Alex we were kitted out by the WVS with small toiletries and other things. Then we got ready to go back to our bases. "Kipper" Garrett bade us all, "Goodbye and Good Luck!" We all cheered and meant it – he had taken us from Hell to Heaven – Thanks Kipper. After the war he was killed in a motor accident, a sad ending to a good man.'

Two Sherwood Rangers escape

Captains Myles Hildyard and Michael Parish were taken prisoner by mountain troops near Sphakia on 1 June and marched back to Suda Bay then to Maleme, where a POW camp had been established. Like many others, they were determined to escape if given the opportunity. Then they heard that all officer prisoners were to be flown off the island and that they would be among the first to go, so there was no time to lose.

'On 7 June, in their blue hospital coats, they set off after breakfast. In a sack they had food, compasses, clothes and a cheque book. They carried a spade and a bucket and tried to look like a

working party. In the village they ran straight into two suspicious German soldiers. They greeted them effusively and pressed unripe grapes on them. "Escape? But how ridiculous! Do you really imagine we could escape in obvious clothes like these?" By 8 June they were out of the plain, moving along gorges into the hills. They found a shepherd who gave them goat's milk. The village of Pangia was the first real taste of civilisation. They were given fresh eggs, chips, hot marrow and salad. A barber shaved them and cut their hair. As they sat in the village café, the locals sent drinks over to them. They found a cobbler to mend their shoes. That night they slept in a bed with sheets and pillows. They kept on the move, sheltering with the Cretans and fed by them. Some houses were clean, some were filthy and alive with fleas. Now and then they came across Allied soldiers who had "gone native" and were living as shepherds. They were weak with dysentery now and falling heavily as they stumbled along the rocky paths.'

Clearly they had to make contact with someone who would get them off the island as soon as possible, and then fortunately came a 'flash of hope' in that they received a note from a Greek officer (Emmanuele Vernikos) who was known as 'the Captain', saying that he was working on a scheme to take them off the island. After numerous adventures they met the Captain who was full of ideas to start and lead a Cretan revolution, 'But how on earth was it to be done, the British wondered, with no shoes, no weapons, no ammunition and no one who knew the country properly? (The local guides seldom had the faintest idea of where they were going!)' However, despite everything and after a number of false starts, on 14 August, the Captain finally found a caique in Mense that he was certain could take them, although, it was by no means plain sailing:

'The caique, when the party arrived, was full of Greeks. Six British soldiers had been turned off as they wouldn't or couldn't pay. There was a mad quarrel as the Captain, who had climbed

aboard, crawled along the bowsprit yelling and brandishing his revolver – which he dropped into the sea. But eventually he got his party on board. The boat, a 20ft caique, was packed and everybody was sick. It was owned by a shoemaker who charged 1,000 drachmae per head passage money and smuggled olive oil and cigarettes. They sailed out. Opposite Antikithera the wind died down and the boat refused to move as the bottom was so encrusted with weed. A glaring sun beat down on bare heads. On the following day a great sea came up with heavy, rolling waves. Most of the Greeks were by now unconscious; those who had a spark of life left in them crossed themselves desperately. The master remarked pointedly that he was a shoemaker not a sailor. At Kithera the Captain went ashore for a bit. He came back confirming the rumours that the island bristled with Germans and Italians; they would have to get the boat round the north cape before daylight. By rowing madly the party managed to round the cape before dawn. The wind had dropped altogether and they sweated in the broiling sun. At last a breeze began to spring up and soon they were scudding towards Greece.'

They reached Greece safely, unloaded the Greek passengers and then sailed across to the island of Elaphonis, went ashore and were delighted to be on dry land again, but it gave them a feeling of being dizzy and light in the head! It was now 22 August. The Captain managed to buy a pink-coloured boat for 60,000 drachmae and they began to row it away from the island at dusk. They now had an Alsatian dog with them, who had attached itself to the previous party, had then been given to the shoemaker owner of the previous boat, but had elected to swim back and join them in their new boat. They rowed by night and managed to dodge the large number of Italian patrol boats in the area. After rowing for some five and a half hours each night, they managed to reach Milos by midday on 27 August. They landed in a little secluded bay, but then disaster struck – while collecting firewood to cook some aubergines they had collected,

Parish fell on the rocks, fracturing his skull and paralysing the nerves of one eye and one ear, whilst his right wrist was badly broken. Hildyard's souvenir Cretan walking stick had to be used as a splint. They managed to carry Parish back to the boat, but found that the blow had affected his sense of the horizontal, so that he could not tell if he was upright or lying down.

> 'They headed for Polino. There was no wind and the current drove them almost to Milos (where there were 550 Germans on the aerodrome). But hard rowing brought them to Polino just as the moon came up. The island was uninhabited – but spread-eagled on the beach they saw a month-old corpse in a British shirt and shorts. They fled from his welcoming grin. They buried the corpse and on 29 August moved on to Kimolos. Here the report was, "No Germans and no Italians – but also no food. We haven't seen bread for three weeks." But there was a port and a small town; they were given some pest-infested pears to eat and they found a doctor who put Parish's arm in plaster, dressed his wounds and got him into bed in a cottage on the cliff.'

From then on things began to get better, especially after the local priest had visited the boat, lit candles and burnt incense, then read Mass, said special prayers for the ship and blessed them all, sprinkling holy water over 'the crew, the boat, the pink sails, the pickled fish and the great basket of blue, red and golden grapes'. Then they set off and made good time with a strong wind which increased to gale force and sent them

> '. . . scudding along to Paros. There they sheltered in a small bay; taking down the sail, it tore; but they were able to mend it by the light of the holy-candle ends. ... On 4 September they saw the mountains of Turkey – surprisingly green. The Captain went ashore first and, in case there should be any skulduggery, pretended that the boat was carrying provisions

and intended to sail on to Cyprus. But he came back with the glorious news that "all was well". They had a bath and meal in a hotel. Serious, thorough-going Turkish officials confiscated from Myles Hildyard "a tiny leather folder I won as a prize for a three-legged race at St Neots, with photos of Toby and John aged 7 and 2 respectively". It was 90 days since they had slipped out of the German camp at Maleme. They returned through Smyrna, Damascus and Jerusalem, to Cairo.' [1]

To Berlin – two different journeys
Sebastian Krug recalled:

'On the night of 28/29 May, the English left Heraklion town and also the district. We were supposed to invade the town on the 29th but now there was no need to do so, we took over the town and the airfield without a fight. On the same day, more paratroopers and mountain troops joined us from Rethymnon. Instead of fighting we had time to lie on the beach, but there was a serious accident – one of the chaps was cleaning his pistol and it went off and killed the man lying beside him.

We were taken by lorry to Maleme and then by plane back to Megara, then by transport from Skopje in Yugoslavia to Berlin. I was a despatch rider with a motorbike and sidecar, so my job was to help lorries which broke down en route and to guide them to their destination.

'On 15 July there was a regimental parade in the Seestrasse in Berlin and the people of Berlin gave us a very warm welcome, after which we were all sent home for a well-deserved leave. While I was on leave, I was asked to give a talk on my experiences. My lecture lasted for two hours and was written down by some members of the audience – I had no idea if they were press or Gestapo, but a short time later I got a signal saying that I must report to my regiment immediately. From our Kreisleiter [2] *I found out what was wrong, I had said something about the Jews and had made a laughing stock out*

of one of the SS men. When I got back to camp I had to report directly to our new commander, Oberstleutnant Nagele and also to the battalion commander Hauptmann Kroh, who had the report in his hand. They both said it was stupid and I have these two officers to thank that it never came to court.'

Sebastian would soon be off to the Grafenwöhr training area and then to Russia. Hitler is said to have considered his Fallschirmjäger to be even tougher than the Waffen-SS and thus had a soft spot for them; however, undoubtedly Sebastian would have stood little chance against the SS no matter what, so he was extremely lucky.

Tom Caselli of Layforce had a very different journey to Berlin, which began by marching from Sphakia, all the way back to Maleme:

'All the villages had suffered aerial bombardment and were badly damaged, and in the Canea and Maleme areas there seemed to be corpses everywhere. We finished up in what appeared to be an olive grove ringed around with barbed wire. Somebody said it had been the former field hospital site, west of Canea ... I have no idea how many there were in the camp, conditions were generally poor and the Germans showed a lack of interest in elementary refinements – no shelters of any kind or sanitation. By now hunger and thirst were the greatest of our problems ... Our guards were the troops we had been fighting and, fair enough, they often turned a blind eye when we went scrounging for edible items. At least when on a working party we got some rations and came back with full waterbottles ... This went on until about the middle of July, then one evening we were told to pack up to move out the following morning. Morning came and we picked up our odds and ends and paraded and marched out surrounded by German guards down to Suda Bay harbour where they gave us two days' rations and filled

waterbottles and we were loaded into the holds of small coastal steamers en route to Salonika. Still being guarded by front-line troops, some of whom were starting their journey home to Germany. Still awfully hot, in the nineties, when we got well away from Suda the guards began to allow parties of us to climb up from the holds to the deck to get some air. I think it took us two or three days to arrive at Salonika.

'When we reached the port, our guards had tidied themselves up and became all regimental. After the boats tied up it seemed ages before we disembarked onto the quay where lines of troops were waiting for us and we were pushed into columns with shouts of "Raus! Raus!", accompanied by nastiness in general and then, closely guarded all round the column, we marched off. Any of the Greek population getting too close or trying to throw anything to us were ruthlessly knocked down out of the way. Some were pushed on to the end of our column and had to remain there. We reached our destination which turned out to be an old 1914-18 Greek Army barracks with several compounds, surrounded by double barbed wire fences and watch towers complete with searchlights. It was long enough before we entered the compound where we were searched, counted and recounted. This was where I "lost" my wristwatch. We were hustled by our nasty guards into another compound, our section was a two storey brick and stone barrack block building without windows or doors … We were reasonably clean when we came into this camp but before long we were flea-ridden and lousy. Sanitation was more or less non-existent, dysentery was soon rife, the building was bug-ridden and, to complete the picture, it was also rat-infested!'

Eventually, about the middle of August, Tom and his companions were moved to Germany, several hundred POWs being marched to the goods yard and loaded into box wagons:

'My recollection is of 50 or more men being crammed in into each one before the doors rolled shut and were secured. It seemed that we stayed there in the heat long enough before the train set off, there was insufficient room for all to lie down, the lucky ones were those who had a back rest against the wagon sides. Ventilation was a problem, there were four blank window spaces, one at each corner high up, well secured with barbed wire. Gradually we began to take a turn to stand and have a look out for a while and report progress. We still had our lice and fleas and in the heat and confined space they drove us frantic. Our journey was to be a slow, stop and start variety and in the event it was to last eight days and nights, taking us through Greece, Yugoslavia, Austria and into Germany ... The rations we had received had not been replenished ... even those who had been frugal had finished theirs and many others were suffering agonies of thirst not having anything to put water in.*

'On the ninth day came "Journey's End" and after a long wait the doors were rolled back with the now inevitable shouts of "Raus! Raus!" from the armed guards and we climbed out in some goods yard ... it was a relief to stand up and get the circulation going but we were still scratching ... still wearing the same Khaki drill uniforms in which we had left Alexandria on 23rd May, uniforms and ourselves unwashed and unshaven, you can guess what we looked like!'

Notes

1. Quoted from *Sherwood Rangers* by T. M. Lindsay, by kind permission of OC 'S' Sqn, Royal Yeomanry.
2. The *Kreisleiter* was the lowest salaried official of the National Socialist party, responsible for administering a *Kreis*.

12

Fighting On

Festung Kreta

The occupied island was divided into two zones, the main German zone and a subsidiary Italian one which comprised the two eastern provinces of Sitia and Lasithi. The garrison here was the Siena Division, whose commander, Generale Angelo Carta, ran his zone with a more liberal and relaxed attitude than did the Germans. His headquarters was at Neapolis, while the German HQ was at Canea, and the first German island commander was Gen Waldemar Andrae, who took over from Gen Student. He was succeeded by another paratrooper, Gen Bruno Bräuer in 1942, then in the spring of 1944 by the hated Gen Friedrich-Wilhelm Mueller, who had gained a reputation for brutality while holding the second senior post on the island as the divisional commander of 22nd Infantry (Air Landing) Division at Arkhanes, south of Heraklion. As will be explained, his brutality had led to him being targeted for abduction, but he was replaced by Gen Kreipe before this could happen, so Kreipe became the target instead. In total the size of the garrison varied considerably from some 75,000 in 1943 to as low as 10,000 just before the surrender in 1945. The crack 22nd Infantry (Air Landing) Division had been sent to Crete in the summer of 1942, much to the annoyance of some senior German officers who considered it was wrong to use such a highly trained division for such a static role.

The Germans had undoubtedly been taken by surprise by the hostile attitude shown towards them from the outset by the Cretan population. Perhaps they had expected the fiercely independent Cretans, who had always been against the established Greek Government, to welcome them as liberators. However, instead they were looked upon just as a new set of invaders, against whom the islanders would defend their homes and their countryside to the last drop of their blood. As the late Alan Clark wrote in The Fall of Crete:

'These men fought in their homeland. Behind them, there is a lasting tradition of gallantry and struggles, up in the mountains and down on the plains. The blood of the guerrilla flows in their bodies. Some of their weapons were long outmoded, guns that had been used in struggles against the Turks, a century ago.'

These fiercely independent people, revolutionaries from the days of Turkish domination, once again made their way into the hills, creating the first resistance centres during the summer of 1941. Their initial tasks included organising the gathering up of those members of the British and Commonwealth forces who had been left on the island but had decided not to surrender. Having collected them from all over the island, the Cretan guerrillas then made themselves responsible for the protection, feeding, clothing and sustaining of these Allied servicemen and, where and when possible, their safe evacuation, so that they could live to fight another day. To do this successfully the guerrillas needed links to the Allied headquarters in Cairo and other parts of the Middle East – via the spy network which was being established. For the next four years, the Cretan Resistance continued to harry the German occupation troops. By doing so they tied up a large number of enemy soldiers on the island and did not cease their activities, despite the harsh reprisals employed by the occupiers – for example, the mass executions and the burning of entire villages which inevitably followed their actions. As one commentator put it, 'Death was at the doorstep of every household,' so they paid high price for their stubborn resistance.

Crete became the perfect place for those cloak and dagger activities which were the ideal occupation of some remarkable English servicemen, about whom numerous films have been made and books written since the war – men like Patrick Leigh-Fermor, Xan Fielding, Billy Moss and Dennis Ciclitira, whose exploits in occupied Crete were made into the film Ill Met By Moonlight in which the late Dirk Bogarde played Leigh-Fermor. Probably their most outrageous exploit was the kidnapping of a German general, as briefly recounted later. However, first let us look at just one successful 'sustaining operation'.

'As we marched through the night on our way to Sphakia, some villages were burning after being bombed by the planes and the people must have known we were leaving. I felt ashamed to desert such gallant people.' That is what one New Zealander, George Weelink, wrote about his last hours in Crete. He goes on to say that he thinks they must be the most loyal people in the world. 'People who were poor, were risking their lives for freedom and helped so many British, Australian and New Zealanders who remained behind in Crete.' [1] One such small group of servicemen were two New Zealanders, an Australian and a young English airman – the late LAC Colin France [2] of No 33 Squadron, whose early hours as a prisoner were recorded in Chapter 7. Later, after he had been a prisoner for some two weeks, he recalled that he had often 'thought about escaping and although I had numerous opportunities, I lacked the necessary courage to do so by myself, especially as I had no knowledge at that time regarding the attitude of the Cretans to escaped prisoners'. Despite these fears, Colin was quick to seize the opportunity when one presented itself. He heard two New Zealanders discussing how they would escape the next day. An Australian was also listening and they both asked the Kiwis if they could join them. Initially the other three were sceptical as they considered Colin too young; however, having seen his stock of food and heard him speak Greek, they agreed.

At 1400hrs on 19 June 1941, they made their break, crawling undetected under the perimeter wire fence after the guards had passed by their sector. The party had nominated NZ Sgt Keith Smythe to be in charge, while the other New Zealander and the Aussie were the 'strong men', leaving Colin as the interpreter and 'general dogsbody'! By this time he had a fair knowledge of essential Greek words but could only make up short sentences. His narrative recalls:

> 'We had only travelled at a fast rate for about an hour when it was decided that we should "lie low" until it became a little darker. At 1700hrs we were on the move again, travelling along a dried-up river bed. We passed through one village that had a garrison of Germans but fortunately for us "Jerry" was out. All the villages we passed through in our flight to the south were very poor but the villagers were extremely kind to us and provided for all our needs in food and clothing. After about two more days, we arrived at the coastal village of Soughia and here we stayed for two days, discussing our plight and plans to leave the island. We had hoped to find a boat but it appeared that the Germans had confiscated all the larger motor vessels.'

Then one day they saw a small dinghy appear in the bay and decided to try to 'borrow' it during the next day. Unfortunately, they were just too late and watched it disappear around the headland that evening. They were determined not to give up so easily and went out looking for it, but although they searched that part of the coast, they saw no further signs of the elusive small boat. By now their food supplies were running low, although they did still have a small amount of tinned food, but decided to keep it in reserve in case they should find another boat. Instead they went 'goat hunting' – easier said than done, and it took them nearly two hours and a considerable amount of effort to catch one! Keith Smythe proved to be a good amateur butcher and cut up some of the smaller joints for dinner. Colin records that it was quite tough, but that there was plenty for the next few days which they kept wrapped in muslin cloth.

'The local villagers were afraid of reprisals from the patrol which was expected, so after a couple of days it was suggested to us that we should leave. Over the mountains we went, this time we were returning to the north side of the island. The Australian informed us that he was leaving our party because he had found himself a job in a bakery in one of the villages we had passed through on our journey from Maleme. It could have been in Nteres, Semprones or Aghia Irini, so we asked him again the real reason why he wanted to leave us. He told us that his boots were worn out and he couldn't walk any further. We could not change his mind, so we said our Goodbyes and left him. Up and down the mountains we went, through Epanochori and Prasses until we reached Orthuni, a small village on the side of a hill, not very far from Therisso. Here an old man invited us to his home, where we were treated as honoured guests for three days. The first meal we had was a banquet and no matter what we said the old man insisted we ate 20 eggs, two plates of chips, three tins of Bully beef, cheese, tomatoes and plenty of wine. We could hardly walk to our beds that night. His niece offered to wash our clothes and the old man provided us with suits of clothing until ours were ready. I had never had an occasion to use my Greek to its full and now this chance was seized immediately. The old man, his three nieces and I conversed for many an hour, well into the night. It was here that I was given the name Nikos and this name has stayed with me until the present day.'

Soon, however, the group split up and Colin found himself travelling alone, until he became friendly with another New Zealander – an ex-cook, who had been living in nearby Therisso, a little mountain village, for the past month, so he knew everyone. He had rushed out of his tent when the

Germans landed, leaving his false teeth behind and had never had a chance to retrieve them, so the villagers called him Fafoutis ('Toothless'). Colin met all the villagers and finally Maria Fyotakis and her brother Eleftheri, who arranged for their family to feed him most days. He spent five weeks there and improved his Greek tremendously, teaching them English in return. During this time he also met some visitors – a Greek sea captain, called Vernikos and two English army officers from the Notts Yeomanry, Myles Hildyard and Michael Parish, whose epic voyage to Turkey I outlined in the last chapter – Crete was certainly 'a small world' in those days! There was talk about radio transmitters and Colin gathered that some were hidden in the village of Loutraki:

> *'Telling Maria that I was going away for a few days was rather difficult as she was very much concerned for my safety as well as for her family's who had sheltered me, an escaped prisoner. Anyway, I managed it and the next day I left for the village which I knew was not too far away ... when I arrived at Loutraki my problems began and I had considerable difficulty in convincing the Greek who held the transmitters that I was not a spy. With the help of a friend who arrived in the nick of time, I managed to drive all doubts out of his mind and I departed the proud owner of a German transceiver and some spare parts. I learned later that as I left the village, a German patrol went in.*
>
> *'On my return to Therisso, I was informed that a German patrol was expected there too. Hiding the radio, I set off with a band of Cretans into the mountains where we were always safe from German patrols. Every Cretan had a rifle of some kind and I felt sorry for any Jerry who pursued us into the mountains at any hour of the day. Two hours later, word came through that the Germans had left the village so we returned, everything back to normal.'*

Two weeks later they were off again into the mountains where they met other escaped POWs, including a red-haired Australian captain called Embrey, who invited them to join the rest of his party encamped in the high mountains. They followed him and found he had a fairly large band of Kiwis, Aussies, Tommies and Greeks, made even larger a few days later by the arrival of Myles and Parish, who told them that Capt Vernikos had managed to obtain two motor boats in which they were hoping to reach Turkey. When the redoubtable captain arrived he was (as mentioned previously) full of plans to start some guerrilla activity. However, as their total armament was one ancient pistol and two equally ancient and rusty bullets, they sensibly decided to abandon the idea!

Colin continued to have a series of exciting adventures all over Crete, managing to keep just ahead of the Germans, whilst being fed, housed, clothed and protected by the brave Cretan peasants. Eventually, while sheltering in a cave near the coast with some others, he heard about a boat which had put in somewhere nearby and taken a number of fugitives on board. Next time they saw a small boat 'chugging along the coast' they chased after it and were delighted when it stopped not far from their cave and they saw the two-man crew talking to their companions:

> *'We continued running until we reached the cave and we were told to carry on to Marithaki – and there was the boat waiting for us. The captain was a Lieutenant May, complete with earring – just like a swashbuckling pirate, also a Rhodesian sailor and two well-armed Greeks. After we had sampled with ecstasy our first Players cigarettes for months, we were told that we would probably leave Crete that night. We all enjoyed a very good dinner that day, although I had a severe case of toothache. It rained during the afternoon, but our spirits weren't dampened; at last we were leaving this island prison with its so hospitable and courageous people.*

'That night, on 26 November 1941 at about 2000hrs, I was invited to go out to sea with them. The Captain secured guns on fixtures aft and forward and then asked me if I could use a Bren gun. I told him that I had only used a Lewis gun, but if he would load then I would do the necessary. This he did. Further out to sea we sailed, then stopped. "Do you hear it?" asked the Captain, "No," said I. "Listen," he said. Then I heard it, the sound of diesels. Up from the bowels of the sea it came; we watched the conning tower break the surface. Then it opened at the top and sailors jumped out before the sea had left the deck. Immediately they loaded the big deck gun and aimed it at us.

We in turn pointed our guns as we sailed towards each other. It was a Greek submarine, the Triton. We unloaded ammunition including hand grenades, cocoa and clothes. Before we returned to Marithaki with our cargo, the Greek crew asked for "Homa" (earth). As soon as the cargo was unloaded all our male companions were embarked and we returned to the submarine handing over to the Greek crew some of the Cretan earth they had requested. At 8.30 we commenced our voyage to Egypt.

'After an uneventful voyage except for some of us being sick after eating some of the rich food which we had not been used to for so long, we entered Alexandria harbour at about 0900hrs on 30 November 1941. It had taken me six months to reach freedom.'

The Kidnapping of Gen Kreipe

Of all the exploits carried out by members of the Special Operations Executive (SOE) on Crete during the German occupation, perhaps the capture of the General Officer Commanding the German 22nd Infantry Division, on 26 April 1944, was the most audacious. The operation began when two SOE officers, Maj Patrick Leigh-Fermor and Capt Stanley Moss, flew, together with two Greek SOE agents, from Bardia on 4 February 1944, bound for the Lasithi Plain in Crete.

Unfortunately, the weather closed in after only Leigh-Fermor had managed to parachute, and it would be another two months before the rest could join him by sea on 4 April. By that time, their original target, the brutal Gen Friedrich-Wilhelm Mueller [3] had been replaced by Gen Heinrich Kreipe. However, it was agreed that the kidnap attempt should still take place. Gen Kreipe was staying at Villa Ariadne, which has featured numerous times already in this book, latterly as the RAMC CRS, where medical orderly Basil Keeble was working and had remained behind as a prisoner to succour the wounded of both sides. Kreipe journeyed by car twice a day between the villa and his HQ which was at Arhanes. Most days he worked from 0900hrs to 1300hrs. From 1600hrs to 2000hrs, he had dinner, then was driven back to his villa. However, on some nights he would remain at the headquarters even longer to indulge his passion for bridge. On this particular evening, he was due to stay for dinner and this fact was discovered and passed on to members of the 'snatch' party, who decided that it would be the perfect time to kidnap him. The abduction would take place during his return journey to the villa, when it would be dark. Also, he would not be immediately missed when he failed to arrive at the villa as his staff there would think that he was still at his HQ playing bridge. And that is exactly how it was done. The kidnap spot chosen was at a T-junction where the Arhanes road meets the Houdesti-Heraklion road and there were high banks on both sides, with ditches in which the kidnappers could hide. The two British officers were disguised as German traffic policemen (both spoke German well) and, officiously waving red lamps and traffic signals, flagged down the car and told the driver that the road was not safe further on. The plan worked perfectly and swiftly the general was yanked out and taken prisoner. He was then 'trussed up like a turkey' and told, when he began to shout, that he was a prisoner of British commandos and that he had better shut up! Getting back into the car, some of the party then drove on, with two men lying on top of Gen Kreipe and threatening him with a dagger, while others took the German driver away. One of the two Englishmen wore the General's cap whilst the car still had the general's flag on it, so any soldiers they passed, stopped and saluted them!

Taking the general on foot into the mountains, they left the car with a note inside which read:

TO THE GERMAN AUTHORITIES IN CRETE.
Gentlemen, Your Divisional Commander, General KREIPE, was captured a short time ago by a BRITISH raiding force under our command. By the time you read this he will be on his way to Cairo. We would like to point out most emphatically that this operation was carried out without the help of CRETANS or CRETAN partisans and that the only guides used were serving soldiers of HIS HELLENIC MAJESTY's FORCES in the Middle East, who came with us. Your General is an honourable prisoner of war and will be treated with all the consideration owing to his rank. Any reprisals against the local population will be wholly unwarranted and unjust.

Auf baldiges Wiedersehen!

PS We are very sorry to have to leave this beautiful car behind.

It was also arranged that the BBC would broadcast a news item saying that a raiding party had carried out the operation and that the general was already on his way to Cairo.

Of course the Germans initially thought that he had been taken by partisans and threatened, in a hastily printed leaflet, to raze all the villages in the Heraklion area and to take severe reprisals against the civilian population. Patrols and recce aircraft combed the hills and mountains, aiming in particular to cover the ground towards the south coast, which was the obvious escape route. In fact they unwittingly occupied the chosen getaway beach, but fortunately the party heard about this and was able to hide in isolated shepherd's huts and to remain hidden while a new escape beach was chosen. In the end, the party took 17 days to reach the new beach, but eventually managed it and were safely taken off. Kreipe had fallen during the journey and had his right arm in a sling. After a difficult and stormy crossing, they reached Mersa Matruh and the general soon began three years of captivity in a POW camp near Calgary, Canada. Both British officers were awarded the DSO for their exploit.

Freyberg thanks the Cretan population

In September 1945, before they went home to 'the land of the long white cloud', the 2nd New Zealand Division returned to Crete to lay wreaths on the graves of their fallen and also to thank the Greek people for helping and sheltering New Zealand soldiers during the German occupation. I am sure that Freyberg spoke for Great Britain and Australia as well, when he said:

> *'The Government and people of New Zealand remember with gratitude all the Greek people have done to help New Zealand soldiers who were left behind when your country was overrun by the German Army in April and May 1941. We are deeply conscious of New Zealand's debt to the Greek nation for their gallantry and self sacrifice in sheltering many of our men.'*

Notes

1. As quoted in Crete 1941 Eyewitnessed.
2. Colin had been reported Missing on 31 May and to his parents in a letter of 5 June 1941. This had been followed up on 6 October 1941 by another letter which advised them that there was little hope of him still being alive – what a wonderful surprise they had in store!
3. Mueller received his just deserts on 20 May 1947, when he was executed in Athens.

13

Conclusions

At first glance, especially to those who had not experienced the modern forms of warfare which the German war machine had perfected by 1941 – such as Blitzkrieg (Lightning War) with its essential ingredient of dive-bombers acting as close-support artillery; or the concept of envelopment from the air by Fallschirmjäger again supported by dive-bombers; or whose practical experience of warfare was still largely based on the static trench warfare of the Great War, then it must have appeared that the defenders held all the aces as far as safeguarding Crete was concerned.

There seemed to be an adequate garrison, which had been on the island for some six months – plenty of time in which to have perfected their defences. Granted they were then suddenly swamped by a large number of additional troops, evacuated from Greece, who lacked heavy weaponry and were even short of basic small arms. Nevertheless, they were battle-hardened soldiers, many being Anzacs, tough, belligerent fighters whose military reputation was second to none. And around the shores was the Royal Navy, undeniably the finest navy in the world, quietly confident of its ability to see off any naval force the Axis could muster against them.

Of course, RAF support was almost non-existent, there being a great shortage of all types of aircraft, especially modern fighters. The RAF lacked the wherewithal to support more than just a handful of aeroplanes on the limited airstrips on Crete, and the nearest airfields in North Africa were far too far away to allow proper coverage of the island. In addition, most

Allied servicemen had yet to experience the full effects of enemy air superiority, especially at sea. The 'icing on the cake' was undoubtedly the presence of a real-life hero as the commander. Gen Freyberg or 'Churchill's Salamander' as he came to be called, was not only an incredibly brave soldier with a Victoria Cross to prove it, but also a highly respected general officer of considerable experience. Surely a few aeroplanes and some crazy paratroops could not beat that lot? And as if to guarantee success there was also the Enigma code-breaking team at Bletchley Park, who had cracked the most highly secret German intelligence device, so that we knew almost to the minute when and where the enemy would make their landings.

Nevertheless, in less than two weeks the defenders had been forced not only to concede and evacuate the island, but also had suffered heavy casualties in killed, wounded and taken prisoner – the approximate figure being 13,800 lost out of a total garrison of some 31,800. Even more worrying, the Royal Navy had had four capital ships (three battleships and an aircraft carrier) damaged, three cruisers sunk and a further six damaged, six destroyers sunk and seven damaged, while 16 small craft – such as MTBs based at Suda – had been lost. That is a staggering total of some 42 ships lost or damaged, together with the irreplaceable loss of over 2,000 well-trained officers and men.

Reasons why
Airpower
First and foremost must be the fact that the British totally underestimated the real power of the Luftwaffe elements that were available for the operation. By using internal lines of communication, the Germans had been able to assemble a massive force of aircraft of all types, ready for the assault. A German treatise on the battle says that between 20 and 31 May 1941, their transport aircraft flew a staggering one and a half million miles and transported a total of 23,464 men, 5,348 weapons containers, 539 guns, 711 motorcycles and over a

million kilograms of stores to Crete, while returning aircraft flew back some 3,173 wounded. This considerable achievement was performed by a total of 650 Junkers Ju52s, of which, by the end of the operation, 143 were destroyed, 120 damaged and eight were missing, the loss of so many aircraft being a measure of the German determination to land troops whatever the cost.

The treatise does not give details of the constant fighter and bomber sorties which took place both in the period leading up to the assault or during the all important two weeks of the battle; however, one just has to remember the constant references to enemy bombing which are highlighted in all the personal accounts in this book, to realise how strong the Germans were in the air at this stage of the war. To quote again from the same German source where it discusses the ways of ensuring successful operations against an island fortress:

'Control of the air above the island is essential for the successful execution of airborne landings. During the Crete operation the British had practically no aircraft based on the island and were unable to improvise effective air cover from North Africa because of the long distance between the air bases in Egypt and the fields on Crete.' [1]

Equally important was the fact that the Royal Navy had to operate under the continual threat of enemy air attack, from bases which were so close to the sea area in which they had to operate, while British aircraft were too far away to provide proper fighter cover. The continual enemy air attacks meant that it was practically impossible for surface vessels to operate in daylight – a similar situation to that which later pertained on land in North-West Europe in 1944-45, when the Allied airpower reigned supreme and the Germans had to severely restrict their movement by day. It was a triumph for air over sea, and makes all the more remarkable the bravery and determination of the Royal Navy to continue to operate under such conditions.

Command and control

The lack of communications between the various garrisons and levels of command on Crete meant that to a great degree they fought their own battles without the support and co-ordination which could and should have been forthcoming from other areas. For example, the loss of the vital Maleme airstrip could have been avoided, or at worst further delayed, if a vital counter-attack had been put in when it was required and not far too late. Knowing now how near the Germans were to aborting the entire operation after suffering such heavy casualties at Maleme, it is easy with hindsight to criticise the senior commanders for not reacting faster. Undoubtedly Freyberg and his senior commanders believed – until it was far too late – that the airborne landings were merely the initial phase of operations and would be followed by a major seaborne landing, therefore they needed to hold a reserve to deal with this major assault.

The changes in command in the run-up to the battle – a staggering seven changes being recorded between Brig Tidbury in January 1941 and Gen Freyberg in April 1941 – certainly did not help, and while there was a plethora of senior 'brass hats' on the Army side, the senior RAF officer on the island until 17 April was a flight lieutenant!

Intelligence

Undoubtedly the German intelligence was downright appalling – they could not have been more wrong about the way in which they would be received by the local population. In addition, their air reconnaissance did not pin-point by any means all of the defensive positions on the island – surprising in view of their total air superiority – and this led to Fallschirmjäger being dropped right on top of defensive positions and suffering unnecessarily heavy casualties. On the other side, the British high level intelligence was so good that the defenders should have known exactly what to expect, but perhaps Freyberg was constrained not to react too obviously lest the Germans discover the truth about Enigma being broken.

Determination to succeed

The dogged determination of the Germans to press on with their attacks once the operation had started, no matter what the casualties might be, undoubtedly was a major factor in their success. However, the sheer size of their casualty figures – the German estimate was nearly 6,000 killed, wounded or missing [2], although the Allies reckoned the true figure as being much higher – Gen Freyberg estimating that 17,000 enemy had been killed and wounded, including 6,000 drowned. Whatever the true figure may be, these losses were particularly severe, especially as they contained large numbers of highly trained Fallschirmjäger who would be very difficult to replace. Indeed, Adolf Hitler was so worried by the losses that he set his face against any future major use of airborne forces, so that the Germans never attempted a similar operation again. 'Crete was the grave of the German Fallschirmjäger,' commented Gen Student in a postwar interrogation, and he was right.

Lessons
British

The following is a list of lessons to be learned from the battle, as detailed by the British HQ MEC in a signal dated 6 June 1941:

(a) Aerodromes being enemy main objectives must be organised for all-round defence (including Pill Boxes), specially as parachutists may drop behind defences. Defences, including artillery, must be in depth. Artillery in sites with cover proved more useful than those in open with all-round fields of fire.

(b) All ranks of all arms must be armed with rifles and bayonets and a high proportion of Tommy guns to protect themselves, and in the case of Artillery, their guns.

(c) By day it should be easy to deal with parachutists, but it must be remembered that parachutists may land at night and secure an aerodrome. Main problem is to deal with enemy airborne troops, and as it is impossible to be strong everywhere, there must be mobile reserves, centrally placed, preferably with tanks.

(d) Defence must be offensive. Immediate action by mobile reserves essential to prevent enemy settling down and in order to secure quick action, good system of intercommunication is vital. Delay may allow enemy air to prevent movement.

(e) During bombing phase, AA and LMGs should remain silent unless required to protect own aircraft on the ground.

(f) AA layout should include dummy AA guns and alternative positions. Positions of AA guns should be continually changed.

(g) Arrangements must be made quickly to render aerodromes liable to attack temporarily unfit for landing.

(h) Equally important to quick action of mobile reserve is position of fighter aircraft support, the existence of which might prevent any airborne landing from succeeding, or at least reduce enemy effort.

'Swings and Roundabouts'

Whilst it does no good to speculate on the effect which the brave, but in the end useless, defence of Crete had on the overall pattern of the war, it is still fascinating to say, 'If Only . . .' A grievous number of brave servicemen were lost on both sides, on the sea, land and in the air, but it is true to say that their loss had only a marginal effect on the outcome of the war. It is also true to say that the British could well have made good use in the months which followed of the large number of ships that were lost and damaged in the battles, while the German airborne troops could have been used to considerable effect in both Iraq and Syria, or to capture Malta, or, perhaps, in the assault on Russia. It is also very easy with hindsight to argue about the way Crete was defended and to highlight the faults in its defence. However, I do not think that there can be any argument that at the time it was the right thing to do. It had to be defended, just as we had to go to the defence of Greece, no matter how it affected our efforts in North Africa. We undoubtedly 'lost on the swings and gained on the roundabouts' so it is true to say that the Allied lives lost were not sacrificed in vain.

Perhaps it should be left to the British Prime Minister to have the last word on the subject, when, in the House of Commons on 10 June 1941, he said:

> *'The choice was whether Crete should be defended without effective air support or should the Germans be permitted to occupy it without opposition ... there are some arguments which deserve to be considered before you can adopt the rule that you have to have a certainty of winning at any point, and if you have not got it beforehand clear out. The whole history of war shows the fatal absurdity of such a doctrine. Again and again it has been proved that fierce and stubborn resistance even against heavy odds and under exceptional conditions of local disadvantage is an essential element of victory.'*

Notes

1. German Report Series Part 4: The Seizure of Crete
2. Official German casualty figures were:

Army		Airforce	
Killed	327	Killed	1,032
Wounded	524	Wounded	2,097
Missing	587	Missing	1,132
Total	1,438	Total	4,261

14

What Is Left To See?

Homage to Crete

In September 1945, representatives of the 2nd New Zealand Division returned to Crete to commemorate the battle. Gen Freyberg paid tribute to those who had fallen:

> *'When our badly equipped forces were driven from the Maleme aerodrome and the slopes west of Canea, the bodies of these men lay on the battlefields where they had fallen. We come, before we depart for our homes, in the name of the New Zealand Division and of the New Zealand Government and of the people of New Zealand, to lay these wreaths on their graves.'*

This was the first of many visits which the veterans and the families of both sides would pay to the battlefields on Crete. For many years now, members of the UK Cretan Veterans' Association (UKCVA), have made regular pilgrimages to Crete to honour the fallen and renew old friendships both among the veterans themselves and also amongst the brave and resilient people of Crete who still remember the wartime days. The Association was officially founded in 1984 by 12 veterans, mainly to organise the 45th Anniversary pilgrimage to Crete. Now, 16 years later, it has been decided that the 60th visit in 2001 would be the last official visit by the UKVCA, although a new society is being established and undoubtedly pilgrimages will continue. The German veterans and their families also visit Crete and have been doing so for many years. As the photographs show, meetings between the two sides now take place in a spirit of friendship and reconciliation.

Suda Bay War Cemetery

The site of the Allied war cemetery was chosen in June 1945 by the military authorities and is at the north-west corner of the bay, about three miles west of Canea and half that distance north of the Canea-Rethymnon-Heraklion road which skirts the southern shores of the bay. To quote from the official Imperial War Graves Commission brochure:

'It is reached by a track which turns off this road and crosses some salt flats, whence a winding path between an olive grove and fields leads to the entrance gate. It lies under the northern hill, sloping slightly towards the sea, with a lovely view across the bay to distant hills. The immediate surroundings are flat and sparsely cultivated, but the cemetery is enclosed by trees and shrubs which give shade and colour, while flowers bloom in the borders along the rows of headstones. Here are buried those who were killed during the operations in Crete, many of whose graves are not identified. This is due to the fact that the German occupying forces moved many of the remains from their graves in the fighting areas into four large burial grounds, which they called British Military Cemeteries, and in doing so lost the identities of the casualties. These four burial grounds were at Canea (the largest), Heraklion, Rethymnon and Galatas. Commonwealth servicemen who died on Crete and whose graves are not identified are commemorated by name on the Athens Memorial which stands in Phaleron War Cemetery, Athens. There are 1,509 Second World War graves in Suda Bay War Cemetery, of which 782 are unidentified. There are also 19 First World War graves and 37 other graves that were moved from Suda Bay Consular Cemetery in 1963.

'The cemetery was designed by Louis de Soissons (1890-

1962), a Canadian by birth, who designed Welwyn Garden City before the war and was the Commission's architect for all World War 2 cemeteries in Italy, Greece and Austria. The forecourt is paved with rosso di Verona marble and travertine limestone. Around and between the stone, pebbles are set in decorative patterns. Inside the cemetery, on the left, is a shelter with walls of the same travertine, in alternate light and dark bands, and with a hipped roof of red Roman tiles. The shelter houses the register box and the historical notice.

'The cemetery is laid out symmetrically in 16 plots, the Cross of Sacrifice in the centre. The shrubberies at the sides of the cemetery include Australasian native shrubs, to reflect the high proportion of New Zealand and Australian graves in the cemetery. The cemetery is looked after by three gardeners.'

The German cemetery

The equivalent German cemetery is at Maleme, on Hill 107, while there is also a memorial to the Fallschirmjäger situated about two miles west of Canea on the left of the main road to Maleme. The German cemetery was inaugurated on 6 October 1974 and contains 4,465 dead. To the west the olive groves slope down to the bed of the wild Tavrontis, while in the distance there is a view of the deep blue sea. The cemetery, which is arranged according to the four main battle areas of Canea, Maleme, Rethymnon and Heraklion, is reached by climbing up steps, and there are benches in the shade of old olive trees that invite one to rest and contemplate. Through an open hall, with a book of names of the fallen, the path leads uphill to the graves which are enclosed by walls. On each stone tablet are the names and dates of two soldiers, while in the middle of the cemetery is a memorial square. Here the names of 300 soldiers who fell on Crete but whose remains could not be found are recorded on metal plates. Many former comrades helped with work on the cemetery, which is sponsored by the German 1st Airborne Division.

Many other memorials

As the photographs show, there are many other memorials to the fallen all over Crete, such as at Sphakia, Heraklion and Galatas, the RAF Memorial at Maleme, and the Royal Artillery at Sternes on the Akrotiri peninsula. There are also many memorials to the Cretan Resistance, for example, the Stavremenos memorial. About 50 miles east of Suda Bay, on the old coast road in Stavremenos, stands a memorial to Australian, Greek and British Servicemen and Cretan patriots. It consists of a flight of paved steps leading to a terrace upon which are two field guns, a concrete pylon and a memorial wall with bronze plaques.

Another example is the Prevelli Monastery plaque. The plaque reads:

> *'This region after the battle of Crete became the rallying point for hundreds of British, Australian and New Zealand soldiers, in defiance of ferocious German reprisals suffered by the monks and the native population. They fed, protected and helped these soldiers to avoid capture and guided them to the beachhead where they escaped to the free world by British submarines.'*

Museums

There is a Naval Museum at Suda Bay and an Army Battle of Crete Museum in Canea. The UKCVA Standards will be laid up in the latter museum in 2001 and will remain there until a new National Museum is built at Galatas, when they will be transferred.

Appendices

1. THE GARRISON OF CRETE, ORDER OF BATTLE AS AT 20 MAY 1941

HQ CREFORCE

Commander:	Maj-Gen Bernard Freyberg VC, DSO, CMG
BGS:	Col Stewart
Staff:	Force HQ: 207 all ranks (inc Signals)
	CRA, CRE, ADST, ADOS and ADMS: 80 all ranks
Naval:	23 all ranks
HQ RAF:	95 all ranks (inc Signals)

Total: **405 (incl Signals)**

HERAKLION SECTOR

Commander:	Brig B. H. Chappel
Staff:	HQ 14 Inf Bde and Sig Sec 173 all ranks
Naval Staff:	22 all ranks
Armour:	Det 3rd Hussars (6 x Light Mk VI tanks) 37 all ranks
	Det 7RTR (5 x A 12 Matilda Mk II hy tanks; two at Heraklion and three at Tymbaki) 33 all ranks
Artillery:	234 Med Bty, RA (13 x 75mm/100mm guns) 200 all ranks
	7 Aust LAA Bty (less one tp + one sect; 6 x Bofors) 105 all ranks
	Tp 156 LAA Bty (4 x Bofors) 63 all ranks
	1 x Sec 15 Coast Regt, RA (2 x 4in guns) 85 all ranks

	2 x Secs C Bty, HAA, RM (4 x 3in guns) 123 all ranks
	Tp 23 LAA Bty, RM (LMGs only) 62 all ranks
Engineers:	CRE and staff 23 all ranks
	Sec 42 Fd Coy, RE 71 all ranks
	Dets 1017 Docks Operation Coy and 1038 Arab Stevedore Coy 96 all ranks
Infantry:	2 Leics 637 all ranks
	2Y&L 742 all ranks
	2BW 867 all ranks
	2A&SH (at Tymbaki) 655 all ranks
	2/4 Aust Inf Bn 553 all ranks
	7 Med Regt, RA (less one bty) Rifle Bn 320 all ranks
	3 Greek 1,100 all ranks
	7 Greek 800 all ranks
	Greek Garrison Bn 800 all ranks
Services:	Coy 189 Fd Amb, RAMC 53 all ranks
	RASC 160 all ranks
	RAOC 52 all ranks
	RAF 220 AMES 51 all ranks
	Airfd det and 112 Sqn 141 all ranks

Sector Total: 8,024 all ranks

CENTRAL SECTOR (RETHYMNON – GEORGEOUPOLIS SECTOR)

Commander:	Brig G. A. Vasey (Lt-Col Campbell 2/1 Aust Bn in comd Rethymnon sector)
Staff:	HQ 19 Aust Inf Bde 67 all ranks
	Sig Constr Sec and Aust Sig Details 104 all ranks

Armour:	Det 7RTR (2 x A12 Matilda Mk II) 12 all ranks
Artillery:	Sec 106 RHA (2 x 2pdr atk) 16 all ranks
	X Coast Def Bty, RM (2 x 4in guns) 87 all ranks
	2/3 Fd Regt, RAA (14 x 75/100mm guns) 190 all ranks
Engineers:	2/8 Fd Coy RAE 151 all ranks
Infantry:	2/1 Aust Inf Bn 581 all ranks
	2/7 Aust Inf Bn 681 all ranks
	2/8 Aust Inf Bn 384 all ranks
	2/11 Aust Inf Bn 645 all ranks
	2/1 Aust MG Coy 170 all ranks
Services:	B Coy 2/7 Aust Fd Amb 52 all ranks
	Dets AASC 105 all ranks
	DADOS Rethymnon, 2/1 Aust Ord Store Coy, etc 150 all ranks
	Provost 77 all ranks
	Airfd Sigs Dets (RN, RAF and Army) 31 all ranks
	Minor Aust units 127 all ranks
Greek Units:	4 and 5 Greek Regts 2,300 all ranks
	Gendarmerie 800

Sector Total: 6,730 all ranks

MALEME SECTOR (INCLUDING GALATAS)

Commander:	Brig (A/Maj-Gen) E. Puttick
CofS:	Lt-Col Gentry
Staff:	HQ 2nd NZ Div 96 all ranks
	NZ Div Sigs 44 all ranks
	CRE 30 all ranks
Armour:	Det 3rd Hussars (10 x Light Mk VI tanks) 75 all ranks
	Det 7 RTR (2 x A12 Matilda Mk II hy tanks) 13 all ranks

Artillery:	Light Tp, RA (4 x 3.7in hows) 87 all ranks
	5 NZ Fd Regt (less Inf Det) 256 all ranks
	[27 Bty in sp of 5 Bde (7 x 75/100mm guns;
	RHQ and 28 Bty in sp of 10 Bde (3 x 75/77mm
	guns)]
	Tp + Sec 156 LAA Bty, RA (6 x Bofors) 94 all
	ranks
	Tp 7 Aust LAA Bty (4 x Bofors) 83 all ranks
	Sec C Bty Hy AA, RM (2 x 3in guns) 62 all
	ranks
	Z Coast Def Bty, RM (2 x 4in guns) 85 all ranks
	Tp 23 LAA Bty, RM (LMGs only) 62 all ranks
Infantry:	4 NZ Inf Bde (Comd: Brig Inglis)
	HQ and Sigs Sec 124 all ranks
	18 NZ Bn 677 all ranks
	19 NZ Bn 565 all ranks
	20 NZ Bn 637 all ranks
	Pl 27 NZ MG Bn 35 all ranks
	5 NZ Inf Bde (Comd: Brig Hargest)
	HQ and Sigs Sec 125 all ranks
	7 NZ Fd Coy (as inf) 148 all ranks
	19 A Tps Coy (as inf) 216 all ranks
	21 NZ Bn 376 all ranks
	22 NZ Bn 644 all ranks
	23 NZ Bn 571 all ranks
	28 NZ (Maori) Bn 619 all ranks
	Two Pls NZ MG Bn 111 all ranks
	1 Greek Regt (at Kastelli) 1030 all ranks
	10 NZ Inf Bde (Comd: Brig Kippenberger)
	HQ and Sigs Sec 36 all ranks
	NZ Div Cav Det 194 all ranks
	NZ Composite Bn (Arty and ASC) 1007 all ranks
	Pl 27 NZ MG Bn 33 all ranks
	6 Greek Regt 1485 all ranks
	8 Greek Regt 1013 all ranks

Services: Medical
5 NZ Fd Amb 154 all ranks
6 NZ Fd Amb 187 all ranks
4 NZ Fd Hygiene Sec 31 all ranks
7 Brit Gen Hosp (incl 2 NZ GH att) 183 all ranks
Patients 7 GH 110 all ranks
NZ Dental Corps 9 all ranks
ASC
HQ NZASC and DID 34 all ranks
Ordnance
DADOS Maleme Sector 16 all ranks
Miscellaneous NZ att Greek units 36 all ranks
NZ Provost Coy 72 all ranks
NZ Entertainment Unit 30 all ranks
NZE Postal 24 all ranks
RAF 252 AMES 56 all ranks
30 and 33 Sqns 229 all ranks
FAA 805 Sqn 55

Sector Total: 11,859
SUDA BAY SECTOR

Commander: Maj-Gen C. E. Weston, RM
COS: Lt-Col Wills
NOIC: Capt Morse, RN
Staff: HQ MNBDO 252 all ranks
Suda Sector Sigs (Army) 42 all ranks
Naval Officer IC Suda and Naval Base Details
315 all ranks
MNBDO Sigs Coy 226 all ranks
Artillery: 'M' Group
HQ 52 LAA Bty, RA 76 all ranks
151 Hy AA Bty (8 x 3.7in guns) 288 all ranks
129 LAA Bty, RA (12 x Bofors) 249 all ranks

156 LAA Bty, RA (less two tps and one sec)
(2 x Bofors) 63 all ranks
Sec 7 Aust LAA Bty (2 x Bofors) 42 all ranks
23 LAA Bty, RM (less two tps) 2 x Bofors 104
all ranks
'S' Group
HQ 2 Hy AA Regt, RM 11 all ranks
AA Hy Bty, RM (8 x 3in guns) 270 all ranks
Sec C Hy AA Bty, RM (2 x 3in guns) 63 all ranks
234 Hy AA Bty RA (8 x 3.7in guns) 288 all ranks
304 Searchlight Bty, RA (20 x lights) 310 all
ranks
Sec 106 RHA (2 x 2pdr atk) 16 all ranks
15 Coast Regt, RA (less one sec) (4 x 6in, 2 x
4in, and 2 x 12pdr guns, 2 x lights) 465 all ranks

Engineers: CRE 32 all ranks
42 Fd Coy, RE less one sec 164 all ranks
5 NZ Fd Pk Coy 120 all ranks
Crete Composite Coy, RE 210 all ranks
1003 Docks Op Coy 126 all ranks
RE Stores Depot 84 all ranks
Aust Engr and AASC Stevedores 360 all ranks
NZ Engr Stevedores 52 all ranks

Infantry: 1 Welch (FORCE RESERVE) 854 all ranks
1 Rangers (9 Bn KRRC) 417 all ranks
Northumberland Hussars (with rifles) 279
all ranks
106 RHA (with rifles) 307 all ranks
2/2 Aust Fd Regt (with rifles) 554 all ranks
Det 2/3 Aust Fd Regt (with rifles) 306 all ranks
16 Aust Inf Bde Comp Bn (2/2 and 2/3 Bns)
443 all ranks
17 Aust Inf Bde Comp Bn (2/4 and 2/5 Bns)
387 all ranks
HQ 11 Searchlight Regt and S Searchlight Bty,

RM 364 all ranks
1 Royal Perivolians (dets of misc British units) 700 all ranks
1 Echelon NZ Div Supply Column (with rifles) 145 all ranks
2 Greek Regt (500 rifles only) 930 all ranks

Services: RASC
231 MT Coy 460 all ranks
101 Pet Coy 257 all ranks
1 Pet Depot 52 all ranks
Two Supply Depots 210 all ranks
Base Supply Depot 70 all ranks
37 DID 32 all ranks
Dets 1 and 26 Fd Bakery 67 all ranks
Misc RASC 110 all ranks
Det EFI 52 all ranks
Ordnance
5 Ind Bde Wksp 104 all ranks
2 Hy AA Wksp, RM 26 all ranks
52 LAA Wksp 51 all ranks
DADOS, OO Docks, Ord Depot, Amn Depot, Misc Ord Depots 630 all ranks
Medical
4 Lt Fd Amb, RAMC 104 all ranks
168 Fd Amb, RAMC 102 all ranks
189 Fd Amb, RAMC, less one coy 106 all ranks
2 Armd Div and 48 Fd Hygiene Secs 52 all ranks
1 Tented Hosp RN 64 all ranks
Dets 2/1, 2/2 and 2/7 Aust Fd Ambs 218 all ranks
Miscellaneous: MNBDO Landing and Maint, Pnr and Labour Groups 300 all ranks
270 Fd Security Sec 21 all ranks
Base Pay and Fd Cash Office 35 all ranks
CMP 64 all ranks

Suda Island det 29 all ranks
RAF details 36 all ranks
Misc Aust Minor Units 140 all ranks
Misc Br Minor Units 175 all ranks
Pioneer and Labour Units: 606 Palestine
Pioneer Corps 442 all ranks
1004, 1005, 1007 and 1008 Cypriot Pnr Coys
699 all ranks
Misc Pnrs 200

Sector Total: 14,822 all ranks
Layforce (landed 24-27 May 1941) 800 all ranks

Grand Total: 42,640 all ranks

Notes

1. Totals include Layforce which arrived during the operation.
2. The figures shown are as accurate as possible, although in a number of cases they are only estimates.
3. 4 NZ Bde was less 20th Bn in Force Reserve, 20th Bn under comd 10th NZ Bde but acting as NZ Div reserve
4. Source is Appendix IV to Official NZ History of WWII Volume CRETE
5. Only about half were properly formed infantry units, the Suda sector having the lowest proportion of armed men (under 1,500). The Greek forces were also poorly armed, as were the Cretan gendarmes and guerrillas.

2. OPERATION 'MERKUR' ORDER OF BATTLE AND CHAIN OF COMMAND OF THE GERMAN FORCES

Luftflotte IV
Commander: General der Flieger Alexander Loehr

Fliegerkorps VII
Commander: General der Flieger Freiherr W. von
Richthofen
4 x Combat Groups
5 x Stuka Groups
5 x single-engined Fighter Groups
1 x twin-engined Fighter Group
1 x long-range Reconnaissance Squadron
10 x Transport Groups assembled under three
transport squadron staffs and ground
formations

The Groups thus comprised:
120 x Dornier Do17 based at Tatoi
40 x Heinkel He111 based at Eleusis
80 x Junkers Ju88 based at Eleusis
150 x Junkers Ju87b Stuka based at Mycenae,
Malai and Scarpanto
90 x Messerschmitt Bf110 based at Argos
90 x Messerschmitt Bf109 based at Malai
Some Fieseler Storch recce aircraft
c650 x Junkers Ju52 Transports
70 x DFS230 gliders

Fliegerkorps XI
Commander: Generalmajor Kurt Student
2IC and CoS: Generalmajor Schlemm
CoS (Operations):   Oberst von Trettner

Chief of Intelligence: Maj Reinhardt

>Corps recce sqn
>Corps tpt sqn
>Motorcycle pl
>41st Sig Bn

7th Parachute Division
Commander: Generalleutnant W. Suessmann
CoS: Maj Count von Uxkuell

Air Transport and Signal units
Sturmregiment Genmaj Meindl
>I Bn Maj Kch
>II Bn Maj Stentzler
>III Bn Maj Scherber
>IV Bn Haupt Gericke

Fallschirmjägerregiment 1 Oberst Bräuer
>I Bn Maj Walther
>II Bn Haupt Burckhardt
>III Bn Maj Karl-Lothar Schulz

Fallschirmjägerregiment 2 Oberst Sturm
>I Bn Maj Kroh
>II Bn Haupt Schirmer
>III Bn Haupt Weidemann

Fallschirmjägerregiment 3 Oberst Heidrich
>I Bn Haupt Freiherr von der Heydte
>II Bn Maj Derpa
>III Bn Maj Heilmann

15th Engineer Bn Maj Liebach
Parachute A/tk Bn Haupt Schmidz

Parachute Arty Bn Haupt Schramm
Parachute MG Bn Haupt Schmidt
Parachute AA MG Bn Haupt Beyer
Parachute Medical Bn Maj Berg
Parachute Motorcycle Tpt Coy
13th and 14th Companies
16th Heavy Weapons Company

5 Gebirgs Division Generalmajor Julius Ringel

Divisional Staff
> 1 (mot) Mapping detachment

Divisional troops
> 95th Reconnaissance Bn (2 x Bicycle Sqns,
> 1 x Hy Recce Coy)
> 95th Anti-tank Bn (2 x atk Coys)
> 95th Mtn Artillery Regt (2 x Bns (each 8 x
> 105mm mtn how); 1 x Bn (12 x 105mm leFH);
> 1 x Bn (mot) (8 x 150mm sFH))
> 95th Mtn Pioneer Bn
> 95th Mtn Signals Bn
> 95th Supply Troops
> 95th Service Troops

Gebirgsjägerregiment 85 Oberst Kraku
> Gebirgs Signals Platoon
> Gebirgs Bicycle Recce Pl
> Regimental Band
> I Battalion Maj Treck
> II Battalion Maj Esch
> III Battalion Maj Ehal

> All battalions have three rifle companies
> (12 x LMG, 3 x 5cm mortars and 2 x 80cm

mortars), one Machine Gun coy (12 x Hy MGs), 1 x Hy Coy (Inf Gun pl – 2 x 75mm inf gun, Sigs pl and Pioneer pl)

16th (mot) Mtn panzerjaeger Coy (12 x 37mm PaK 36)
Inf Gun Section (2 x 15cm inf guns)
Light supply Colm (horsed)

Gebirgsjägerregiment 100 Oberst Utz
Gebirgs Sigs Pl
Gebirgs Bicycle Recce Pl
Regt Band
I Battalion Maj Schrank
II Battalion Maj Friedmann
III Battalion Maj Ehal

Organised as for Gebirgsjägerregiment 85

In addition, for Operation 'Merkur', the division had Gebirgsjägerregiment 141 attached from 6th Gebirgs Division (comd: Oberst Jais)

Total Strength: **22,040**
(as landed by parachute, glider or troop transport)

Maleme: by parachute and glider 1,860; by troop carrier 13,980
Canea
(inc Ayia Valley): by parachute and glider 2,460
Rethymnon: by parachute and glider 1,380
Heraklion: by parachute and glider 2,360

3. KNIGHT'S CROSS WINNERS IN CRETE

1   Olt Josef Barmetler
2   Olt Karl Becker
3   Graf Bluecher – KIA
4   Maj Bruno Bräuer
5   Olt Reinhard Egger
6   Lt Wilhelm Fulda (glider pilot)
7   Olt Alfred Genz
8   Hptm Walter Gericke
9   Olt Andreas Hagl
10   Oberst Richard Heidrich
11   Maj Ludwig Heilmann
12   Olt Harry Herrmann
13   Hptm von der Heydte
14   Ofw Wilhelm Kempke
15   Olt Hans Kroh
16   MG Eugen Meindl
17   Dr Heinrich Neumann
18   Oberst Bernhard Ramcke
19   Olt Arnold von Roon
20   Hptm Gerhart Schirmer
21   Ojr Erich Schuster
22   Maj Edgar Stentzler
23   OTL Alfred Sturm
24   Lt Rudolf Toschka
25   Olt Horst Trebes
26   Lt Helmut Wagner
27   Fw Heinrich Welskop

Bibliography

Books and Magazines

Beevor, Antony: *Crete, the battle and the resistance;*
John Murray Ltd, 1991.

Clark, Alan: *The Fall of Crete;* Anthony Blond, 1962.

CRETE – *A Tribute from New Zealand;* published by the
New Zealand Army.

Davin, D. M.: *Official History of New Zealand in the Second
World War 1939-45 – CRETE;* Dept of Internal Affairs,
Government of New Zealand, 1953.

Davis, B. L.: *Uniforms and Insignia of the Luftwaffe Vol 2
(1940-45);* Arms and Armour Press, 1995.

Detwiler, Donald S., Editor: *World War II German Military
Studies, Volume 13, Part VI The Mediterranean Theater;*
Garland Publishing Inc, 1979.

Guedalla, Philip: *Middle East 1940-1942, a study in air power;*
Hodder and Stoughton, 1944.

Hadjipateras, Costas N.: *Crete 1941 Eyewitnessed;* Efstathiadis
Group, 1989.

Heydte, Baron von der: *Daedalus Returned – Crete 1941;*
Hutchinson and Co Ltd, 1958.

Howell, Edward: *Escape to Live;* Longmans Green and Co,
1947.

Laffin, John: *British VCs of World War II – a study in heroism;*
Sutton Publishing, 1997

Lewin, Ronald: *Ultra goes to War;* Hutchinson and Co, 1978.

Lindsay, T. M.: *Sherwood Rangers;* Burrup, Mathieson and Co
Ltd, 1952.

Lucas, James: *Storming Eagles – German Airborne Forces in
World War Two;* Arms and Armour Press, 1988.
Hitler's Mountain Troops; Cassell, 1992.

Pack, S. W. C.: *The Battle for Crete;* Ian Allan Ltd, 1973.

Psychoundakis, George: *The Cretan Runner;* John Murray Ltd, 1955.

Richards, Denis: *ROYAL AIR FORCE – 1939-1945, Vol 1 The Fight At Odds;* HMSO, 1953.

Sheffield, Maj O. F.: *The York and Lancaster Regiment 1919-1953;* Gale and Polden, 1956

Stewart, I. McD. G.: *The Struggle for Crete;* OUP, 1966.

Trevor-Roper, H. R, Editor: *Hitler's War Directives 1939-45;* Sidgwick and Jackson, 1964.

Underhill, Brig E. W.: *The Royal Leicestershire Regiment 17th Foot: A History of the Years 1928-1956;* published by the Regiment, 1958.

BR 1736(2) *Naval Operations in the Battle of Crete 20th May-1st June 1941, Battle Summary No 4;* Historical Section Admiralty, 1960. (Originally graded RESTRICTED, downgraded to UNCLASSIFIED under PRO ADM 234/320.)

Parnassos Bulletin Vol 7 No 4 dated May 1991; Parnassos Cultural Society Inc, of 1315 Prince of Wales Drive, Ottawa, Canada K2C 1N2.

Tracklink; The Magazine of the Friends of the Tank Museum, Number 47, September 1999.

Archival Sources

The Queen's Own Hussars Museum, the Notts (Sherwood Rangers) Yeomanry Museum, the Black Watch Museum, the Yorks and Lancs Museum, the Argyll and Sutherland Highlanders Museum, the RAMC Museum and/or from their respective RHQs, as shown in the various chapter notes. Various RAF Squadron Associations as shown in the chapter notes, including: 30 Squadron RAF, 'Highlights and Personal Experiences from the Squadron's time in Greece and Crete, November 1940-May 1941' (Supplement to Newsletter 2/87).

Cretan Crazy Week, a memoir by F. C. C. Graham, written at
   Latimer, 4 April 1948 and held by the Imperial War
   Museum.
Kameradschaft Sturmregiment – programme of 40th
   commemoration held at Lich 3-4 June 2000.

Private manuscripts of recollections belonging to:
   John C. Croft, Rex Hey and the late Colin France.

Index

Battle of Crete